Computers in the Fashion Industry

Computers in the Fashion Industry

Patrick Taylor

**THE LIBRARY
LONDON COLLEGE OF FASHION
20 JOHN PRINCE'S STREET
LONDON W1M 0BJ**

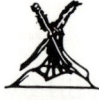

Heinemann Professional Publishing

Heinemann Professional Publishing Ltd
Halley Court, Jordan Hill, Oxford OX2 8EJ

OXFORD   LONDON   MELBOURNE   AUCKLAND   SINGAPORE
IBADAN   NAIROBI   GABORONE   KINGSTON

First published 1990

© Patrick Taylor 1990

British Library Cataloguing in Publication Data
Taylor, Patrick
   Computers in the fashion industry.
   1. Great Britain. Fashion industries. Applications of computer system
   I. Title
   338.476870285

ISBN 0 434 91916 0

Printed and Bound in Great Britain by
Redwood Press Limited, Melksham, Wiltshire

Contents

Preface		vii
1	The world of fashion	1
2	Dedicated fashion computer systems	22
3	Computer basics	37
4	Surveys and sizing	48
5	Computer-aided design (CAD)	67
6	Pattern-design systems (PDS)	89
7	Computer grading with CAM	107
8	Layplanning with CAM	120
9	Computer bulk cutting	135
10	Computer-aided production machinery PRESSING	160
11	Computer-aided management and production control	182
12	Projection into the future	201
13	List of computer hardware and software companies	208
Index		213

Preface

Computer technology has now established itself in all areas of the fashion industry, and the manufacturer is facing ever-increasing pressure to adopt some degree of computerization. When faced with the array of computer systems offered, the clothing manufacturer is often at a loss to know which one to choose! The salesmen and demonstrators in the computer companies will, of course, be totally biased in favour of their own product – firstly, because they will be protecting their livelihood, and secondly, because, hey have not had experience of any other systems with which to be able to compare their own. If they have used other systems, they still will not feel free to give a prospective customer an unbiased answer to questions related to comparative performance of systems.

It is hoped that this book will throw light on the various aspects to be taken into account when approaching the problems involved when considering the adoption of a computerization. Having used several systems, I feel in a position to give an unbiased view of their performance in relation to the function that they have been designed to perform, and to describe the basis of their operation. However, it is not the object of this book to compile a detailed comparative merit table of all the systems on offer.

My background consists of many years in the clothing industry, starting in the cutting room as a stock cutter through to grading, pattern cutting and design, and finally settling for production pattern cutting. Subsequently, I have spent many years teaching these subjects, first at Leicester Polytechnic and then at the London College of Fashion.

The contents of this book are the result of experience gained by a typical 'computer systems user', who has a background in clothing technology and is in no way a product of the computer industry.

Included in the book are a large number of photographs showing the hardware of prominent manufacturers. Not all manufacturers' products have been included for reasons of space, but there is a considerable representation. This has been done to give a visual reference with regard to all the leading companies' products.

It is hoped that this book will not only be of use to the clothing industry, but also to sixth-formers interested to know what the fashion industry has to offer and students who are currently studying fashion and clothing subjects such as design, pattern cutting, management and production technology. Also, last but not least, the book will be relevant to anyone interested in the field of fashion and anyone who, for any reason, opens its pages.

Patrick J. Taylor

Chapter 1

The world of fashion

For the reader who knows nothing about the fashion industry, I will start by outlining the main areas and explaining some of the terminology, as well as giving job descriptions of the key posts of employment. Refer to the flow charts (Figures 1–4) for an overview of the following descriptions.

The retail sector

The buyer
The retailers are the outlets for the supply, and the supply must match the demand as near as is possible. The person responsible for this is the retail buyer, who is employed by the retailer or chain-store owner to anticipate the requirements of the market in advance, and order from the manufacturer the correct merchandise for that store to sell and at the right price.

The buyer has a heavy responsibility. It is his or her job to predetermine accurately the type and style of garment, its colour, price bracket, and quantity to be sold.

In the case of an individual shop, the buying is invariably done by the owner; however, for a larger company running a country-wide chain of stores, several buyers may be employed, each one being allocated a type of garment, such as:

1 Lingerie
2 Blouses

3   Skirts
4   Day dresses
5   Evening dresses
6   Swimwear
7   Children's clothes
8   Accessories

A buyer may be allocated more than one type of garment to buy, but he or she will need considerable experience in those fields before being trusted with the very large amounts of money that are involved. He or she will have had previous successful experience in buying that particular type of wear, and know the different manufacturers that produce it. A buyer will have to know how garments are assembled, and be able to outline specifications regarding make, finish, and washing properties, etc.

But, most important, will be the ability to choose the style, cloth and colours that will sell. This has to be done a season in advance, which is usually about six months. This, of course, is very difficult and bad mistakes can be made. A buyer can order and take delivery of a large quantity of goods costing thousands of pounds, only to find that the market has shifted, leaving the buyer with 'dead' merchandise on their hands, and with no other option but to sell it off at bargain prices.

A buyer is told beforehand how many items of a specific type can be ordered, and roughly how much it will retail for. They are then allocated a quantity of money and told when to have the garments in the stores ready for sale.

The experience for this type of operation is gained by being an assistant to an established and experienced buyer – there is no other way of entering this field. No retailer will trust anyone, other than a buyer with at least five years' experience assisting a known buyer, with the heavy responsibility of stocking their shops with merchandise worth a great deal of money.

The training required to become an assistant buyer will be gained on a clothing technology course at a college of fashion or clothing technology. The student buyer will have to study and practise designing, pattern construction and garment assembly, plus other allied subjects including dedicated computer systems designed for clothing production. These systems will include the networked computers installed in the stores that monitor details of sale and reorder requests, etc.

The fashion buyer has a most difficult task as the winds of fashion are so unpredictable. There are categories of clothing that are not so affected by the whims of fashion and are more predictable, such as types of underwear, men's suits and jackets, work wear, uniforms, etc. But most clothing is affected by fashion to some degree. It is therefore safer for the buyer to order what has sold well last season, but with slight variations in style and trimming detail.

This means that the same styling will tend to be perpetuated from year to year, but at the same time this is dangerous because taste can suddenly change and leave the company with a large quantity of unsaleable goods which invariably end up in one of the markets – jobbed off at cost price or less, or as a genuine sale item in the shop. So the buyer is always in danger of making mistakes; if buyers could accurately predict what will sell next season, they would be worth their weight in gold and be sought after by everyone.

A buyer will usually experiment by including in their ranges styles that are a little way out in relation to their particular market, in order to test the water for next season. Buyers are always on the horns of a dilemma. If they order a lot of styles in small quantities, they find that by the time it becomes apparent which ones are selling, there is not the time to restock and reorder from the manufacturer (a) because other retailers will be in the same boat and be trying to reorder the same good sellers, and (b) the manufacturer is perhaps not flexible enough to resupply in time to catch the fleeting market, which is always weather controlled, or the necessary cloth is not available for that style.

The store will then be left with the task of moving a lot of styles in small quantities that are not selling very well. On the other hand, the buyer can buy in large quantities of stock only covering a few styles that have previously sold well. If the market has not shifted, then everything goes to plan and all is success; if the market has changed, it is failure – which can mean the buyer may lose his or her job. So the buyer has to be very acute and continually feeling out the market from the data feedback which is available from the retail computer system.

There are two main seasons in the fashion world: summer and winter. Also, there are two mid seasons, spring and autumn, which are smaller and less important, and are slotted in between the main ones.

There are also two types of retailers. There is the large operator like Marks & Spencer, who manufacture their own products, using contractors. And there are the small, more flexible retailers who work from hand to mouth, which means that they can buy in small quantities from the wholesaler as the demand requires. The larger and more cumbersome companies cannot move their production quickly enough to operate in that way, because they are dealing with such large quantities and have to plan well ahead regarding cloth and style design and fixing delivery dates. All this involves large sums of money, and cash-flow considerations become very important. But with the proper use of computer systems, large companies can speed up these processes, and become more efficient and quicker to respond to market demands.

The buyer will be responsible for having the products in the shop at the right time and also running quality-control checks on the garments before they are delivered to the stores.

Quality is a relative concept. It mostly relates to the weather. If the weather is behaving as it should and a style or styles are selling like hot cakes, then nobody looks too closely at the quality, and it all gets pushed through to catch the sales. But if the sales are sluggish, then quality becomes very important. First, for the obvious reason that customers tend to be more choosy when there is a glut of goods in the shops, and less so when the sun is blazing or it suddenly turns cold and they have to have that garment in a hurry. And secondly, the retailer is reluctant to take delivery of garments from the manufacturer if they know that they cannot sell them, and therefore refuse to accept them on the grounds of poor quality or any other excuse they can find. Many small manufacturers have been placed in real difficulty because of this.

As has already been said, the large manufacturers produce two main collections, winter and summer, and two mid-season collections. They invite all the buyers from the various retailers to attend the shows, which continue for approximately three weeks. Each manufacturer tends to specialize and cater for a particular segment of the market, and the buyer gets to know the manufacturer that they prefer for any specific type of styling. So they plan their visits between the various houses, placing their orders for the various styles that they require, until they have spent their cash quotas.

In the eyes of the manufacturing houses, the buyer is 'the one who can do no wrong', and is treated accordingly. The degree of this accord is directly related to the amount of money the buyer has control of.

The retail sector will also carry out market-research projects to ascertain the depth and density of a given area of demand. The relevant factors involved will be:

1 Age group
2 Price range
3 Size and shape
4 Cloth
5 Colour
6 Type of garment
7 Styling

The buyer will undoubtedly play a key role in this, helping to frame the survey and outlining the data that will be useful for the buying department.

Wholesale manufacture

The showroom

The showroom of a fashion house is always located in the centre of a trading area, together with the head offices, accounting, directors' offices, board room and design department. The factory or manufacturing units are invariably set away from the cities, where land, rents and wage levels are lower. They may even be in another country.

The showroom is run by a manager or manageress, usually a manageress with two or three assistants, usually female. The showroom area is attractively furnished with a walkway or equivalent in the centre, where the models can display the garments. It is here that the buyers from the various retail houses are invited to view the current fashions as interpreted by the individual wholesale manufacturing houses.

For the important buyers from the large chain organizations, a time is offered for them to view alone, while the small shop owners are invited in groups.

There are other permutations, such as menswear, which is not high fashion, and which may have other arrangements slightly different to the female fashion scene; for example, the men's suit manufacturers may be the retailers as well. In this case, styling only changes in detail from season to season and no fashion shows are needed, unless the manufacturer is operating in the fashion sector of the menswear market. The latter is distinct from the traditional attire sector, and will also require fashion shows which will follow the same pattern as the womenswear sector. Also, in the case of small fashion wholesalers who work on a week-to-week basis, they will show their new designs to the buyers as they are produced.

For the large manufacturers, the summer and winter ranges will consist of approximately seventy new styles for each season and twenty plus for the mid-season ranges. The buyers will place their orders, stating numbers required, sizes, cloth design and colour for a given style.

As the shows progress, it gradually becomes apparent which styles are selling well and in what size, colour and cloth design. Also, it gradually becomes apparent whether the company is going to have a good season or not. That is, are sales high, average or low? The atmosphere in the showroom during showing is always tense, made so by the directors who have a lot at stake, probably having invested considerable money in advance on securing cloth for the coming season with the fear that there will not be enough orders to keep their factories going at full capacity. When, and if, it becomes apparent that the orders are flowing in at a good rate, then the atmosphere changes and all is sweetness and light.

The orders are fed into a computer system re style number, number ordered, sizes, cloth style number and retailer, colour, trimmings and accessory requirements, and delivery dates – and perhaps other details. Having done this, the manufacturing process can be put into motion – bearing in mind that the manufacturing process can never stop, being designed to be in profit over a precise turnover quantity.

The design department

The designer and pattern cutter

The product process begins with the 'working sketch', which is, of course, produced by the designer. But it will be necessary, at this point, to jump over the designer to the 'pattern cutter'. The term 'pattern cutter' implies a mindless cutting of shapes in paper. This could not be further from the truth. Who was responsible for inventing the term is not clear, but it was almost certainly the employer who, it can only be assumed, had reasons for degrading the position.

In fact, the pattern is the hub, around which everything else rotates. The creator of the pattern is therefore also of primary importance.

The ability to take a sketch and construct the pattern, which when cut out in cloth and made up will accurately represent the style in proportion, silhouette and size, requires a long training and in many areas. A better title for the 'pattern cutter' would be 'pattern designer' or 'pattern engineer'.

Pattern cutters are in fact the most important technicians in the total process, and when enough experience has been acquired, they are considered technologists capable of setting up various aspects of the production process – such as sizing surveys, stand design, grading systems, and advising in other production areas.

There are two types of pattern technicians: the one that works in the design department (sample room), and the one that produces the final production pattern. The production pattern has to be perfected in size, style, shape and accuracy and is cut in a heavy durable card or plastic, and sometimes in metal. In contrast, the prototype pattern is cut in paper, which is cheaper and more easily filed. Also, the prototype will probably be cut about and altered and even discarded, the style not being considered suitable to be included in the final range to be shown. If it is in the final range, then the pattern – along with a repeat sample – is sent to the production pattern cutter to produce a perfected pattern, out of which will be cut the bulk orders.

This requires more experience, and in general is a higher-paid position than the design-department technician, who has to produce the first prototype pattern for the designer from the original working sketch. The working sketch will have to be drawn as near to scale as possible, and carry information needed for pattern construction. If the sketch is not in scale, it cannot be properly interpreted. A fashion sketch is not in scale, because the body has been distorted in order to enhance its proportions and make the design more attractive. This misleads everyone and has no place in a design room. The place for these sketches is in a fashion magazine.

There are two pattern-construction techniques; one is called 'flat pattern cutting' and the other 'modelling'. A good pattern technician will be expert in both. Also, the pattern technician will have the ability to make up or machine the cut-out garment; this skill need not be to a very high standard, but sufficient to be able to understand the manufacturing processes and advise where necessary.

The manufacturing model that is being outlined here refers to a large mass-production organization, which by definition produces cheap- to medium-priced products.

The smaller companies will not be able to carry, for example, a pattern technician for sample room and another for the production pattern construction. One technician will do both jobs, and even be the designer as well.

Also, there is the top end of the market or the higher price bracket. This is the so-called 'couture house', which produces individual garments for clients, or very limited numbers of a given style. These companies will have a slightly different structure, but the job specifications will be similar.

It is appropriate at this point to return to the 'designer'. The modern designer has to be expert in all aspects of production. Because of this, he or she must be trained as a pattern cutter first, and therefore able to produce patterns for their own designs – and, if necessary, to be able to make them as well. This implies that the designer can anticipate production processes and design styles that are capable of being mass produced to the given price bracket.

It is much easier to design when not limited by price, cloth costing and skill limitation. This is the case in the couture sector, where each garment is almost individually built. In the mass-production unit, a designer is limited in all areas of production and has to be much better informed and in all ways more ingenious to be able to produce saleable styles at a price.

The term 'designer pattern cutter' is the one used when a designing post is advertised. The designer is a busy person and, although capable of making their own patterns, they very often do not have the time. Designers require an assistant pattern technician to help them, but it is still essential that the designers themselves are expert pattern cutters. No large mass-production company will employ a designer without a pattern-cutting background.

The designer is required to produce at least eight new styles per week over a period of about three months, in order that from approximately one hundred designs sixty to seventy can be chosen to show.

This is not easy; designers can dry up and no fresh ideas appear. They are free to attend showings elsewhere, or tour the shops for inspiration, or whatever is necessary, but they must produce the ideas come what may. They carry a heavy responsibility. They must, with the help of the directors, choose the fabrics that they wish to use in the coming season. For this they must call in the textile representatives, who will bring their current range of designs from which the designer will choose. Sample lengths of approximately 5 metres will be ordered for immediate delivery for the design and construction of the prototype. Usually about one hundred sample lengths will be ordered, which will give the designer scope to begin the new range.

The first task is to make a working sketch on a specification sheet outlining all requirements such as zip length, cloth price, interlining, trimmings such as button-style price and source, embroidery, pleating, etc. Embroidery and pleating companies have to be called in where necessary, and designs and prices negotiated. Then the pattern must be constructed, either by the designer or assistant pattern cutter.

The designer has to be available to:
1 See buyers
2 See the directors
3 See reps of various kinds
4 Supervise the making of all the new designs
5 Make patterns
6 Create new designs and working sketches
7 Attend shows

8   Travel abroad when asked
9   Attend meetings with the production manager to discuss production problems on the different styles
10 Buy sample cloth, trimmings, etc. and keep records of all prices and sources
11 Be reponsible for the design department and the staff

There are probably more responsibilities, but these are enough to indicate the range of activities that have to be dealt with. At this point it is necessary to indicate that the design processes can be carried out on a computer. These computers are called 'dedicated computer systems'. This means that they are designed to perform a specific set of functions relating to a limited area, in this case 'clothing product design'. They come under a general heading of CAD/CAM.

CAD, which stands for computer-aided design, is used in the design departments of fashion houses and textile manufacturers. These will be fully described in later chapters.

Textile design

The textile designer is usually freelance, and may specialize in either woven fabric or printed fabrics. In either case, they should have a background training in the area they intend their fabrics to be used. Certain knowledge is required regarding check, stripe and pattern repeats in order to make the fabric economical in use, and easy to match, whether for furnishing or fashion.

The textile manufacturer is in a similar position to the garment fashion manufacturer, in that they also do not know what designs will sell in the coming season. Consequently, they cannot foresee which cloth to weave or print in advance, and in what quantity.

Fashion designers, when choosing sample lengths to design for, will choose the ones they think will sell; in other words, the ones they like. The cloth manufacturer will get some idea of what is popular with the designers, but designers are very often wrong in their predictions — as are the buyers, and indeed anyone who is in the predicting game.

The answers to this do not become apparent until the customer begins to buy. Then there can be a mad scramble to make the cloth and the garments that are selling well. This usually means that everyone is after the same cloth and styles of garment. Some larger companies will commit themselves to ordering large quantities of cloth in advance, and stipulate that they want sole use of that particular design. They would then be required to place a minimum order with the textile manufacturer and pay for it in advance. This would ensure that no competitor will be able to use that design.

This, of course, is very risky, but if it works then all is well. It means a heavy cash commitment in advance, which makes for very nervous directors.

All this points to the fact that the cloth design can be as important as the garment design. Indeed, with some styles the garment is sold on the strength of the cloth, which can be something quite simple and exclusive.

Another area that has to be organized by the dress designer is finding suitable freelance models to show the new range of clothes. These models have to be a specific size, as near to a size 12 as possible for womenswear, unless it is for outsize, when a size 18 is used; for men, usually a thirty-six inch chest is preferred.

In the larger companies, an inhouse model is employed full time, and is available to show garments between shows and to model the new designs coming from the design department, both for fitting sessions and showing to directors, sales staff and production manager regarding selection into the final collection.

The sample cutter

This member of the design department team will lay the pattern on the cloth, matching stripes, checks or print patterns where necessary, and interlocking the pattern pieces in order to get as economical costing as possible.

The 'costing' is the amount of cloth used and the result is what is termed a 'layplan'; this is a plan of the pieces on the cloth. This is recorded, along with the material costing on the specification sheet which will have the working drawing on it, with all the other relevant information. This 'spec sheet' is put in a large envelope with the pattern and a swatch of the cloth, and then filed.

The style is then cut out by the sample cutter and passed, with the sketch, to the sample machinist. The sample cutter must of course be a very accurate cutter, using shears or an electrically driven cutter. He or she must also be an expert layplanner. There is also a computer program that will enable layplanning to be carried out automatically, but more of that in Chapter 8. If this is available, then it will be the sample cutter's job to operate it.

This computer will come under the heading of CAM, which stands for computer-aided manufacture.

The sample machinist

The sample machinist is the most experienced, accurate and intelligent operator of 'making-up' machinery that is available.

Sample machinists' expertise and knowledge of the manufacturing process is of great value in assessing the degree of difficulty, time and cost of garment assembly, which will indicate whether a design is suitable for mass production and, if not, how it might be altered to make it so.

They advise on the most suitable 'order of assembly' of the style in question, and can break down the machine process into its separate procedures.

The samples that they make are precisely made, and when and if necessary they have to change details by unpicking, recutting and, where required, fitting to individual models.

They can and do advise on the details of pattern construction, and a harmonious relationship between the pattern technician and sample machinist is essential.

Mass production

Orders from the retailers must be processed on a computer regarding:

1 Style
2 Number ordered
3 Cloth
4 Sizes
5 Delivery date
6 Customer

When this has been done, a priority list is produced and sent to the 'production manager' at the factory as a basis for planning the future output.

Production manager (PM)

The production manager is in total charge of the production area, or factory, which can be located anywhere. With the use of computers and 'modem' (telephone linkage of computers), the mass-production process can be remotely controlled, if necessary from another part of the planet.

The PM is responsible to the directors for the entire operation. This is a highly paid position and requires a deep understanding of production techniques, plus a superficial insight into all areas.

Some of the best PMs come through the pattern-engineering sections, where the most extensive experience is gained in all aspects.

They liaise with the designer at an early stage in order that time is not wasted on impractical styling – impractical, that is, from the production standpoint.

They employ senior staff for middle management and supervisory positions. They must be able to plan appropriate production procedures and be up to date on the latest technology. In fact, 'the buck stops at the PM'. All that follows is their domain.

The first request from the production manager to the design department is for the duplicate sample and prototype pattern of the top half-dozen styles on the 'priority list'. These are sent to the production-pattern department in the factory. The patterns can be sent via modem, to a corresponding computer workstation in the pattern room.

Here the pattern engineers or technicians will start from scratch and produce a 'production pattern'. This will be cut out in a production sample room by a cutter, and be assembled by a production sample machinist who will assess it regarding degree of difficulty, time taken, breakdown of assembly and the accuracy of the pattern.

It will then return to the pattern room to be checked for style balance, fit and size, and the designer will be shown each style before it goes into production to judge whether or not it has been accurately copied.

If all is well, the sample garment and perfected production pattern are sent to the grading department to have the pattern graded into the other sizes that are specified on the cutting order docket.

The grader

The setting up and designing of a size chart and grading system are the province of the pattern technologist or production pattern cutter. The grading of a pattern to other sizes ideally should be carried out by the pattern technician, but it is a time-consuming process and the peaks of grading activity follow the two major shows when the production pattern cutters are at their busiest, so a position of grader has been introduced to deal only with grading. The grading technician is not trained in pattern construction and is taught, usually by the pattern technician, a technique of grading, that is of applying increases in a lawful way to the base pattern that has been perfected in the production-pattern department.

The technology of sizing is a subject on its own, and will be covered in more detail in a subsequent chapter.

The grader has to work carefully and with great accuracy and be able to cut cleanly round the pattern card or plastic. The final result is a complete set of patterns; it may be from size 8 to 18 or only 10 to 16, depending on the style and the range of sizes covered by the company. They may specialize in outsizes or short or tall figures, etc.

under the heading of CAM, 'computer-aided manufacture'. This would be done by the grader. The actual mental activity of grading is the same using the computer as doing it manually, but the copying and cutting out of all the other sizes is done automatically by the computer and saves an enormous amount of time. Computer grading will be covered in depth later.

Layplanning

The layplanning department is comprised of a long narrow room in which there is a long table or tables, at least 6 metres long and, if there is space, 10 metres (or 6 to 10 yards) – the longer the better. The width of the table will be wider than the widest cloth produced. Two metres or 2 yards is ideal. There is usually one head layplanner (or marker maker) and one or more assistants, depending on the size of the company.

This also is a very important part of the process, since the main aim of this department is to minimize the usage of cloth, by arranging the pattern pieces within the width of the cloth so that they interlock as closely as possible. This can save a large amount of money, particularly if the company is large and has a high turnover. A lot of time is spent in this area struggling with styles to reduce the cloth costing that the garment was originally priced on, which costing came from the design department. The original costing is based on one garment, but the layplanner will be making a costing based on multi-garment lays; this will reduce the amount of cloth required.

Once the graded patterns have been cut out they are sent with the sample garment to the layplanning department, accompanied by the cutting docket.

The first step is to contact the cloth stock-room manager to see whether the cloth for the style in question has arrived from the textile manufacturer. If it has, all well and good; if not, then trouble is brewing for someone. If it has all arrived, then the stock-room manager will have the pieces of cloth checked for width and, if it is a repeat print, stripe, or check design, and a sample width is cut off and sent to the layplanning room, along with the width measurements.

The layplanner, or marker maker, has no pattern-cutting expertise, but has an overall experience which they get from working in the cutting room as stock cutters.

Their function is to arrange the pattern pieces, within the width of the cloth being used, on to white paper in the most economical way possible, and then draw round each piece. This will be called 'the marker', which will be laid on the top of the 'lay'. The lay is the cloth that has been cut into the same lengths as the marker, and laid one on top of the other, sometimes as much as one hundred layers thick. This lay can be up to 8 inches high. The marker is then placed on top of the lay and secured. It is then cut out by the stock cutter, using an electrically driven straight knife. But more of that later.

The marker or layplan can be quite long, comprising several garments perhaps of different sizes, and the lay of cloth is made up of all the colours and sizes designated on the cutting docket. Layplanning can also be done on a computer, either manually or completely automatically.

The computer uses a layplan program, which is also a part of the CAM system. This can reduce the area of floor space needed for layplanning and can reduce staffing numbers, but there will always be a need for a good layplanner as he or she usually have the edge over the computer auto systems when it requires minute savings of cloth, such as in jean manufacture, where vast amounts of cloth are used.

The computer will be worked by the layplanner, and the resultant marker will be printed off on a large plotter. More of this later.

The bulk-cutting department (or cutting room)

This is a large area comprising several long tables, up to 10 metres (yards) long and 2 metres (yards) wide. The number of tables will depend on the size of company. It will be run by the cutting room manager, who is in charge of the stock cutters.

The manager is responsible for the quality of the cutting, the speed and timing of the cut garments to the production area and the employment of, and if necessary the training of, cutters. They are given a cutting schedule and are responsible for implementing it. They collect the markers from the layplanning department along with the cutting docket and sample garment. They then contact the cloth stock-room manager and ask that the consignment of material for that style be sent to the cutting room. Having received the cloth, they allocate the cutting of it to a team of spreaders and stock cutters.

In a large company the laying up of the cloth is done by a lay maker or cloth spreader. These people have a special skill in laying the cloth up, layer upon layer, making an accurate lay, with the leading edge straight and vertical, also ensuring that the cloth is not stretched and creating internal stresses in the lay, which will distort the cutting. If a mechanical spreader is available, then they must operate it and understand its workings.

The lay is then cut out by the stock cutter. This is highly skilled and carries a weighty responsibility. An electrical hand-operated knife is used, either a 'straight knife' or a 'round knife'. The one has a long narrow straight blade that goes up and down and the other has a round or circular blade that rotates. Both are dangerous and are used with great care. There is one other kind of knife called a 'band knife', which has a continuous flexible band blade driven round a roller system. These also are highly dangerous and are treated with great respect.

The stock cutter has to be expert at using all kinds of knives. Accuracy is the primary concern and then speed. This skill is learned in the cutting room as an assistant cutter.

In the smaller companies the laying up and the cutting will be done by the stock cutter, and also the separating. 'Separating' is the separation of the different colours and sizes from the cut lay into bundles ready for the production line.

The bulk cutting can also be done by a 'computerized bulk cutter'. This will replace the stock cutter, who will no longer be needed. Details of this follow in later chapters.

Production area

Assembly

There are two types of assembly methods.

The first is where the machinist is given a bundle containing all the component parts for a number of garments, and also the zips and relevant size and style tickets to be sewn into the finished garment. The machinist (operator) has then to assemble (close or machine) the whole garment. The garment is costed as a whole unit and the operator is credited with the number of units in the bundle.

The second method is where the assembly is broken down into parts, and the machinists are organized into a sequence where each part is assembled by a different operator, until it emerges as a complete unit at the end. Each operation is costed and credited to the individual machinists.

The first method is used in small factories and high-class work. It has disadvantages in that the quality of assembly will vary according to the skill of the individual. Also, the speed of output will vary for the same reason. If the operator is paid 'piece work', which means paid for each garment satisfactory completed, then quality can suffer because the machinist is rushing to complete as many as possible. The slower ones will earn less and perhaps do better work. This situation can cause friction in the workforce, and for that reason some employers pay their machinists on a weekly basis. This also has its drawbacks, in that the quality can be good, but the output slow.

The second method, of sectional assembly, will always be used by large manufacturers because the advantages far outweigh the disadvantages. This method ensures a higher and consistent quality and faster output.

The reasons for this are that each operator, having only a small part of the assembly, can perfect that operation as it is repeated immediately over and over again, so that speed and accuracy can be attained quickly. If the sectioning of the work is done with intelligence then no bottlenecks should occur because of slower operators. In any case, a machinist who has a slower reaction can soon speed up under the pressure of repetition. Because of the increased speed and better quality, the garment will be cheaper and will sell better.

The main disadvantage is that the work satisfaction is lower, highly pressurized, and can be monotonous – with little, if any, relationship between the workers. But good money can be earned if the price costing is right; if the price is too low, then trouble will ensue.

There are various types of machines used for assembly, or 'closing', as it is sometimes called.

The machine used will depend on the type of material. Fabrics fall into three main categories:

1. *Woven.* This has warp and weft and is in general terms the most stable; in other words, it will not stretch out of shape.
2. *Knitted.* This is the most unstable material, because it can stretch in all directions and does not recover its shape.
3. *Elastic weaves.* These have warp and weft, and either or both can have predetermined elastication built into the fabric. This type of material, when stretched, will fully recover its original shape, and so can be considered to have variable stability.

For woven fabrics, a lockstitch machine will be used. This means that the stitch is comprised of two thread sources which lock round each other and cannot be pulled undone – as in a chainstitch, which will unravel if the loose end is pulled because there is only one thread which loops round itself. These are the same as the domestic ones, except that they are much more powerful and very fast.

For stretch fabrics, such as knitted and weaves with elastic qualities, either a swing-needle or a lockstitch overlock machine can be used, which enables the cloth to be stretched without breaking the stitch. There are various attachments that can be used on these machines that enable the machinist to carry out operations that would normally be slow and difficult to perform quickly and cleanly. Typical of these operations are gathering, hemming, binding, etc. Some of the machines are semi-automated, which means that the attachment will follow a predetermined stitch path, which can be electronically controlled.

Finishing

This area contains many different types of machine, called 'special machines'. These will include overlockers which finish the cut edge of the cloth to stop it fraying; buttonhole and button-sewing machines; welt pocket machines; multi-needle machines; and many other specialized devices that have been developed for detail finishing.

Operators are specially trained on these machines, and usually are proficient in more than one type, so that they can be moved to a different machine if required.

Pressing

Pressing is a highly developed area of production, and in no way can be termed 'ironing'. Like all the operators in production, the presser is very skilled.

There are two types of pressing. The first is done during assembly and is called 'under pressing'; this is where parts of the garment are pressed that cannot be properly done when the garment is finished. The other is the final finishing press. This is usually done using a mixture of 'hand iron' pressing and 'hoffman' pressing, which is a specialized steam and vacuum press that gives a very clean finish. There are also other presses that have been developed to shape and press specific parts of the garment, such as shoulders and sleeve heads, and whole jacket fronts. When the garment is pressed and hung up on a hanger, it is put on a stand or figure shape, the correct size, and inspected by quality controllers and 'passed'. If it is not satisfactory, then it is returned for correction. Then it is cleared of fluff and dust with a compressed air device, put in a plastic dust cover, and sent to the warehouse ready for dispatch.

The warehouse

The warehouse is a large, high enclosed building where all the finished stock is kept. The garments are put on rails, sometimes several stories high, in categories of style, colour and size. When an order is ready for dispatch to the retailer, then the warehouseman will collect all the garments on to a rail and load them on to a van for delivery, or send them to the packing department to be boxed and sent via other means to their destination. A large part of the movement of garments and garment parts around the factory can be done using overhead transporters. These systems can be controlled by computers. This will be fully explained in later chapters.

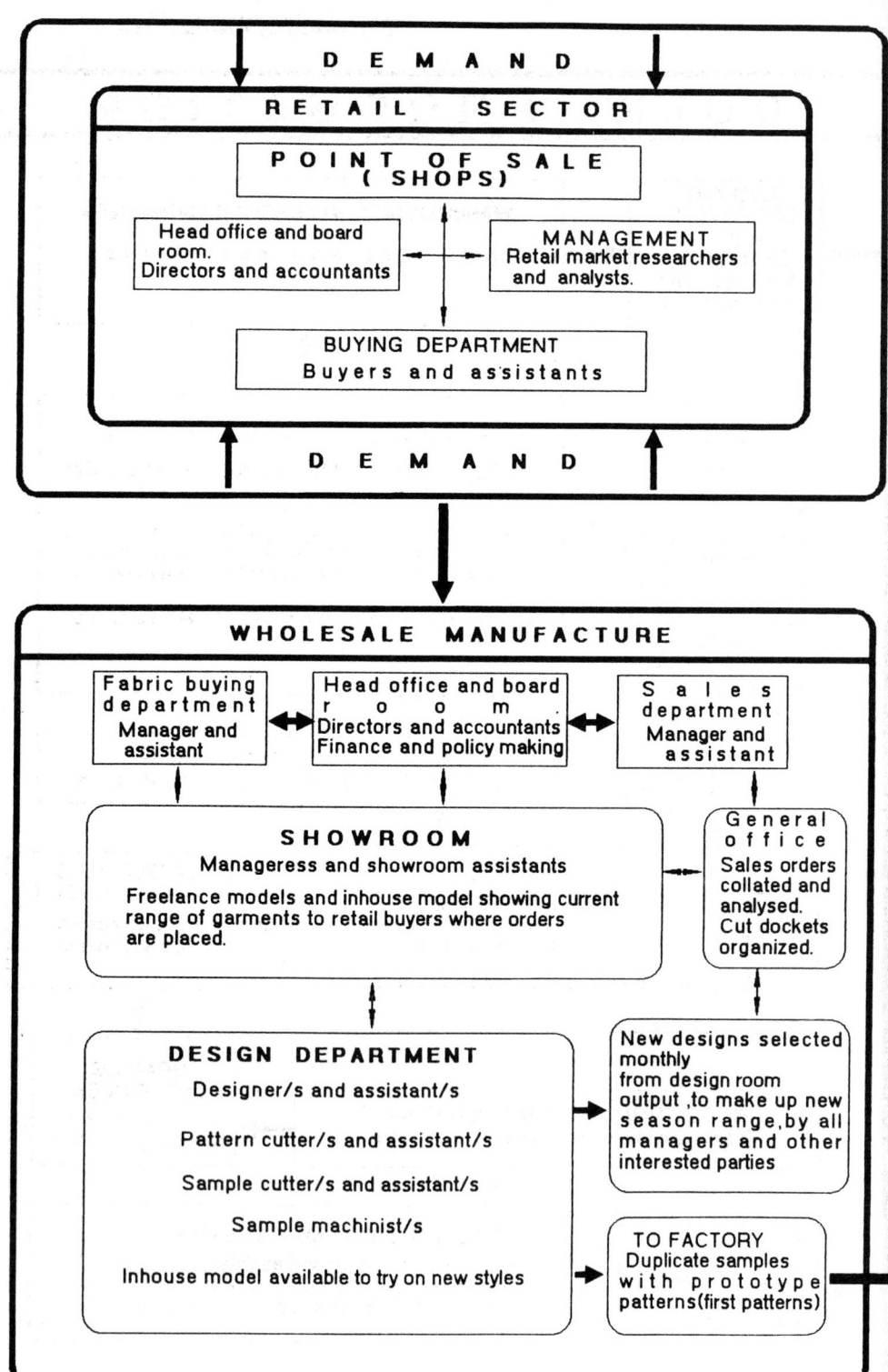

Figure 1 *Department and personnel chart for the retail sector and design and sales departments of a typical large wholesale fashion house*

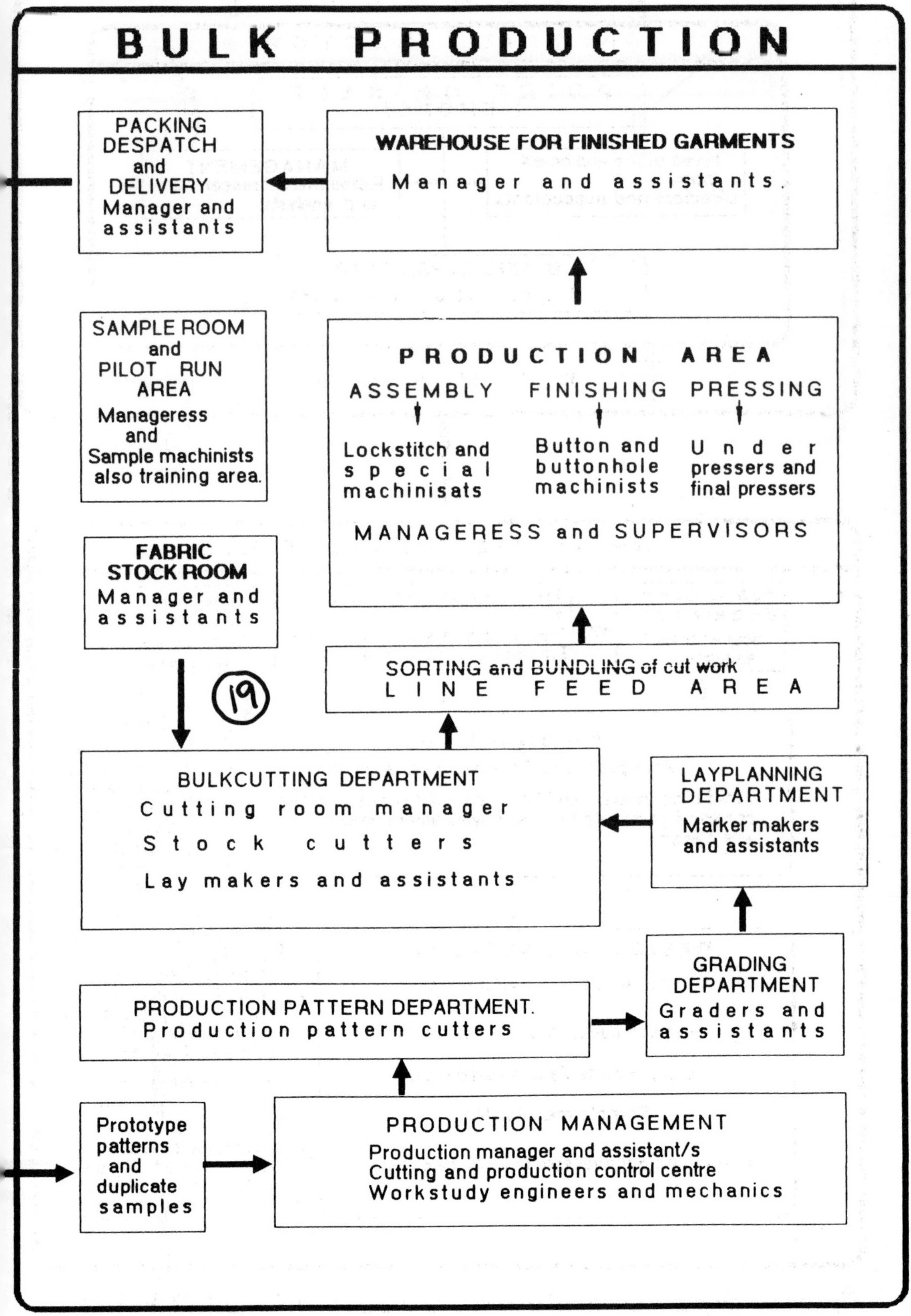

BULK PRODUCTION

PACKING DESPATCH and DELIVERY
Manager and assistants

WAREHOUSE FOR FINISHED GARMENTS
Manager and assistants.

SAMPLE ROOM and PILOT RUN AREA
Manageress and Sample machinists also training area.

PRODUCTION AREA

ASSEMBLY	FINISHING	PRESSING
Lockstitch and special machinisats	Button and buttonhole machinists	Under pressers and final pressers

MANAGERESS and SUPERVISORS

FABRIC STOCK ROOM
Manager and assistants

SORTING and BUNDLING of cut work
LINE FEED AREA

BULKCUTTING DEPARTMENT
Cutting room manager
Stock cutters
Lay makers and assistants

LAYPLANNING DEPARTMENT
Marker makers and assistants

GRADING DEPARTMENT
Graders and assistants

PRODUCTION PATTERN DEPARTMENT.
Production pattern cutters

Prototype patterns and duplicate samples

PRODUCTION MANAGEMENT
Production manager and assistant/s
Cutting and production control centre
Workstudy engineers and mechanics

Figure 2 Department and personnel chart for a corresponding production unit

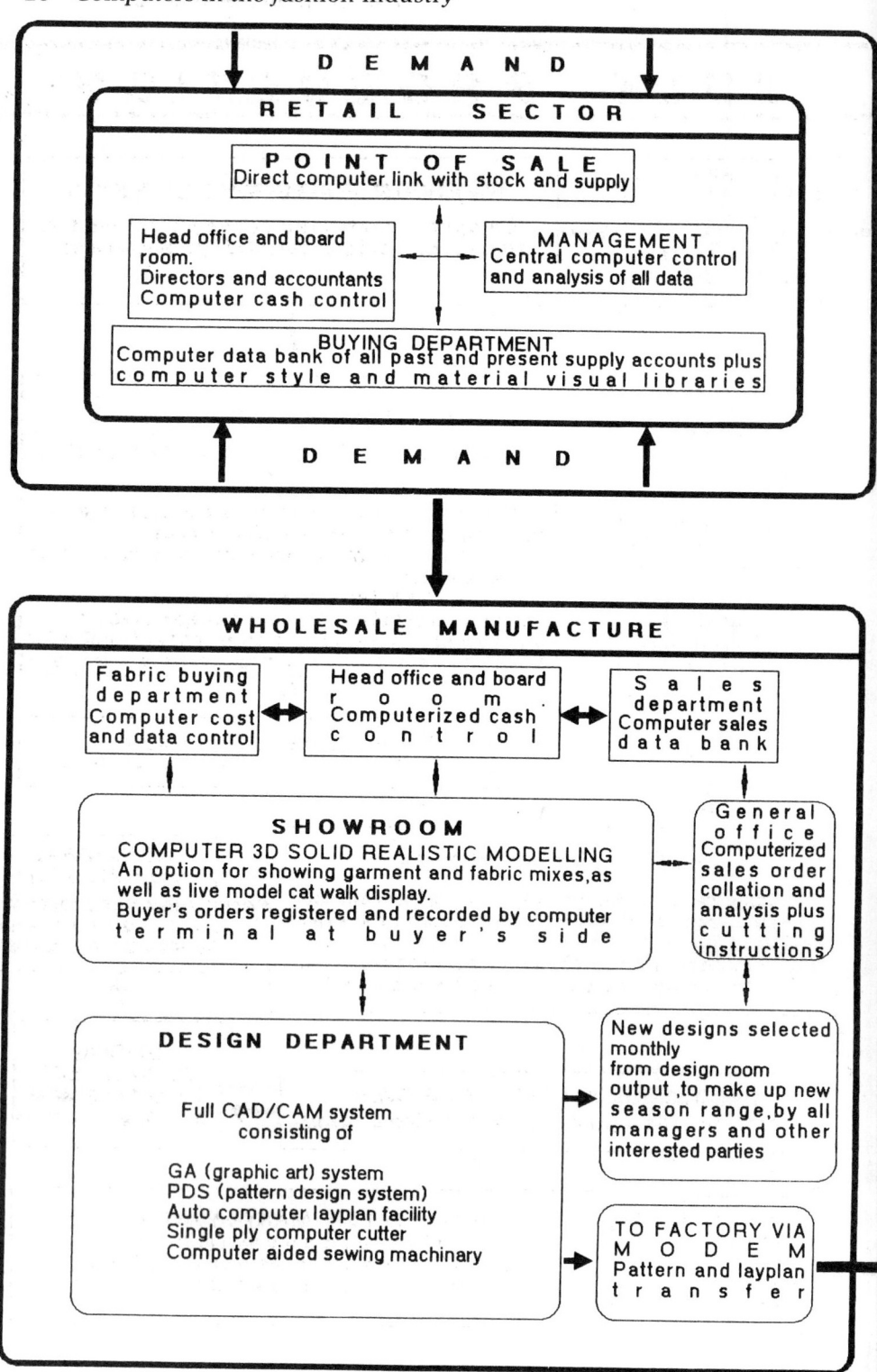

Figure 3 *Computerization of the retail- and fashion-house departments*

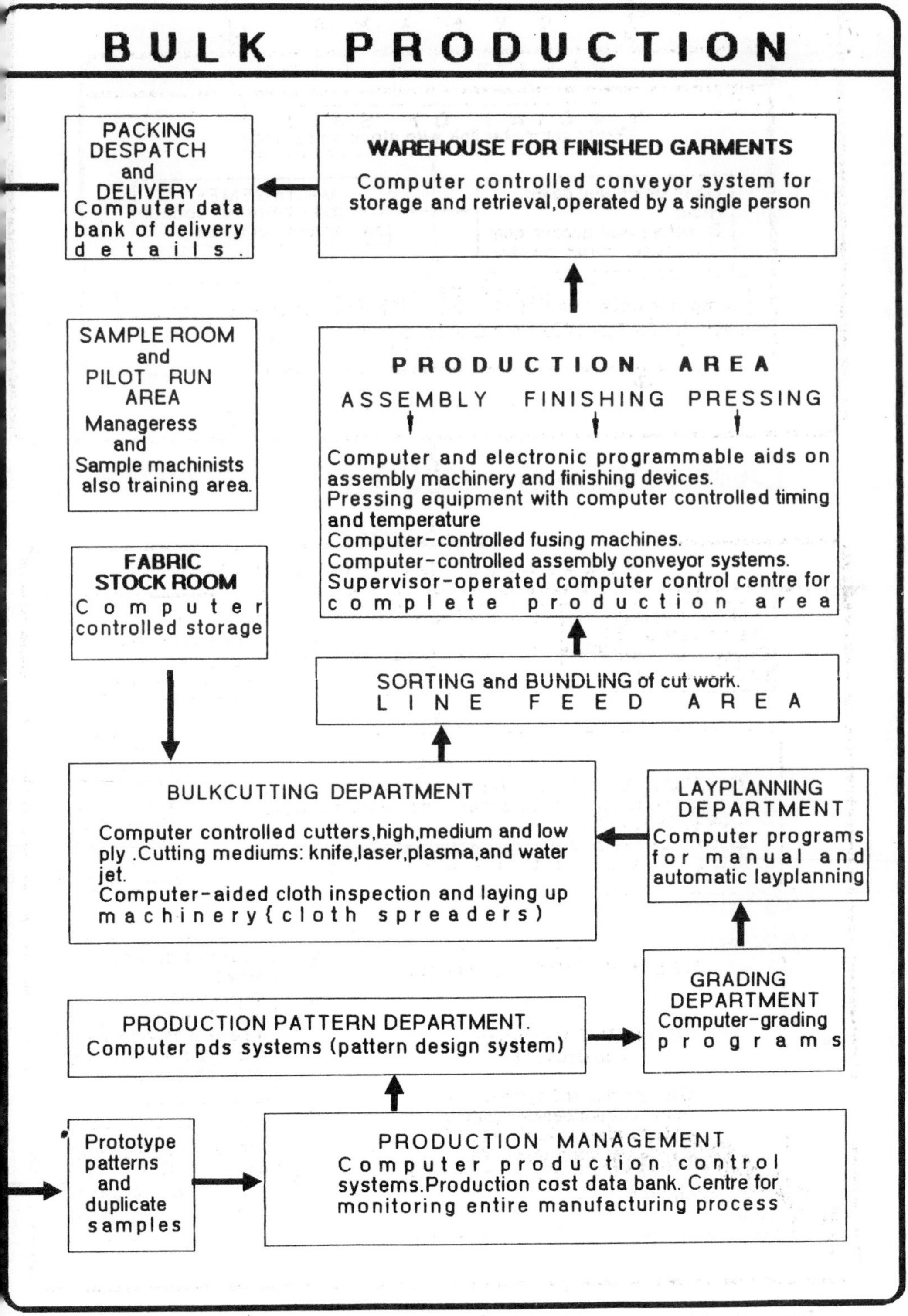

BULK PRODUCTION

PACKING DESPATCH and DELIVERY
Computer data bank of delivery details.

WAREHOUSE FOR FINISHED GARMENTS
Computer controlled conveyor system for storage and retrieval, operated by a single person

SAMPLE ROOM and PILOT RUN AREA
Manageress and Sample machinists also training area.

PRODUCTION AREA
ASSEMBLY   FINISHING   PRESSING

Computer and electronic programmable aids on assembly machinery and finishing devices.
Pressing equipment with computer controlled timing and temperature
Computer-controlled fusing machines.
Computer-controlled assembly conveyor systems.
Supervisor-operated computer control centre for complete production area

FABRIC STOCK ROOM
Computer controlled storage

**SORTING and BUNDLING of cut work.
LINE FEED AREA**

BULKCUTTING DEPARTMENT
Computer controlled cutters, high, medium and low ply. Cutting mediums: knife, laser, plasma, and water jet.
Computer-aided cloth inspection and laying up machinery (cloth spreaders)

LAYPLANNING DEPARTMENT
Computer programs for manual and automatic layplanning

PRODUCTION PATTERN DEPARTMENT.
Computer pds systems (pattern design system)

GRADING DEPARTMENT
Computer-grading programs

Prototype patterns and duplicate samples

PRODUCTION MANAGEMENT
Computer production control systems. Production cost data bank. Centre for monitoring entire manufacturing process

Figure 4   Computerization of the production areas

Chapter 2

Dedicated fashion computer systems

A complete CAD/CAM system would comprise:

1. Graphics package for art design work
2. Imput hardware, digitizer, scanner
3. Interactive hardware workstations
4. PDS software
5. Grading software
6. Layplanning software
7. Output plotters and printers (alpha numeric and thermal colour for illustrations)
8. Single-, medium- and high-ply computer-driven bulk cutters
9. Production and management control software
10. Computerized sewing and pressing equipment
11. Overhead transport system

To equip a factory with a full system, as above, would cost about £350 000 or more.

The first seven items would cost from £60 000 to £100 000, the last three would cost at least £250 000. These are only rough estimates as prices change with time.

All of these areas are dealt with fully in their own chapters.

Origins

The famous American, Howard Hughes, was the first man to initiate a development program involving computer-driven devices relating to two-dimensional applications; this means any drawing or cutting processes carried out on flat surfaces.

This was started at the Hughes Research Company in 1960. In that year, a working laser was publicly demonstrated. Eight years later, in 1968, Hughes, working with Genesco, successfully developed a computer-controlled machine using a laser beam to cut cloth at speeds and accuracies far in excess of conventional means.

It became apparent that this technology would lend itself to the manufacture of clothing. With the help of Autographics, a company with generations of garment-manufacturing experience, Hughes designed a system that would streamline the two difficult processes called 'grading' and 'layplanning'.

This was called the AM1 system, and was the first CAM system available to the manufacturer of clothing. It was driven by a powerful Hewlett Packard mainframe computer.

The AM1 was perfected and sold by Hughes Apparel Systems over the next ten years, up to 1978–9 when they were bought out by a company called Gerber, also American. Gerber specialized in the development of computerized bulk cloth-cutting machines, and had devised a system that they had patents and copyrights on. The Hughes AM1 system, which was CAD/CAM up to layplanning, used Gerbers for bulk cutting. Gerber continued to perfect the AM1, and also produced a streamlined version called the AM5. Both of these were mainframe Hewlett Packard, and as from recently they also offer an IBM-based machine which is cheaper and lends itself to a fuller integration with other devices and software.

Not many of these systems were bought in the ten years from 1968 to 1978, mostly because they were too new and unknown, but also because they were very expensive – being about £100 000 – which even today is a large sum of money.

There were two other companies emerging around this time. They were the Camsco Company in the USA and Lectra Systems, a French company. Lectra began development in 1975 and marketed their first system in 1978. They also specialized in the development of the laser cutter, and marketed a laser with their system that would cut patterns in card and also single-ply cloth or leather.

Both of these companies produced CAM systems (grading and layplanning) and were developing CAD software to be incorporated in the main system (graphics and garment pattern construction software).

Camsco were bought out by Gerber in the early 1980s. The main reason for this was to cut down the opposition and absorb it into one large concern, as at that time the market was not as strong as it is today.

That left two large companies to operate in a not very large market: Gerber and Lectra. After an intensive sales programme by these two companies, the demand began to increase, and in the mid-1980s, it attracted the attention of other computer manufacturers who began to muscle in on what looked like being a fast-developing market. A Spanish company called Investronica made a strong entry into the arena. They produced a mainframe system that equalled the others in quality and price, but the casual observer could be forgiven for thinking it was a copy of the Hughes/Gerber system. It is a fact that Investronica make all their own hardwear and have written all their own software programs, and to say that someone copied someone else is irrelevant since there are no other basic options in design to the ones that were originally laid down by the Hughes company in the 1960s. Lectra systems also look the same in concept as the original Hughes system. The differences can only really be in the design interpretation of the details.

The main bone of contention for Gerber was the general adoption by all the companies of the basic design of their bulk-cutting concepts, of which they had copyrights. They contested this in the courts but ran a losing battle, and now all the competition uses similar solutions to the basic problems of bulk cutting.

Other manufacturers to appear, most of which are still around, are:

Microdinamics	USA	Macpi	ITALY
CDI	USA	Cybrib	UK
Seco	SWITZERLAND	Datamonster	SWEDEN
Cuttex	W. GERMANY	Concept 11 (Ormus)	UK
Bullmerwerk	W. GERMANY	Moda cad (Macintosh)	USA
Eurolog	W. GERMANY	Polygon	USA
Texograph	W. GERMANY	Shima Seiki	JAPAN
Assyst	W. GERMANY		

It is doubtful whether the demand is large enough to support all of these new computer manufacturers. Only the best will survive. Gerber, Lectra and Investronica seem the most likely candidates to be around in another ten years, but of course no one can foresee the future fortunes that lay in wait for the computer manufacturers of today.

Factors in system selection

When a clothing manufacturer is faced with choosing a system, the most important factors are:

1. Advanced and tested technology.
2. System reliability.
3. A good maintenance and software update facility, plus a reasonable guarantee that the supplier will be in business for at least as long as the projected period for system renewal.
4. The chosen system must be easy to use and be simple to learn.

These systems contain a very wide range of programs, and are complex because of this fact. Each of the software programs has to be understood and mastered, and then the means of linking them to enable interaction between the functions. This also is a complex process to understand; inevitably, it takes time to gain control of the whole system. The manufacturers will tell the buyer that their system is easy to master and, when asked, the instructors will say the same. The instructors at least will mean it. Having worked the system for months on a daily basis, they know it so well that it comes very easily to them. However, they have long forgotten how much they had to struggle to get to where they are at present when they tell clients it is simple. The author, being a teacher, is very familiar with this situation. Everyone forgets the learning process and the inevitable time and struggle it takes to grasp things, and how easy it is to say 'it is easy'! Some of the newer companies can afford to admit that systems have not been easy to use, since the bosses of these new companies have usually worked for the larger companies and have decided to strike out on their own. They start from scratch with all the experience of hindsight and a clean slate, enabling them to produce a more streamlined system with the latest innovations in technology. This has produced systems that are designed to be more 'operator friendly'. In contrast, the older software has been cluttered up with continuous requests by companies for additional bits and pieces; this has resulted in a mountain of options that the novice has difficulty in finding their way around in, and distinguishing what is important and what isn't.

In the late 1980s the market opened up considerably, and clothing manufacturers began to get cold feet at the prospect of not being computerized and being left behind by their competitors. They were feeling compelled to jump on the computer roundabout, probably not realizing that once on it they could never get off again.

Most of the original systems were and are mainframe, but are now nearly all offering cheaper options of IBM-type architecture running on 32 bit processors of the intel 80286 and 80386 family. The aim of this new move towards IBM hardware is to facilitate a degree of integration between the various software programs that cover most of the areas of designing, manufacturing and management in the clothing industry.

The main difficulty at the present time is that there is no standardization in either hardware or software. Pieces of one system cannot be interfaced with parts of another. This may be done on purpose, which only gives a doubtful advantage to the computer manufacturer and places the buyer at a distinct disadvantage.

The other area that would benefit from a degree of standardization is in menu design. All menus are constructed differently, and each item on a menu has to be understood in order to make it work correctly. Consequently, when moving from one system to another the whole process of learning each item must be gone through and the menu structure understood and memorized. This is sometimes made more difficult because of bad translations from the original language.

Menus, particularly PDS systems (pattern-design systems), are very big and confusing, with sub menus and sub sub menus. It can take weeks before the program is reasonably mastered and some areas are never understood, as they are not needed very often, if at all, and the operators find their own way of getting round problems sometimes by some other long-winded route.

There is definitely a strong move to standardize some areas, so that a reasonable degree of CIM (computer integrated manufacture) can be realized, but for other areas it is probably just a dream.

The other problem that is beginning to loom up is the availability of trained staff. There is bound to be a period at the beginning when the availability of experienced computer operators is at a premium. This will cause some difficulties for employers and good opportunities for a few enterprising clothing technologists.

Training courses for clothing CAD/CAM systems are included in the purchase price of the system, and are run by the computer manufacturer. These vary in length from one to two weeks' full-time tuition and are supported by a telephone help service. It is generally accepted that the learning period is approximately ten times the length of the training time. Thus, to become fully competent, two weeks times ten equals twenty weeks of continuous operation; this should produce a minimum qualification period. This figure describes a systems manager requirement. Specialized operators, such as a layplanner or a grader, would require less time, and a pattern cutter and designer would need longer than the previous two jobs, depending on the individual concerned.

So far, there are no courses offered in colleges devoted to dedicated CAD/CAM systems. The main reason for this is that the college hierarchy has not fully understood the implications of the situation, having itself not had intensive experience of computer operation. College officials are therefore not in a position to make realistic assessments of the needs of students for the future. That is not to say that there are no CAD/CAM systems in colleges; there are some, but they are mostly window dressing and stand gathering dust. This is because the staff are not properly trained, and have no opportunity to operate a system on a day-to-day basis. Because of the complexity of these systems, there needs to be continuous use in order not to forget the essentials – which happens very quickly.

The fact is that these systems do not lend themselves to teaching large classes of students, because they usually only have two or three workstations. Therefore the teaching tends to be very time intensive and individual for a hands on experience, or only a demonstration for student appreciation.

There is, at the time of writing, a demand for training on these systems, by individuals (pattern cutters, graders, designers) who are already in industry and who wish to equip themselves with the necessary expertise in order to qualify for the new type of positions that are becoming available. Computer companies themselves only train employees of the purchaser.

It is therefore necessary that colleges world-wide, who have these systems, offer short concentrated courses on the various programs that are relevant to the demands current in their areas and ensure that their teaching staff are sufficiently experienced and fluent in all areas and on all systems. This will entail setting up specialist departments with all the current hardware and staffed by lecturers whose only task is to teach this subject on a day-to-day basis.

Teaching pattern cutting, grading and layplanning on computers is a different subject entirely, and needs a system of networked workstations where up to twenty students can sit down with their own machine and be taught with its aid and to have access to semi-animated demonstration programs to learn from in their own time. To date, this type of teaching software has not been made, probably because of the limited demand for it; but the demand could be quite extensive if it were extended to schools, where at the present only sewing and needlework is taught.

When a company converts to computers they take a big step into the unknown. It constitutes a major upheaval. There is a large financial outlay, and a period of chaos when everything needs to happen at once.

Staff must be trained and all data, patterns, designs, layplans, production schedules, sales delivery dates, etc. must be integrated in the system in an orderly way, so that it can be easily manipulated and managed.

This requires the training or the employment of a systems manager. The smooth and easy running of the system will depend on how the manager sets the system up in the first place and will determine whether the system can be easily taken over by another manager in the future.

At the same time, the designer, pattern cutters, graders and layplanners have to learn how to work efficiently on the system. The transfer to computers is usually done in stages, but it still is a difficult thing to do. To go the whole way and introduce bulk cutting and overhead transport is even more difficult, and requires very special planning and preparation.

It will be necessary to run dual processes in some areas, to retain the original manual operation with its equipment and floor space, while at the same time introducing the computerized equivalent. This gives time to test the equipment and train staff to use the computers.

This would be necessary, for example, in layplanning and bulk cutting. It would ensure the continuous running of the factory in the changeover period, but, of course, would entail extra financial expenditure. It would also provide an opportunity to compare the two processes in action, and assess the existing staff regarding their adaptability and aptitude in the new field of computers. Computers put new and different pressures on employees; some cannot cope with the new technology, particularly older people. Having to remember large amounts of command coding, and sometimes complex procedures, is often beyond the scope of many older – and sometimes young – employees. They have to continue to function efficiently at their job and at the same time learn a complex new field of activity. The tools that they are so used to – their moving functions, hands and legs – are suddenly almost redundant, and they are faced with the task of learning to use a very alien and difficult piece of electronics. They mostly will be required to sit and use a few fingers and stare at a video screen for long periods, which in itself can cause severe strain on the eyes and produce aches in the head and various other parts of the body.

Many things can and do go wrong when learning a new and complex system. Things that should take a few minutes can take hours, as a result of continuous mistakes and the resultant strain and tiredness. The boss will get nervous and bad tempered and begin to wonder if he or she has made a big mistake. Having listened to the computer salesman's reassuring smooth talk for weeks, you can be lulled into a false sense of security for the future smooth running of everything. Added to this is the new menace of system breakdown – just when all the eggs have finally been placed in one basket (the computer) and total reliance invested in it. The complete business is entrusted to a machine that keeps everything on a disk. This machine must be super reliable and the disks must be backed up (copied) and put in a safe place at the end of each day, away from thieves and fire. All the patterns, markers and working data will be committed to disk, and sometimes only one person knows exactly how to extract and manipulate the information efficiently. Bosses, who are not usually computer literate, will have to place great trust in certain employees.

These systems are not an absolute necessity for all companies, particularly the smaller ones. A manufacturer who runs a small unit may be able to profit by computerizing a section of their operation, or using a computer service facility, of which a few are appearing. These computer centres, in the past, have not been a big success, but one or two have survived and made a reasonable profit. It has depended on where they were situated and what type of clothing manufacture was at hand.

It would be unwise for all manufacturers to feel that they must join the rush to computerize their operation. However there are cheaper systems available – that is, around £25 000 or $75 000, if that can be called cheap. A small company would find that amount a heavy expenditure, and may live to regret it if they have not calculated exactly what they require and searched the market for the precise equipment at the best price with a not-too-crippling maintenance contract. Until a company gets a system under its roof and begins to play with it, it does not know precisely the system's capabilities, or indeed their own. They cannot totally rely on advice from the computer people, as it will, by definition, be slanted. When the truth is known it may be too late, and a lot of time and money will have passed under the bridge.

There is a definite resistance in some areas to the introduction of computers, mainly because it will erode the manual skills and sensitivity of the designer and artist; also, it takes away the fulfilling skills of using pencil on paper and cutting with shears and straight knife, which provides the direct feedback that manual work has. The computers' advantages are great, as will be obvious from reading the other chapters, but there are some very sad losses in the sphere of human activity.

Dedicated fashion computer systems 31

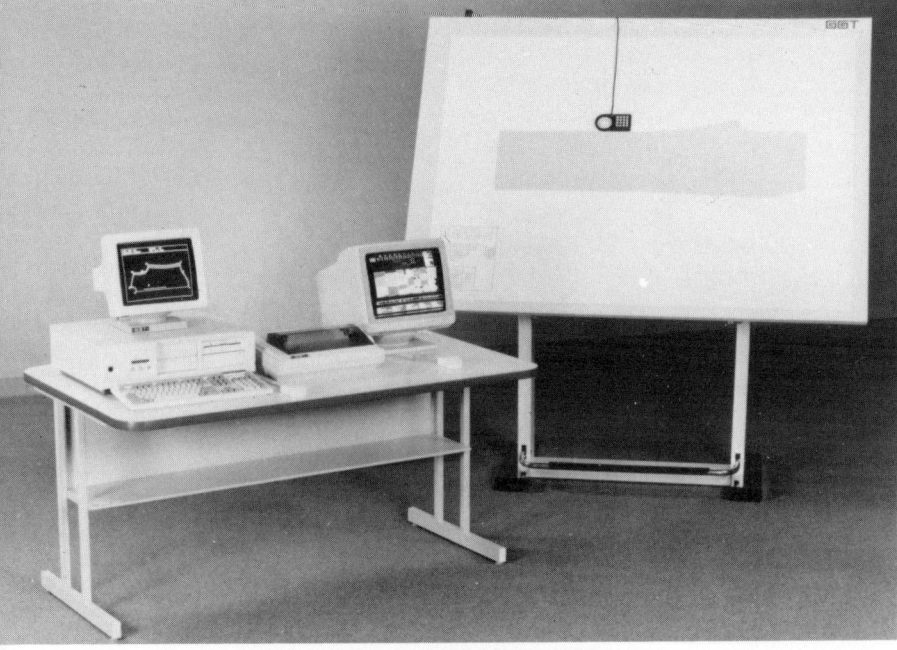

AccuMark 300 is an automated design, grading and marking system.
Menu-driven, this GGT system is modular and includes specialized software for
pattern digitizing, pattern design, automatic pattern grading, interactive marker
making and full-scale pattern and marker making
  (Courtesy Gerber Garment Technology, Inc.)

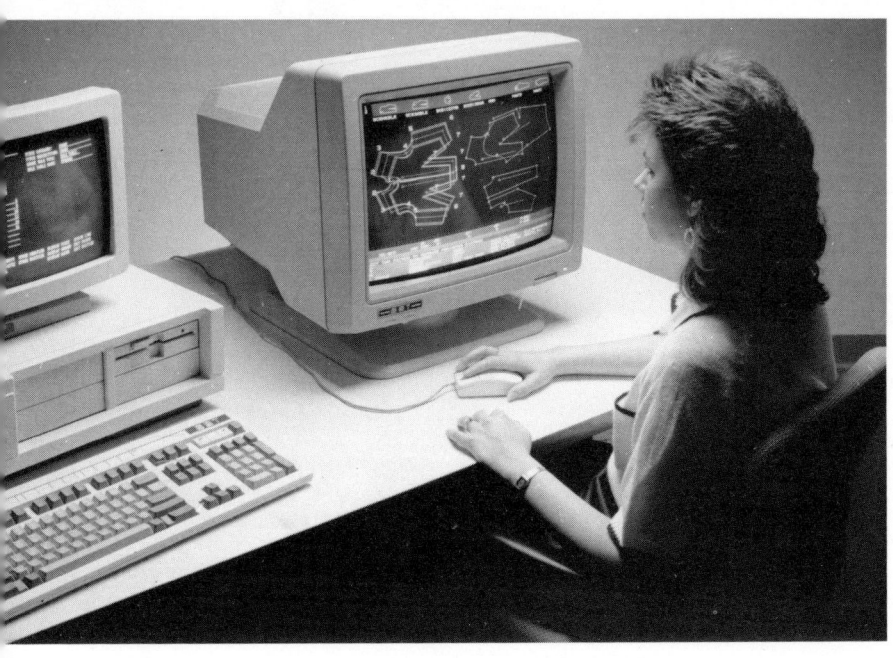

AccuMark PDS (standard with AccuMark 300 systems) computer-aided pattern
design system
  (Courtesy Gerber Garment Technology, Inc.)

32 Computers in the fashion industry

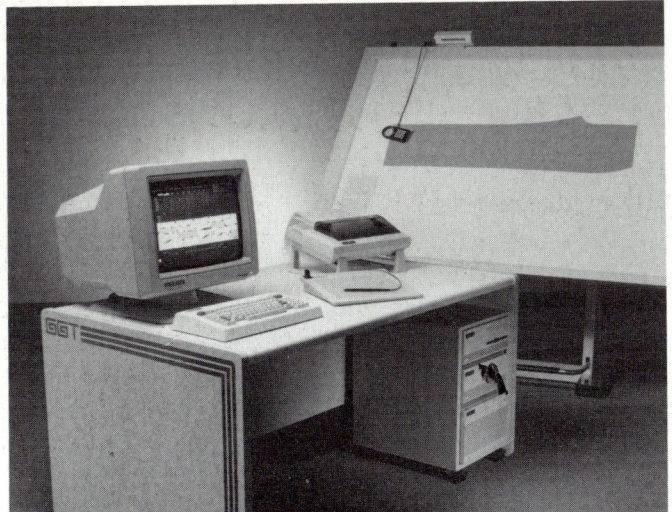

AM-5 Series 3200 grading and marking system available from GGT. It blends a powerful computer with multi-tasking, multi-user functionality to increase throughput and quality
(Courtesy Gerber Garment Technology, Inc.)

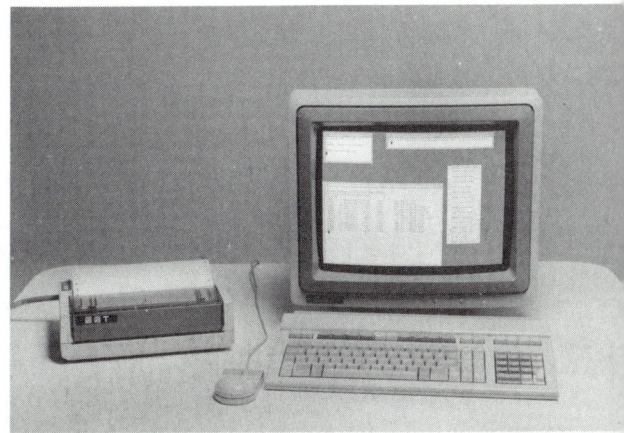

AccuMark 700 File Server provides high-speed networking and data storage to the GGT family of comuterized systems, as well as third-party systems
(Courtesy Gerber Garment Technology, Inc.)

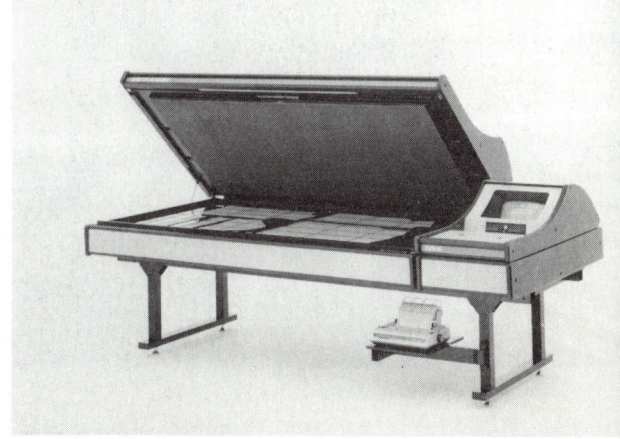

The Cybrid Linx low-cost integrated system including GA and PDS systems
(Courtesy Cybrid Ltd)

Dedicated fashion computer systems 33

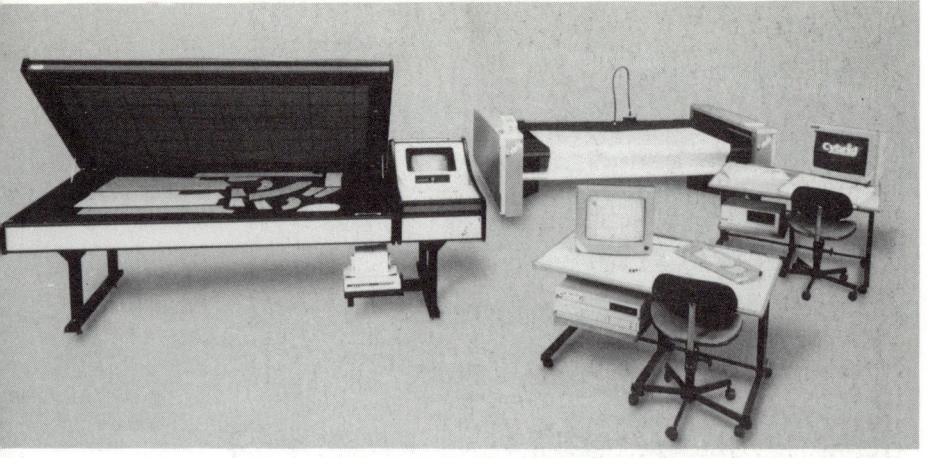

Full Cybrid low-cost CAD system
(Courtesy Cybrid Ltd)

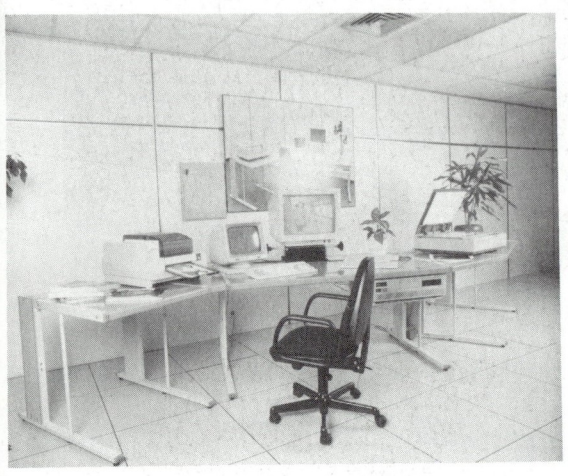

Complete design and sketch system
(Courtesy Investronica UK)

34 Computers in the fashion industry

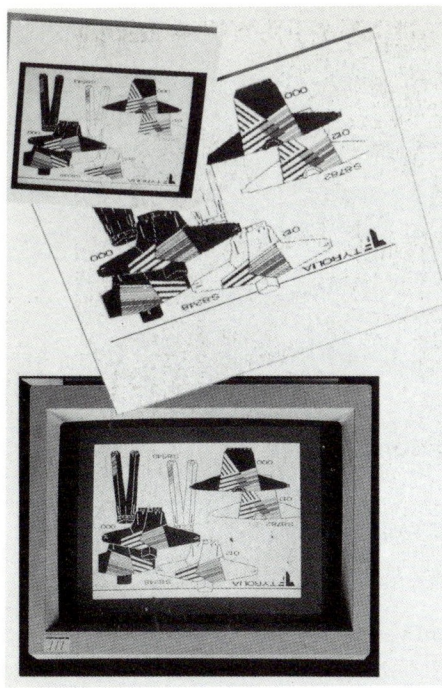

*GA artwork with CAD
(Courtesy CIM
Microdynamics Ltd)*

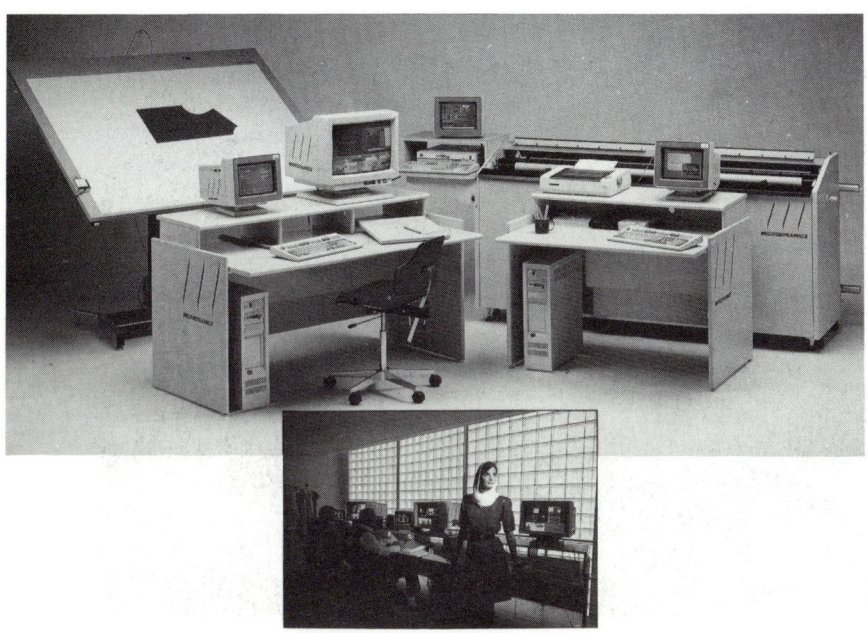

*Full CAD system
(Courtesy CIM Microdynamics Ltd)*

Dedicated fashion computer systems 35

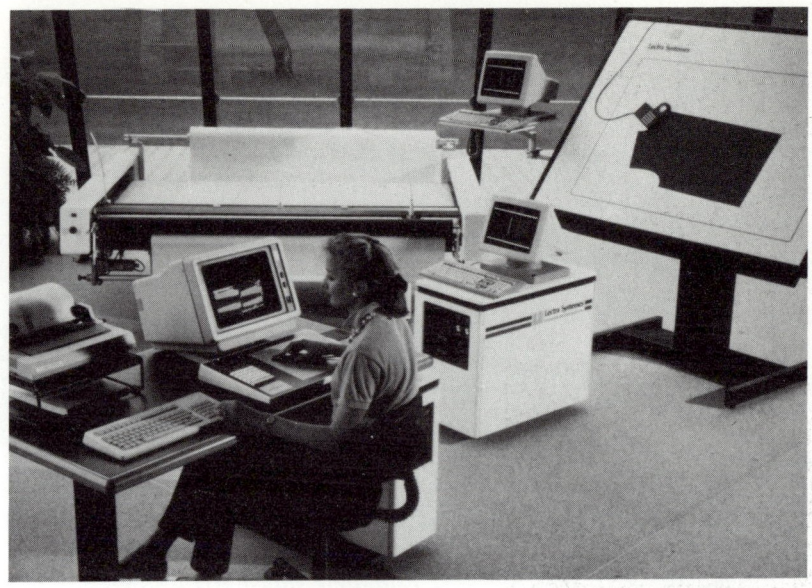

*Full CAD system
(Courtesy Lectra Systems)*

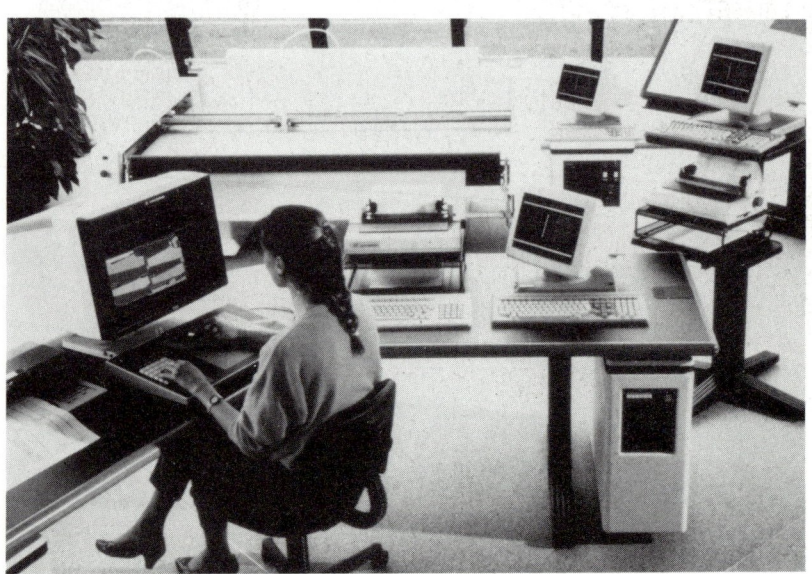

*Full CAD system
(Courtesy Lectra Systems)*

36 Computers in the fashion industry

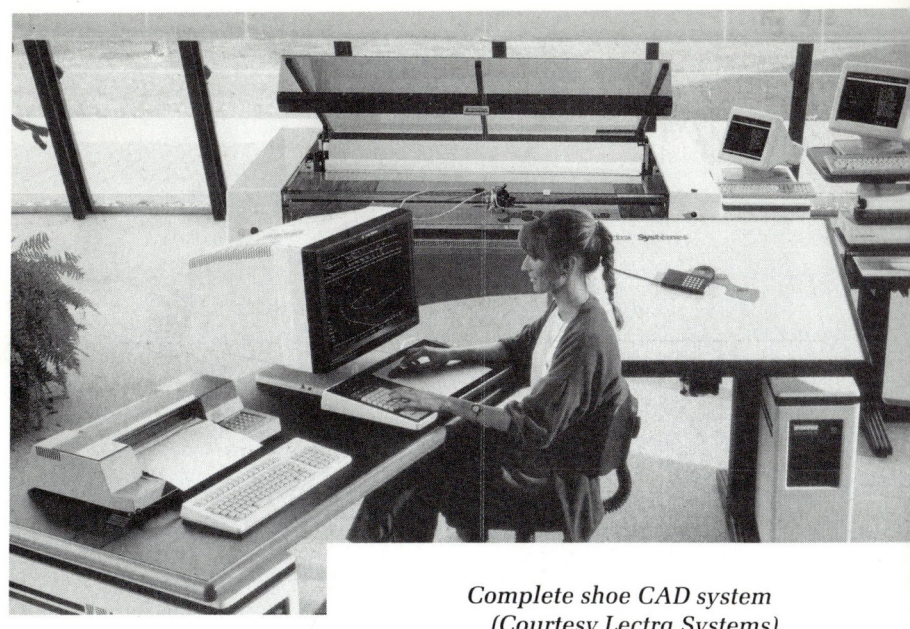

*Complete shoe CAD system
(Courtesy Lectra Systems)*

Chapter 3

Computer basics

This chapter is definitely not for the computer hack or any kind of computer expert. It is strictly for the potential operator of a system who, like the car driver, wishes to get from one place to the next and is not too concerned about what goes on under the bonnet.

Having said that, it is of course an advantage to understand the basics and be familiar with some of the jargon. This chapter aims to outline a few basic principles and translate the commonly used words. This will probably be more useful to the older generations rather than younger readers, most of whom will have some computer knowledge from their schooling.

Before starting, there are two cornerstone words that need explanation. These are 'hardware' and 'software'.

Hardware are all the bits that are touchable and have weight and substance. Software are all the programs that operate the hardware, and are kept on some form of memory device such as a disk or tape.

In the human being, the body and the brain are the bits of hardware, and the education and learning that have been placed in memory are the software. So the two are inseparable. If something is wrong with the software, then the hardware will behave illogically or unpredictably.

Compared to the human being, the computer hardware and the programming that is possible at the present time are just toys and are, by comparison, crude to say the least.

As with the human being, the computer consists of three parts:
1   Input
2   Storage and interaction

3   Output

In the human, the input consists of

1   Light into the eyes
2   Sound into the ears
3   Smell into the nose
4   Taste into the tongue
5   Pressure and temperature and sensation into the body
6   Air into the lungs
7   Food into the mouth
8   Life force to drive the other factors

Once these substances have entered through the input devices into the body and brain, they are stored and then manipulated in various ways, interacting with each other according to chemical and electrical processes and controlled by a program or education. The results of this interaction cannot remain inside, so they need forms of output.

In the human, the output mechanisms are:

1   The voice
2   Movement of the body
3   Carbon dioxide and other gases
4   Excretion

Points 1 and 2 have vast variations, and constitute all human behaviour. The mechanical movements of the body, facial expression and the programs that drive them are amazing in their ingenuity and complexity, and the human characteristic of speech and song make the range of expression quite vast. All of this manifestation takes place in an atmosphere of feeling and emotion which colours it at all times.

This is all created and maintained by a life force that is beyond understanding, unlike the computer which is what could be called 'dead'. The computer has no self-awareness or feeling; it cannot initiate anything, but only respond according to the input and devices for output that are built into it by human beings. Its only food is electricity.

What impresses us about the computer – and for some, what makes it appear to have a will of its own and capable of remarkable feats – is firstly the amazing 'word and number' crunching ability with a stable memory of vast capacity. This, plus an ability to calculate and manipulate huge figures that would take a team of humans a lifetime to resolve. It can also be programmed with complex maths and geometric formulae which it can then go on and elaborate on its own. This gives an awesome impression of power, but all the results that it produces are mechanically arrived at by following lawful logic paths which cannot be broken without making nonsense of the process. It does this with such speed that once-distant aims can be made to be almost immediately attainable.

Man's software or programming, which we call our education and learning and which is elaborated by usage or experience, is infinitely more complex. If a list is made of all the different types of learning and subject-matter that is input into the average person in their lifetime, and then added to that the fact that all of this is more or less interactive or integratable with its self, then a picture of mind-blowing ingenuity and complexity emerges.

Computer input and output devices

These can be grouped into three main areas:

1. Physical energy (movement)
2. Sound energy
3. Light energy

Input

The most common form of input is through the keyboard, which is an 'alpha numeric' (numbers and letters) configuration. This relies on physical energy to depress the keys, each of which has its own code which will energize a pattern of light dots on a cathode ray tube (VDU, video display unit) corresponding to the letter or number. So in this case the input required physical energy and the output was in the form of light on a monitor. Another input method is using an electronic pen to allow freehand drawing and painting. Alternatively, a 'mouse' can be used instead of a pen, which is a hand-held selector that uses a rolling ball and two buttons to draw or choose items with a pointer on the screen. Similar to this is the 'digitizer', which is used for outlining any two- or three-dimensional shapes and putting them into the computer memory. (These are described in greater detail in later chapters.)

These all depend on physical movement to allow input to occur. The use of robotic devices sometimes requires the copying of complex human movements by manually using the robot arm to do the job, while recording the movements in the computer memory so that they can be played back – thus reproducing the movement exactly. This is done for spraying paint and welding metal, and other similar processes.

Used with robots are touch-sensitive devices that help the robot to orientate itself in relation to another object. They input the robot's position in the field of activity.

All of these rely on movement to input data for processing and then for output.

The next form of input uses light. These are in the form of scanners. There are two-dimensional and three-dimensional types, one for the flat patterns used in all kinds of manufacture and the other for recording solid objects for various reasons. There is also a photographic scanner for copying coloured photos and drawings into the computer for manipulation.

Lasers are also used in light-sensitive receivers to guide forms of mobile robots; in other words, a crude form of seeing.

The last medium is sound, which is used to input and record voice and speech where oral commands are used in controlling processes. Also, sound is used for various musical applications, which are known as 'midi' functions.

These cover the main areas of input, but there are others where research is being carried out and will gradually make their influence felt in the computer technology of the future.

So far, smell and taste have not been experimented with, probably because of the complexity of recording chemical reactions and the lack of real application for these functions. However, one can never predict what the future will hold.

Output
The output devices linked to physical movement are various. The main one is the printer, which copes with all alpha/numeric requirements. These are of two main types. The first is 'dot matrix' (9 and 24 dot configurations), where the letters and numbers are made up of tiny dots. The second type is the 'daisy wheel', which has a rapidly rotating wheel of letters and numbers, that produces a high-quality definition.

There is a third category called 'laser printing', which is very flexible and produces a high-quality output; it uses light as the medium, but is more expensive than the other two.

For colour output there are two types. The first is the 'ink jet' printer, which uses five basic colours, including black, and squirts it on to the paper through tiny holes. This is a fairly crude form, and is used mainly for graphs and similar diagrams where basic definition is required in colour. But it is being developed to produce finer definition and may become a medium for accurate illustrations.

The other colour printer is called a 'thermal printer'. This endeavours to copy the exact colour, as in a photograph. This technology is still being perfected and the output is steadily improving.

The other form of line output is the 'plotter'. This usually uses a ballpoint pen to draw out any plan or draft, either in full size or to any desired scale. These are either 'flat bed' or 'drum plotters'. One is flat like a table and the other stands upright (thus taking up less space), but they both do the same thing.

The same type of configuration can be used for all kinds of cutting; instead of a pen, a cutting device of some kind is used. The cutters can be reciprocating blades, laser beams, water jets, circular knives, and gas or electric arc cutters for metal work.

All kinds of robotic configurations are used to output movement for various tasks.

The main and obvious output is using light, which is in the form of the cathode ray tube or the video screen; this does not need any explanation.

Sound is used in various ways, which again are fairly obvious: speech synthesizers and midi addons, plus various warning and indicator sounds which come out of most computers.

All of these input and output devices are very crude and limited in comparison with animal functions, in particular the human animal with its highly developed logic ability. Leaving aside the emotional aspects, it will be impossible to imitate, in a convincing way, all the characteristics of animal and human behaviour. No doubt someone will endeavour to produce some kind of replica for amusement that will mimic bad temper or happiness, like grumbling while doing the washing, or any of the facets that have been dreamed of on the television in programmes such as *Lost in Space*, etc.

Memory

The faculty of memory is the foundation on which all processes rely. This does not only apply to computers, but is also a fundamental part of the human machine. The computer is a crude copy of a very small part of the human organization.

Nothing could be carried out or accomplished without a means of fixing or capturing part of the 'now', and storing it by some means for reference and comparison with already stored words, numbers, pictures, sounds, smells, tastes, sensations, movements, and any other that can be thought of. These stored data and experience are an inseparable and indispensable part of the interactions that take place in the 'now'.

The human being has many types of memory, such as those mentioned above, and all of those categories of memory are connected and overlay each other by association. For example, when in the kitchen while food is being prepared, there are different impressions coming in through the various senses and being stored, as it were, on one tape. There may have been an argument while preparing the food and a cup of boiling gravy spilt, burning someone's hand. This would mean that there were feelings of pain and emotions of anger superimposed on the other sense inputs, so that all the various impressions are memorized superimposed on each other; when one thing is brought to the attention, other things come also – even if they are not required – as if they were all stuck together. This little kitchen episode can be lived through again in part by trying to re-run it on the inner display facility that exists in the human brain. It will not be an exact reproduction, as the human memory is affected by erosion of time and overlays of other memories. This kind of memory is not reliable as far as detail is concerned – perhaps all that is remembered is the anger associated with the smell of cooked chicken, plus the expression on the face of the other person in the argument. Another form of human memory that is more reliable, unlike the above, is the storage of body movements and their coordination. Once the process of riding a bike, for example, has been resolved and stored, then it is never forgotten or distorted. It is the same with walking or running; it would be inconvenient to have to learn to walk each day, and this also applies to talking. These processes take a lot of effort initially to refine the timing and relationship of the various movements, but once perfected they are never forgotten, and are continually reinforced and elaborated from day to day.

Another form of memory is pure data storage in the form of words, or names and numbers. In the human being this faculty varies in reliability from person to person; some have good storage and recall and others have a poor ability. The erosion by time also varies, usually the older the person the shorter the memory recall, perhaps because the memory is not so deeply imprinted in the older person. This, in computer jargon, is called alpha-numeric data – in plain English: letters and numbers.

All this has been mentioned so that there is some orientation regarding memory and makes it possible to proceed with a bit more clarity. It will help in understanding the interaction between the person and the computer and to distinguish the various computer memory functions and their application.

Before anything can be stored, an input device is necessary. In the human there are several, known as the senses: sight, hearing, smell, taste, and a facility for measuring and assessing, through touch, pressure, texture and temperature. All of these have a negative and a positive side; that is, they blend from the painful through neutral to pleasurable.

All of these devices respond to the energy that they are designed to receive, and the response is frozen or impressed on a substance that is sensitive to this energy and which will not quickly degrade or change its nature. In this way, a trace of the past can be stored and re-run, interacting with the energy of the present and producing phenomena.

In the brain they are retained on living matter that has limited stability, outside the brain they are inscribed on stone, wood and paper, which have varying resistance to time. In the computer they are inscribed on a magnetically sensitive surface using electro/magnetic impulses. These impressions will last indefinitely without change, unless unwanted magnetic fields come within the range of the sensitivity of the substance.

The computer has two main types of memory. The first is called RAM, short for 'random access memory'. This memory uses silicon chips as a means of storage. This is a small rectangular piece of silicon with intricate circuitry, many of which reside inside the computer as a permanent part of the machine. The more RAM chips there are, the more powerful the computer is assumed to be. The reason for this is that it can remember more things at one time and is therefore more useful. The drawback with this kind of memory is that it only functions as long as the computer is switched on; when the current is off then the chip empties and is ready to be used afresh. There is another type of chip called a ROM, short for 'read only memory'. These chips do not lose their contents when the current is switched off. These usually contain a piece of software or program, which will be described later.

There are two other forms of storage used with computers; they are tapes and disks. These are used for permanent storage, which means that once they are imprinted they retain the impression indefinitely. The disk has an advantage over the tape in that the storage on a tape is sequential, which requires that the tape is run through until the data that is needed appears. In contrast, the disk data is picked out by a selector head in what is called 'real time' or 'now' without having to plough through unwanted material; it thus saves a great deal of time.

There are two types of disk: floppy and hard.

'Floppies' are small in size and small in capacity. They are called floppy because the early ones were 5.5 inches and floppy or bendy. More recently, a smaller (3.5 inches) but stiffer disk is being used. The capacity of these disks is either a half or one kilo/byte. There is work being done on high-capacity floppies, of up to 10 mega/bytes, but they are not available at the time of writing.

The 'hard' disk is a larger disk, and has a much greater memory or storage capacity. It is usually incorporated inside the computer, and is an integral part of the system. It will have a memory of up to 60 mega/bytes or even more. This is the main storage system for permanent computer memory.

Floppy disks are inserted into the disk/drive of the computer. This is a device designed to spin and read the disk, and then put its contents on to RAM chips ready for manipulation.

There is some memory jargon that ought to be explained:

BIT   BYTE   KILO/BYTE   MEGA/BYTE

A 'bit' is the smallest unit of memory that a computer operates with. It is an 'on' or an 'off', a one or a two, a plus or minus. The computer at its heart consists of thousands of switches. These switches are either on or off and the sequence of these on/offs are the memory patterns that represent data. The on/offs are recorded in a mathematical language called 'binary', which only counts up to 2 and then starts again — as opposed to counting in tens and starting again.

This fits in well with the on/off switch. A bit is therefore a computer letter which carries a piece of information. The word 'bit' is a shortening of 'binary digit'. If the decimal system were to be used, then ten different electrical current strengths would be required to operate the computer. This would make life very complex and would make computers less reliable because the control of those ten current values would be critical, and any minute variation could sabotage everything.

A 'byte' is a computer word, or a chunk of information made up of 4 bits, two of which give 8 bits or 2 bytes, and so on up to a 64 bit chunk. And so a computer can be an 8 bit computer or a 16 bit computer, etc.

The computer will only operate with the size of byte that it is designed for. The smaller the number of the bits processed in one piece, the less power the computer has, since the amount of data that can be conveyed will depend on the number of bits. It is like having a piano with only 4 notes; the number of tunes is limited in relation to a piano with 8, 16 or 32 notes. But the complexity and cost of the computer increases rapidly in relation to the need for high-numbered bytes. The CPU (processor) is designed to handle a certain number of bits at a time, 8, 16, 32, or 64, and it sends them down a road, wide enough to take either 8, 16, 32, or 64 width bytes; this road is called a 'bus'. A computer is sometimes designed with a 32 bit processor and a 16 bit bus, so that it must send the information down the bus in two goes. This is done for the sake of keeping costs down. This would be called a 32/16 bit machine. The measure, then, of the power of a computer is determined first by the amount of

RAM it has, and secondly by the size of the bus and processor byte handling capability.

A 'kilo/byte' is 1000 bytes and is called 'K' for short, so 64 K is 64 000 bytes. A 'mega/byte' is 1000 kilo/bytes. So a powerful computer would be described as 'a 32 or 64 bit computer with one to four mega/bytes of RAM and a 60 mega/byte hard disk'. There are other forms of memory that have been designed for computer use. They are expensive and are not in general use.

Software

Given all the input and output facilities, how are they made to operate in a useful way? What controls these functions? Basically, they are run by a set of instructions written in a computer language.

The root language of the computer is 'machine code'. This is based on the binary system, 'bits and bytes', but writing instructions or 'software' at this level is long and laborious, and the implementing of the commands through the keyboard is done in non-associative alpha/numeric code. This code is difficult to remember for the average user, although it is the fastest because it goes direct to the processor without having to be interpreted into a high-level language.

The set of instructions (program or software) is usually put on to a disk for storage. This can be a hard disk or a floppy. When required for use, the floppy disk is put into the disk drive of the computer or the hard disk is accessed and the computer transfers the instructions into the RAM chips (computer temporary memory) ready for the CPU (central processing unit) to read the instructions and use them to carry out the commands.

The CPU is the heart of the computer, as it processes all the commands and generally coordinates the inner workings of the whole system; it may have a sister or brother processor that is designed to carry out specific functions, such as looking after all the sound effects. This will take the pressure off the main processor, and enable it to function faster and more efficiently. The CPU will be designed as an 8, 16, 32, or 64 bit processor, and will run at a designed speed, which is measured in megahertz. The faster it runs the better, as it will get through its work quicker. A 64 bit CPU running at 24 MHz is a very powerful chip, and will require a large and complex package of hardware to back it up. This will be expensive, and thus such machines are only used where specialized functions are required – such as flight simulators, for training pilots, as simulating a flying process requires a powerful computer. These computers are usually mainframe or mini computers, which are the most powerful type of machine available.

For the more mundane and common applications, a cheaper and less powerful computer will suffice. These are usually called PCs – or personal computers. This title was first used by IBM, the largest computer manufacturer in the world, but has been since used by all the other computer manufacturers, who make what is known as 'IBM clones'. These are machines that are basically the same as the IBMs, as they run on the same CPU and have the same internal architecture, and therefore can run all the software programs that have been written for the IBM computers. A computer will only be bought if it has programs written for it, as each software program must be written for a particular CPU and will not run on any other. If a manufacturer produces a superb computer but nobody has written any software for it, then they probably will not sell any machines.

PCs are stand-alone workstations but can be linked to others by 'networking' within the same building or linked by 'modem' (telephone) to other computers world-wide.

There are other computers that are not called PCs, but which are similar in function. They are based on different CPUs and have their own software written for them. For example, there are the Amiga and the Atari ST which are based on the 68 000 CPU, and also the Macintosh, which also uses the same chip. There are others and still more in the pipeline, but they will all be stillborn if the manufacturer does not arrange for software to be available at launch.

As said earlier, the large computer systems are linked world-wide by modem, and can be accessed by each other provided the code of entry is known. These codes are secret and known only by the privileged few. But they can be broken into by computer hackers who use computers to break down the codes. This is the equivalent to the modern-day bank robber; he sits at home at his computer, breaks into the bank computer system and transfers a hefty cash balance into his own account.

Computer languages

As previously stated, the basic language of the computer is machine code, which uses bits and bytes. When writing software in this language, a deep understanding of computer inner construction is required and a great deal of patience.

In order to speed things up and make life easier for the programmer, a high-level language is used. This comprises chunks of machine code, already, as it were, predigested. The names of some of these computer languages are (there are many others):

Basic. This is an acronym for 'beginners all-purpose symbolic instruction code'.
Fortran. This is an acronym for 'formular translation'.
Cobol. This is an acronym for 'common business orientated language'.
Algol. This is an acronym for 'algebraic oriented language'.
PL/1. This is a multi-purpose language with the advantages of both fortran and cobal.

Each of these languages is designed to facilitate the programming of specialized areas, and more are being devised as new areas are coming into the domain of computers.

Graphics

This area deals with monitors or VDUs (visual display units) or CRTs (cathode ray tubes).

The pictures on these screens are made up of dots that can be lit up or turned off and can be either white, red, green or blue (RGB).

The definition or clarity of a picture is described by the word 'resolution': low resolution, medium resolution or high resolution. The highest resolution or clearest picture is determined by how many dots or 'pixels' can be produced on the screen. The more pixels per centimetre the better the picture is defined; it is clearer with more detail.

A computer may be designed to operate in all of the resolution modes. But if the monitor is not capable of high resolution, then those modes cannot be fully exploited.

If what has been outlined is understood, then it will prove sufficient knowledge for the user. If more is required, then the experts must be accessed.

Chapter 4

Surveys and sizing

It would be impossible to study the clothing industry, and the part computers play in it, without going into the area of sizing in some detail.

Since nearly everything in modern-day life is mass produced, surveys of all kinds need to be carried out to establish averages, which in turn indicate the gravity centre of a demand. In the given case, we need to look at the size and shape of the human body. Analysing a population's size and shape is a very complex exercise and, unless linked closely with an aim, can get out of control and become an end in itself.

The aim in this case is first to find the statistically average size, height and shape, and secondly to establish an acceptable sizing system for general use.

At present, there is no international sizing code; each country has set up its own system of sizing. It would be advantageous if all countries used the metric system and had a common sizing code. America, for example, is still using the imperial measurements. Even in the British Isles, where the metric system is in force, imperial measurements are still used in the pattern departments by the older generation, who, because of their seniority, force it on to younger employees in spite of the fact that the latter have used metric measurements from infant school onwards. If this continues, the imperial system will be perpetuated in design and pattern departments, while everywhere else will be metric.

There probably never will be an international sizing code, as the surveys in the different countries highlight different characteristics in the relationship of the major body measurements. Also, the survey data can be interpreted in different ways when designing a sizing system for general use. The fact is that everyone has their own size, just like a finger print, and by definition it is impossible to mass produce garments to fit everyone.

The problem of sizing in mass production increases with the degree of fit: the tighter or closer the garment is to the body the greater the need for more sizes; the looser garments will look acceptable on more people so fewer sizes will suffice. For example, foundation garments such as corsets and bras need as many size options as is economic to produce, but a sari will fit anyone. So between these two extremes exist all the sizing requirements.

When designing a size chart it is always advisable to base it on close-fitting clothing, which means placing the sizes as close together as possible; this will lend itself to all degrees of fit as two sizes can be coupled together to indicate the range of body size that a garment will be suitable for.

There is a minimum increment that can be safely put between sizes; this should not be less than the tolerance added to the body measurement for movement and comfort on the major girth that is indicated on the sizing ticket.

Setting up a survey

The following is a list of the areas to be studied:

1 The aim of the survey
2 To survey growing bodies or grown ones
3 Which sex
4 Define the age group
5 What measurements to take
6 What instruments to use
7 The team of measurers
8 Geographic area to be covered by the survey
9 Analysis

1 Aim of the survey

There are two basic reasons for surveying the size, shape and weight of the body. The first is for medical reasons, such as growth rates related to age and diet, etc. The second is for reasons related to clothing and ergonomics.

When related to clothing production, the main questions revolve around:

(a) The average size and height
(b) Sizing systems
(c) The number of sizes required to fit satisfactorily a given sector of a population
(d) The designing of model forms (stands) to conform with the sizing system adopted as a result of the survey

2 Surveying growing bodies or grown ones

For the mass production of children's clothing, the survey will be measuring mainly the size of the skeleton in relation to the age and weight. Any size chart constructed for the growing body will mostly reflect the bone-structure changes, and will therefore be primarily based on height increments. The girth increases will be relatively small in relation to the height changes.

Allowances for fat and muscle can be made by including girth options within each height category.

The mass production of clothing for children and teenagers is a complex area, and clever designing will be needed to reduce the problems that rapid growth creates.

When the bone structure has finished growing, the problem of sizing revolves around muscle development and the putting on of fat. This area is easier to handle than the growth area, but still poses a big problem for the manufacturer of close-fitting garments.

3 Sex

Children's clothing up to the age of seven or eight is largely bisexual regarding size and shape. It is necessary to develop separate size charts and model stands for older children.

There is a large amount of sizing data available for adult men owing to the fact that surveys have been carried out by the armed forces in order to establish sizing systems for their own use in manufacturing uniforms. Added to this is the inherent method of assessing size and shape that is used in the tailoring industries, which entails taking many measurements from the individual and in so doing a large databank has been established. There is less data available for adult women and the collecting of data is more difficult owing to women's greater resistance to the invasion of their privacy.

4 Define the age group

There may be a specific age group that is of interest, in which case it will be necessary to isolate it and study it separately. Age has a considerable effect on size, and if a wide age spectrum is surveyed and the data averaged, then a different picture will emerge as opposed to the results of a small age band.

It is always advisable to break up the data into age groups of ten years, starting from the point at which growth stops. In this way, average sizes can be established for each group and, if necessary, the overall average figure type can easily be calculated.

When a survey of growth is carried out, the data will be averaged out according to height, usually at 5- or 10-centimetre intervals.

When surveying growth areas, defining averages by age is not advisable; it can be very misleading owing to the large variances encountered.

The most reliable results can be arrived at by coupling the height to the weight. In theory, from these two the major girth measurements could be calculated.

In fact, when surveying adults it is also necessary to divide the data into at least three height groups in each age category, in order to arrive at a usable sizing system.

5 What measurements to take

Measuring the body is not an easy matter, as it is a very complex shape and varies infinitely within the limits of normality. Obviously, the more measurements on the body that are taken then the better the final definition of shape and size will be. But there are two main difficulties. First, the body has very few precise landmarks from which to measure, and secondly, the individual measurements will vary in their interpretation of where these landmarks are.

Measurements of the body can be divided up into three main categories:

(a) girth measurements;
(b) height measurements;
(c) width and depth measurements.

If enough measurements are taken, they will give a fairly accurate picture of the size and height of a human being; the actual shape and stance, though, will be open to guesswork.

To get even a rough indication of shape would entail taking many measurements from each individual based on triangulation, and would make the survey very difficult and extremely expensive – bearing in mind that at least 3000 people must be measured if a usable statistic is to be arrived at. In fact, a sample nearer 10 000 would be preferable.

So it is possible to gather data related to size and height but very difficult to define the shape with any degree of accuracy. The following list shows the the measurements that ideally should be taken, using the instruments commonly available:

1. Weight
2. Height
3. Chest girth
4. Bust girth
5. Waist girth
6. Hip girth
7. Thigh girth
8. Bicep girth
9. Neck girth
10. Wrist girth
11. Knee girth
12. Calf girth
13. Ankle girth
14. Rib cage girth
15. Elbow girth
16. Armscye girth
17. Head girth
18. Hand girth
19. Upper hip girth
20. Top head/nape
21. Nape/waist
22. Waist/hip
23. Waist/knee
24. Waist/floor
25. Nape/bust
26. Nape/c.f. waist
27. Shoulder length
28. Outer arm length
29. Inner arm length
30. Front waist length
31. Bitrochanteric width
32. Bust width
33. Scye depth
34. Scye width
35. X/back
36. X/chest
37. Body rise
38. Abdominal/seat diameter
39. Interacromion width
40. Shoulder angle
41. Crotch length
42. Head width
43. Head depth
44. Top head/chin

6 What instruments to use

There are two instruments used for taking body measurements manually. The tape measure is used for taking the girth measurements, and the length and width measurements are taken with an anthropometer.

Until recently, there was no other means of measuring complex three-dimensional objects, but with the advent of computers and other electronic developments it is now possible to scan shapes, using light, and record as many measurements as are needed to build an accurate computer image. This is therefore an ideal instrument for survey work.

This makes it possible to establish the average shape of the different parts of the body as well as of the whole: for example, the shoulder area, which is so important to the pattern technician when balancing the garment. The weight of the garment is taken on the shoulders; if the pattern shape is not correct, then the garment will not hang properly.

Another part of the body that requires more statistical detail is the seat and stomach area. This has always been a difficult part to fit correctly for mass-production trousers and jeans. The techniques used for scanning a live body have to overcome variations due to movement during scanning. The scanner has to take several measurements at each point, and then average them to produce the mean. This movement will be caused by breathing and balance adjustments while standing in the scanner.

The other difficulty arises because of the soft nature of flesh in the case of the female. Support garments are usually worn and, for reasons of propriety and also to get some standardization of support, some form of body stocking would need to be worn. For men and children a body stocking would not be necessary, as a swimming costume would suffice.

One other difficulty remains: that of the arms, which overlap the body and mask its shape. This is not easily overcome, since moving the arms out if the way changes the shape of the trunk and shoulders. This is not desirable, since a relaxed normal position of the shoulders is one of the main reasons for the shape survey. One way to overcome this would be to raise one arm sideways to get the torso shape on that side, and superimpose it on the other side by reversing it for the computer image and visa versa for the other side.

There is quite a lot of work going on developing methods of recording and measuring three-dimensional shapes, as this kind of facility would be of great use in the retail sector also. (This will be covered in a separate chapter.)

7 The team of measurers

If the survey is to be carried out without electronic assistance, then a team of measurers will have to be employed and instructed in the methods of taking measurements.

Depending on how many measurements are to be taken on each sample will determine how many are needed in the team.

Before any measurements can be taken, the cardinal points must be marked on the body to be measured.

This is best done by one experienced person so that the points are as consistently placed as possible; also, it is desirable to confine each member of the team to taking three or four measurements. This will enable each team member to refine the process and reduce the field of error that is inevitable in an exercise of this kind.

The size of the team will depend on the amount of money available, as will the numbers to be measured in the survey and also the number of measurements to be taken from each sample.

8 Geographic area to be covered by the survey

Getting to the sample is no easy matter. Asking people to strip off, put on a body stocking, and have thirty or more measurements taken is not the most enticing prospect.

Some kind of incentive or reward is necessaary to make the operation a possibility. This inevitably will cost money.

A measuring centre would have to be set up and people invited to offer themselves for measurement and given some form of recompense. One large retail company has set up a survey using their own shops as centres, offering their customers vouchers to be spent in their stores if they are willing to be measured. This is an ingenious way of doing it. Previous survey projects were not so lucky as to be in that position. They have had to resort to going to large factories in working hours, and paying for the time and space and hoping that the workers would welcome a little light relief from their labours in order to be measured.

There are other options, of course, but it is clear that all is not plain sailing in this area.

There do seem to be local physical characteristics – a tendency to be taller or thicker hipped for example – so it is necessary to spread the sample evenly across the country. Also, there are racial characteristics; these may distort a survey and decisions have to be made regarding this factor: whether or not to omit them from the final analysis or to exclude them from the start.

9 Analysis

It is essential that enough data is collected, and spread evenly over the age range and the girth sizes. If there is insufficient data, then the survey will not be of much use.

Ideally, the sample should be similar to the following example.

Adult female survey

The age group to be split into five-year increments, starting at the age of sixteen. Eight hundred sample in each age group; each 800 to be divided into eight hip girth categories, starting at 82 cm with 5.0 cm increments.

Age	Hip cm	Number in sample
16/21	82/86	100
	87/91	100
	92/96	100
	97/101	100
	102/106	100
	107/111	100
	112/116	100
	117/121	100
	Total	800

This is to be repeated for the age groups:

22/27
28/33
34/39
40/45
46/51
52/57
58/63   This will give a total sample of 6400

Any hip sizes below and above the ones listed will be relatively rare, and best not included in the final data.

A statistic has to reflect a true average, where the individual is either, 'it' just below or just above.

It will be illustrated what a statistic should not be. Take the example arrived at of the average income of a population, where there are 30 per cent very rich and 70 per cent very poor; this will result in a statistical average income that represents nobody. These kind of statistics are often used to hoodwink the unwary and can in the long run give statistics a bad image, whereas averages can be very useful if truthfully arrived at.

For this reason, it is best to omit extreme figure types, of very short and fat or very tall and thin, and vice versa. The most useful way to break down the data on the 6400 sample would be to average each hip category in each age group. This would result in sixty-four averages, over forty measurements. To build a basic size chart, the three major girth measurements would be used and their relationship will reveal the essence of the sizing system that can be adopted for use on a general scale. The major girths are:

hip;
waist;
bust.

Usually, the hip is used as the size indicator; when a garment does not have a hip, then the bust is used. The waist usually follows the hip increases.

It follows that for each age group there will be eight hip categories, with average bust and waist relating to each hip size. These data will show how much to increase the waist and bust with each hip increment.

It may be that the waist and bust increase at the same rate as the hip, or it may indicate that the bust increases at a faster rate than the hip, or vice versa. But it will only relate to that age group. Other age groups may throw up a different pattern.

Of course, the option of hip increments are open; some may prefer a smaller increment of 4.0 cm or a larger one of 6.0 cm. A mixture of hip increments can be used, but it complicates the already complicated situation.

If it seemed appropriate, averages of bust and waist could be calculated for a complete age group, rather than each hip category. This would give eight statistical averages.

The overall statistical average can be extracted by using all the data, but just how useful these results would be is questionable.

Lastly, the division of the data into height groups is required. For adults, it has been found adequate to use only three categories: short; medium; tall.

This will provide three sets of girth-size charts with different vertical measurements. The most important vertical measurements are nape to waist and outer sleeve length on the top or above the waist; the skirt length for the area below the waist; and for trousers it will be the body rise and inner or outer leg measurements.

These are just suggestions, and not meant to be the only way of breaking down the data. They are intended to open up the area for questioning and counter proposals. The most difficult type of garment to market regarding fit is the 'close fitting one piece', where there are three critical major girths to fit accurately: the bust, waist and hip. A woman will rarely match the three major girths exactly in any sizing system. Most women tend to be a mixture: one size above the waist and another below the waist. With garments that fit closely around the hip, a women is fortunate if she can find a good fitting top to go with it; often, a top of different size will need to be purchased. Where the skirt is full and does not fit the hip area closely, then the waist measurement will be the active ingredient and will decide the size to be chosen.

Above the waist, the bust will determine which size is selected where the garment has a loose waist fitting; if the waist is close fitting, then it will depend on the individual – whether they have a bust larger or smaller than the bust/waist ratio in the size code for that country's sizing system.

Another important area is the chest/bust ratio. The chest and bust are important where styles are strapless. The survey will show the statistical average ratio of these two girths and produce what is called the proportionate bust measurement. When the bust is smaller than the norm, it is called a minus disproportionate bust, and when larger than the norm it is a plus disproportionate bust.

Where support garments such as corsets and bras are concerned, then a separate sizing code is required which will give a wide selection. This uses another girth measurement which is the ribcage. This is related to the bust girth. Options on this ratio are offered in the form of cup sizes, usually A, B, C and D. The cup B size corresponds to the proportionate bust in the bust/chest ratio. A cup is a minus disproportion and the plus disproportions are C and D. There is an international sizing table for this area, which has been widely accepted.

The more sizes that are offered the better from the public's point of view, but manufacturers will not be able to offer vast size choices because it will not be economic to do so. It will be left to the manufacturers to specialize in the various figure types, that is, short, outsize, tall, slim, etc. Most manufacturers cater for the medium height and the overall statistical average hip/bust configuration.

This is where most of the population fans out from and offers numerically the richest pickings. This is the main reason why only a small proportion of the population can get a reasonably well-fitting skin-type garment, unless it is a stretch fabric. Stretch fabric brings another factor into the situation, and can simplify some areas of sizing such as swimwear, leotards, and various knitted garments.

Size charts

There is a distinct difference between the recommended standard sizing code and the individually designed size charts that each manufacturing company will produce for its own products.

The country's standard recommends a set of parameters within which it advises companies to operate, so that the population can expect some degree of continuity. Usually, there is a recommended minimum and maximum measurement laid down for each size. The psychological ploy that most companies use in this situation is to make their products as large as possible within the recommended code, that is, to work to the maximum end of the size in order to fool the buyer into believing that they are smaller than they think. This, it is hoped, will entice the buyer to seek their product again in the future. But the danger here is that it tends to escalate, with companies vying with each other to produce large versions of a size. This eventually exceeds the recommended measurements, thus destroying the standard. This results in a size inflation, where a 10 becomes a 12, and so on.

Each company will specialize in a size range and design their own size chart, which their products will be constructed to follow. This size chart is based on body measurements, which in turn are taken from the current survey. The grading system will be based on the increments of this chart. There is a distinction to be made here regarding size charts. There are two types, one is based on body measurements and the other is to indicate the finished garment dimensions. The latter is used for quality and size control, whereas the body chart is for the use of the pattern technologists and technicians.

Size chart design

The main factors that control the design of size charts are:

1. The degree of fit
2. The range of sizes to be covered
3. The age group
4. Fabric characteristics

The size chart that will be used by the technical staff will contain as much data as possible, up to forty measurements – the more the better. It will show the incremental changes between sizes; these can be equal or variable. This chart will contain information needed for the design and construction of the pattern and the grading increments for the grader.

1 The degree of fit

As was said earlier, the closer the fit of the garment, the more size options will be required with closer size increments.

A size chart can be constructed for height only if required. This chart, for example, could be based on one set of girth measurements, and have several height options. A company might decide to cater only for a girth size corresponding to a 12 and offer very short, short, medium, tall, and very tall. It is unlikely that a company would offer such a narrow size range, but it illustrates the idea of designing size charts for specific size areas.

Size charts may be designed for girth only, where the height remains constant throughout and the rest of the measurements are related to the girth changes.

The most common configuration is for a combined height and

girth size chart, where the height increases with each increment of girth. This is logical when dealing with growing bodies, but does not make much sense when applied to adult sizes. The factor that always has an influence is that if a garment is too long or too big it can always be shortened or reduced in girth, but if it is too short or small then the sale is lost. This also leads the manufacturer to make the garments as large as possible within the given size recommendation.

The degree of fit will influence the size of increment between each size, and thus determine how many sizes are offered between the two extremes of the major girth that are being used.

A size chart might offer small, medium and large. The small being a combined 10 and 12, which will fit hips from 87.0 cm to 92.0 cm. The medium will be a combined 12 and 14 to fit hips from 92.0 cm to 97.0 cm. The large will be the 16 and 18 to fit hips 97.0 cm to 102.0 cm. This is just an example, where three sizes are offered where six usually are offered over the same girth range.

2 The range of sizes to be covered

The range of sizes offered by the company depend on the type of clothing made and the company's policy.

It is possible that a size range starting at an 82.0 cm hip and ending at a 122.0 cm hip will be offered. It is unlikely that many, if any, styles will lend themselves to such a large span of size, so that styles will be designed for specific size ranges within a company. It is usually a large concern that will offer wider size options, since it would require a large output to economically justify such a large size range. With the help of computer systems, larger size options are an economic possibility; and with the greater flexibility that computers bring, larger styling options are also possible. But smaller companies, unless they use computers, will only be able to offer small size ranges, probably from size 12 to 16 will be the norm, in the medium height range of 162.0 cm (5 ft 4 in) is usual.

3 The age group

This is, of course, influenced by company policy, and this will determine everything that follows.

The main consideration here is: Which age group commands the greatest financial clout? Which area is the most interesting to the directors?

Children and babies are the most difficult regarding sizing because of the growth factor and the large number of sizes that must be offered. The financial returns in this sector are debatable, since a lot of specialized expertise is needed in various areas. This tends to break the market into smaller pieces and constitutes, in the eyes of some, an unwanted degree of risk in relation to the returns.

The wealthiest group would appear to be the unmarried in the eighteen to twenty-five age range. The married area of the market in the child-bearing age (up to 40 years), when the children absorb a lot of the family income, is not so lucrative for the fashion field. Above that age, up to 65 years and retirement, is good, but falls off rapidly after that. There is, however, a new phenomena appearing; this is the large numbers of well-off retired persons. In Germany, it has become necessary to survey above the sixty-five age group, whereas no one bothered beforehand.

In conclusion, it seems that the ideal operating zone is the statistically average size in the eighteen to twenty-five age group.

4 Characteristics

There is really only one factor here that has any great influence on sizing, and that is the degree of stretch.

Where a material is designed with a 'recoverable' stretch characteristic, then close-fitting garments can be designed with larger spacings between sizes and fewer sizes.

Where the material is not stable − that is, it will not recover its original size after stretching − then it is best treated as if there is no stretch at all.

With garments such as leotards and swimwear, small size ranges are sufficient, since the material will adapt to a wide variety of shapes and sizes. Also, larger people tend not to wear them.

3D Electronic scanners

This opens up new possibilities for the future. The main advantage is in collecting survey data. It will mean that there will be no need to train and employ a team of measurers. Secondly, the amount of data collected is almost limitless, since the scanned figure can be stored in computer memory, and the three-dimensional image generated on the screen can be rotated to view from any angle including above and below. The facility to measure the image from any point in real scale will be possible, and thus permit detail analysis when and where required. To be able to store each individual figure scan, and in this way build up a large reference library, will be invaluable. There would also be a computer option to superimpose figures on each other for comparison.

The model-form (stand) manufacturers could benefit greatly from this technology in designing and constructing more realistic stands for use in pattern departments and production areas for quality control. Another step could be taken in developing a device to reverse the 3D data; this would enable the constructing of the figure shape in fibreglass for the individual, instead of having to cover the subject in plaster of Paris and then cut them out of it to use as a female cast. Other disciplines will undoubtedly find a use for this technology, and so a steady development can be expected along these lines in the future. More will be said about 3D scanning in Chapter 6. It may open up the way to making fashion garments to individual measurements collected at the source, but that remains to be seen.

*Body measurements for medium bust development:
Increments are based on an increase of 5 cm girth and 2.4 cm height*

Area		10	12	14	16	18	20	22	Increment
1	Height	159.6	162.0	164.4	166.8	169.2	171.6	173.0	2.4
2	Weight (Pounds)	102	118	134	150	166	182	198	16lb
3	Hip	87.0	92.0	97.0	102.0	107.0	112.0	117.0	5.0
4	Bust	81.0	86.0	91.0	96.0	101.0	106.0	111.0	5.0
5	Waist	61.0	66.0	71.0	76.0	81.0	86.0	91.0	5.0
6	Chest	77.4	81.0	84.6	88.2	91.8	95.4	99.0	3.6
7	Top hip (11.0 cm from waist)	81.0	86.0	91.0	96.0	101.0	106.0	111.0	5.0
8	Ribcage (under bust)	66.0	71.0	76.0	81.0	86.0	91.0	96.0	5.0
9	Neck	35.0	36.0	37.0	38.0	39.0	40.0	41.0	1.0
10	Bicep	24.7	26.5	28.3	30.1	31.9	33.7	35.7	1.8
11	Elbow	23.7	25.5	27.3	29.1	30.9	32.7	34.5	1.8
12	Wrist	15.2	16.0	16.8	17.6	18.4	19.2	20.0	0.8
13	Thigh	49.8	53.0	56.2	59.4	62.6	65.8	69.0	3.2
14	Knee	32.6	34.0	35.4	36.8	38.2	39.6	41.0	1.4
15	Calf	31.6	33.0	34.4	35.8	37.2	38.6	40.0	1.4
16	Ankle	22.3	23.0	23.7	24.4	25.1	25.8	26.5	0.7
17	X-chest	29.8	31.0	32.2	33.4	34.6	35.8	37.0	1.2
18	X-back (12cm down from nape)	31.8	33.0	34.2	35.6	36.8	38.0	39.2	1.2
19	Shoulder length	11.7	11.9	12.1	12.3	12.5	12.7	12.9	0.2
20	Scye width	10.1	11.0	11.9	12.8	13.7	14.6	15.5	0.9
21	Scye depth	17.5	18.1	18.7	19.3	19.9	20.5	21.1	0.6
22	Bust width	17.8	19.0	20.2	21.4	22.6	23.8	25.0	1.2
23	Nape to bust	32.6	34.0	35.4	36.8	38.2	39.6	40.0	1.4
24	Nape to waist over bust	51.8	53.0	54.2	55.6	56.8	58.0	59.2	1.2
25	Nape to waist centre back	40.4	41.0	41.6	42.2	42.8	43.4	44.0	0.6
26	Nape to hip	62.1	63.0	63.9	64.8	65.7	66.6	67.5	0.9
27	Nape to knee	97.5	99.0	100.5	102.0	103.5	105.0	106.5	1.5
28	Nape to floor	137.9	140.0	142.1	144.2	146.3	148.4	150.5	2.1
29	Sleeve length (outer)	57.1	58.0	58.9	59.8	60.7	61.6	62.5	0.9
30	Sleeve length (inner)	43.1	43.5	43.9	44.3	44.7	45.1	45.5	0.4
31	Abdominal seat diameter	21.3	23.0	24.7	26.4	28.1	29.8	31.5	1.7
32	Hip width	30.2	31.8	33.4	35.0	36.6	38.2	39.8	1.6
33	Body rise	27.9	29.0	30.1	31.2	32.3	33.4	34.5	1.1
34	Shoulder angle (degrees)	20.5	20.5	20.5	20.5	20.5	20.5	20.5	NIL
35	Outside leg	100.5	102.0	103.5	105.0	106.5	108.0	109.5	1.5

Conversion from metric to imperial

0.3 cm = 1/8 in
0.6 cm = 1/4 in
0.9 cm = 3/8 in
1.2 cm = 1/2 in
1.5 cm = 5/8 in
1.8 cm = 3/4 in
2.1 cm = 7/8 in
2.5 cm = 1 in

Figure 5 *A typical women's body measurement size chart for combined height and girth covering a wide range of dimensions. This would be used by the pattern and grading technicians*

Growth size chart

6.0 cm height increments

INFANT AND CHILDREN UNISEX

Age	3m	6m	9m	12m	18m	2	3	Grade Incr	4	5	6	7	Grade Incr
cm													
Height	62	68	74	80	86	92	98	6.0	104	110	116	122	6.0
kg													
Weight	7	8	9	10	12	14	16	1–2	17	19	21	23	2
Body	43	45	47	49	51	53	55	2.0	57	59	61	63	2.0
Chest G.													
Block	51	53	55	57	59	61	63	2.0	64	66	68	70	2.0
Body	45.4	46.6	47.8	49	50.2	51.4	52.6	1.2	53.8	55	56.2	57.4	1.2
Waist G.													
Block	52.4	53.6	54.8	56	57.2	58.4	59.6	1.2	59.8	61	62.2	64.4	1.2
Body	46	48	50	52	54	56	58	2.0	61	63.4	65.8	68.2	2.4
Hips													
Garment	54	56	58	60	62	64	66	2.0	66	68.4	70.8	73.2	2.4
Body	19	19.6	20.2	20.8	21.4	22	22.6	0.6	23.6	24.4	25.2	26	0.8
X. Back													
Block	20	20.6	21.2	21.8	22.4	23	23.6	0.5	25.6	26.4	27.2	28	0.8
X Chest	19	19.5	20	20.5	21	21.5	22	0.5	23.8	24.6	25.4	26.2	0.8
Body	8	8.5	9	9.5	10	10.5	11	0.5	12	12.8	13.6	14.4	0.8
Scye depth													
Block	9.5	10	10.5	11	11.5	12	12.5	0.5	14	14.8	15.6	16.4	0.8
Nape to													
Waist	19	19.8	20.6	21.4	22.2	23	23.8	0.8	24.5	26	27.5	29	1.5
Shoulder													
Length	6.2	6.5	6.8	7.1	7.4	7.7	8	0.3	8.2	8.5	8.8	9.1	0.3
Sleeve													
Length	23	24.5	26	27.5	29	30.5	32	1.5	34.5	37	39.5	42	2.5
Body Rise	12	13	14	15	16	17	18	1.0	19	20	21	22	1.0
Thigh Girth	24.6	25.8	27	28.2	29.4	30.6	31.8	1.2	33	34.5	36	37.5	1.5
Body	22.4	23	23.6	24.2	24.8	25.4	26	0.6	26	27	28	29	1.0
Neck G.													
Block	23	24	24	25	25	26	27	0.6	27	28	29	30	1.0
Body	14.2	14.8	15.4	16	16.6	17.2	17.8	0.6	18	18.6	19.2	19.8	0.6
Bicep Girth													
Block													

GIRLS

Age	8	9	10	11	Grade Incr	12	13	14	15	Grade Incr
cm										
Height	128	134	140	146	6.0	150	154	158	162	4.0
kg										
Weight	25	29	33	37	4	43	47	50	52	4–2
Body	66.2	69.4	72.6	75.8	3.2	76.4	79.6	82.8	86	3.2
Chest G.										
Block	74.2	71.4	80.6	83.8	3.2	75.4	78.6	91.8	95	3.2
Body	59	60.6	62.2	63.8	1.6	64	65	66	67	1.0
Waist G.										
Block	64	65.6	67.2	68.8	1.6	68	69	70	71	1.0
Body	71.8	75.4	79	82.6	3.6	84.8	87.2	89.6	92	2.4
Hips										
Garment	76.8	80.4	84	87.6	3.6	89.8	92.2	94.6	97	2.4
Body	27	28	29	30	1.0	31	32	33	34	1.0
X. Back										
Block	29	30	31	32	1.0	33	34	35	36	1.0
X Chest	27	28	29	30	1.0	31	32	33	34	1.0
Body	15.2	16	16.8	17.6	0.8	18	18.4	18.8	19.2	0.4
Scye depth										
Block	17.7	18.5	19.3	20.1	0.8	21	21.4	21.8	22.2	0.4

64 Surveys and sizing

Nape to Waist	30.5	32	33.5	35	1.5	36	37	38	39	1.0
Shoulder Length	9.4	9.7	10	10.3	0.3	10.6	10.9	11.2	11.5	0.3
Sleeve Length	44.5	47	49.5	52	2.5	53.5	55	56.5	58	1.5
Body Rise	23	24	25	26	1.0	27	28	29	30	1.0
Thigh Girth	39	40.5	42	43.5	1.5	46	49	52	55	3.0
Body	30	31	32	33	1.0	34	35	36	37	1.0
Neck G.										
Block	31	32	33	34	1.0	35	36	37	38	1.0
Body	20	21	22	23	1.0	24	25	26	27	1.0
Bicep Girth Block										

BOYS

Age	8	9	10	11	12	13	14	15	Grade Incr
cm									
Height	128	134	140	146	152	158	164	170	6.0
kg									
Weight	24	29	34	39	44	49	54	59	5
Body	67	70.2	73.4	76.6	79.8	83	86.2	89.4	3.2
Chest G.									
Block	77	80.2	83.4	86.6	89.8	93	96.2	99.4	3.2
Body	61	63	65	67	69	71	73	75	2.0
Waist G.									
Block	65	67	69	71	73	85	77	79	2.0
Body	70	73.2	76.4	79.6	82.8	86	89.2	92.4	3.2
Hips									
Garment	75	78.2	81.4	84.6	87.8	91	94.2	97.4	3.2
Body	28	29.4	30.8	32.2	33.6	35	36.4	37.8	1.4
X. Back									
Block	30	31.4	32.8	34.2	35.6	37	38.4	39.8	1.4
X Chest	27.2	28.6	30	31.4	32.8	34.2	35.6	37	1.4
Body	16.6	17.4	18.2	19	19.8	20.6	21.4	22	0.8
Scye depth									
Block	19.6	20.4	21.2	22	22.8	23.6	24.4	25	0.8
Nape to Waist	31	32.5	34	35.5	37	38.5	40	41.5	1.5
Shoulder	11	11.4	11.8	12.2	12.6	13	13.4	13.8	0.4
Length Sleeve									
Length	45.5	48	50.5	53	55.5	58	60.5	63	2.5
Body Rise	21	22	23	24	25	26	27	28	1.0
Thigh Girth	38	40	42	44	46	48	50	52	2.0
Body	30	31.2	32.4	33.6	34.8	36	37.2	38.4	1.2
Neck G.									
Block	31	32.2	33.4	34.6	35.8	37	38.2	39.4	1.2
Body	21	22	23	24	25	26	27	28	1.0
Bicep Girth Block									

G = Girth

Conversion from metric to imperial

0.3 cm = ⅛ in
0.6 cm = ¼ in
0.9 cm = ⅜ in
1.2 cm = ½ in
1.5 cm = ⅝ in
1.8 cm = ¾ in
2.1 cm = ⅞ in
2.5 cm = 1 in

Figure 6 *A children's size chart combining body and block-pattern measurements. The block pattern is a basic pattern that follows the contours of the body and includes tolerances that enable normal body movements. Its dimensions will therefore be greater than the body measurements. The block pattern is the starting point for all style developments from the designer's fashion sketch. This chart will also be used by the pattern and grading technicians*

Man's shirt

Size designation (neck size)		Girth when fastened						Length from collar seam at centre				Length from top edge of sleeve to bottom				Length of collar from centre of buttonhole to centre of button		Length of cuff from end to end, long sleeves		Girth at bottom of short sleeves		Girth of shoulder across bottom of yoke		Depth of armhole		Width across elbow	
		Under-arms		Waist		Bottom edge		Back		Front		Long sleeve (including cuff)		Short sleeve													
cm	in	cm	in	cm	in	cm	in	cm	in	cm	in	cm	in	cm	in	cm	in	cm	in	cm	in	cm	in	cm	in	cm	in
31	12½	99	39½	88	35¼	100	40	82	32¾	74	29½	58	23¼	23	9¼	31	12½	22	8¾	35	14	36	14½	22	8¾	17	6¾
32	13	104	41½	94	37½	106	42½	84	33½	75.5	30	60	24	23	9¼	32	12¾	22	8¾	37	15	39	16	23	9¼	18	7⅛
33	13½	104	41½	94	37½	106	42½	84	33½	75.5	30	60	24	23	9¼	33	13¼	22	8¾	37	15	39	16	23	9¼	18	7⅛
34	14	104	41½	94	37½	106	42½	84	33½	75.5	30	60	24	23	9¼	34	13¾	22	8¾	37	15	39	16	23	9¼	18	7⅛
35	14	110	44	100	40	112	44½	84	33½	75	30¼	62	24¾	24	9⅝	35	14	24	9½	39	16	42	17	24.5	9¾	19	7½
36	14½	110	44	100	40	112	44½	84	33½	75	30¼	62	24¾	24	9⅝	36	14½	24	9½	39	16	42	17	24.5	9¾	19	7½
37	15	110	44	100	40	112	44½	84	33½	75	30¼	62	24¾	24	9⅝	37	15	24	9½	39	16	42	17	24.5	9¾	19	7½
38	15½	116	46½	106	42½	118	47¼	86	34½	76.5	30½	64	25½	24	9⅝	38	15½	26	10½	41	16½	45	18	26	10½	20	8
39	16	116	46½	106	42½	118	47¼	86	34½	76.5	30½	64	25½	24	9⅝	39	16	26	10½	41	16½	45	18	26	10½	20	8
40	16½	116	46½	106	42½	118	47¼	86	34½	76.5	30½	64	25½	24	9⅝	40	16½	26	10½	41	16½	45	18	26	10½	20	8
41	16½	122	48¾	112	44½	124	49½	86	34½	76	30½	66	26¼	24	9⅝	41	16½	26	10½	41	16½	48	19¼	27.5	11¼	21	8½
42	17	122	48¾	112	44½	124	49½	86	34½	76	30½	66	26¼	24	9⅝	42	17	26	10½	41	16½	48	19¼	27.5	11¼	21	8½
43	17½	122	48¾	112	44½	124	49½	86	34½	76	30½	66	26¼	24	9⅝	43	17½	26	10½	41	16½	48	19¼	27.5	11¼	21	8½
44	17½	128	51¼	118	47¼	130	52	88	35¼	77.5	31	68	27¼	25	10	44	17½	28	11¾	43	17½	51	20½	29	11½	22	8⅞
45	18	128	51¼	118	47¼	130	52	88	35¼	77.5	31	68	27¼	25	10	45	18	28	11¾	43	17½	51	20½	29	11½	22	8⅞
46	18½	128	51¼	118	47¼	130	52	88	35¼	77.5	31	68	27¼	25	10	46	18½	28	11¾	43	17½	51	20½	29	11½	22	8⅞
47	18¾	134	53½	124	49½	136	54½	88	35¼	77	31¾	68	27¼	25	10	47	18¾	28	11¾	43	17½	54	21½	30.5	12¼	23	9¼
48	19¼	134	53½	124	49½	136	54½	88	35¼	77	31¾	68	27¼	25	10	48	19¼	28	11¾	43	17½	54	21½	30.5	12¼	23	9¼

Figure 7 *A size chart based on garment dimensions. This is used in quality control for checking the finished size of the garment – in this case, a shirt. It will also ensure that the correct size label has been sewn in*

	Age groups					
Area	18/29 years		30/44 years		45/64 years	
	cm	in	cm	in	cm	in
1 Height	161.0	5'4½"	160.0	5'4"	157.0	5'3"
2 Weight (lbs)	126.6		134.5		143.8	
3 Hip	95.0	38	97.5	38	102.4	41
4 Bust	89.5	35¾	93.0	37¼	99.0	39½
5 Waist	64.0	25½	68.9	27½	76.4	30½
6 Chest	84.0	33½	86.4	34½	90.0	36
7 Top hip	85.0	34	88.8	35½	95.3	38¼
8 Ribcage	74.0	29½	78.0	31¼	84.0	33½
9 Neck	38.0	15¼	38.5	15½	39.0	15¾
10 Bicep	27.6	11	28.9	11½	30.4	12
11 Elbow	27.0	10¾	27.3	11	27.8	11¼
12 Wrist	16.5	6½	16.8	6½	17.0	6¾
13 Thigh	54.0	21½	56.2	22½	60.0	24
14 Knee	35.0	14	35.4	14¼	36.0	14½
15 Calf	33.5	13¼	34.0	13½	34.5	13¾
16 Ankle	23.0	9	23.7	9¼	24.0	9½
17 X/chest	31.8	12½	32.5	12¾	33.3	13
18 X/back	33.3	13¼	34.0	13½	34.7	13¾
19 Shoulder length	11.7	4½	11.7	4½	11.7	4½
20 Scye width	11.4	4⅜	11.9	4¾	12.4	5
21 Scye depth	18.4	7¼	18.8	7⅜	19.2	7½
22 Bust width	19.5	7¾	20.0	8	21.0	8¼
23 Nape to bust	34.8	13¾	36.0	14¼	39.0	15⅜
24 Nape/waist over bust	52.0	20½	52.0	20½	52.0	20½
25 Nape to waist C.B.	38.2	15	37.8	14⅞	37.0	14⅝
26 Nape to hip	60.0	23¾	59.5	23½	58.0	23
27 Nape to knee	95.6	37¾	95.0	37½	93.8	37
28 Nape to floor	137.8	54½	137.0	54¼	135.0	53⅜
29 Sleeve length (outer)	58.4	23	58.0	22⅞	57.7	22¾
30 Sleeve length (inner)	44.8	17¾	44.2	17½	43.3	17⅛
31 Abdominal seat diam	24.0	9½	25.4	10	27.9	11
32 Hip width	33.0	13	33.7	13¼	34.9	13¾
33 Body rise	29.0	11½	29.7	11¾	30.9	12⅛
34 Shoulder angle (degrees)	20.2	20.2	20.2	20.2	20.2	20.2

Figure 8 This chart shows the statistically average size for women in three age groups covering thirty-four dimensions. This data was taken from the British survey carried out in the early 1950s, thus the older age group were born around the turn of the century and the younger group in the early 1930s. These dimensions are still valid today except in the area of height, which has increased a little. Also, the standard waist measurement used in the 1980s is about 3.0 cm larger than in the 1950s

Chapter 5

Computer-aided design (CAD)

General principles of design

The computer is capable of storing and manipulating a wide spectrum of data and, because of this, is suited to many areas of designing.

It can be used to store all the forms used by the designer. These are:

1 Language
2 Mathematics
3 Two-dimension geometric forms
4 Three-dimension solid forms
5 Colour
6 Sound

The storage capacity of a computer can be as large as is necessary, and access to it can be very rapid.

The other facility that the computer offers is the easy manipulation and the mixing of this data or knowledge. And finally, it offers the varous output facilities for the results.

The computer is a very powerful tool in the hands of any designer, and is obviously suited to many aspects of design, but to some, the fine artist in particular, it has its limitations.

The artist spends years mastering his or her own body, perfecting the difficult skill of observation, both of shape and colour, perspective, and tonal values and their relationship to each other, and learning how to transfer that observation through their body via a brush, pen or pencil to the paper or canvas. It is in the moment of transfer through the tool to canvas or paper that the quality of whatever the artist is experiencing is transferred and captured permanently.

It is the quality of transfer that the computer lacks. It is clumsy and sterile in comparison to the human touch. Subtle energies of this kind cannot pass through a computer as the electronic stylus is dead to pressure and variation and even, if it were, the cathode screen is not capable of interpreting and representing such fine variations. There is work being done to make the electronic pens more sensitive and to increase the resolution of the screens, and maybe in the future the computer will be able to register the finer qualities that pass through the artist's hands.

Even so, the computer will never match the direct and immediate feel and feedback that the artist feels through the pencil, brush and palette-knife, or the satisfaction and fulfilment of using the simple tools and feeling the paint flow from the brush on to the canvas.

With the computer, the artist has to struggle with a complex machine that stands between them and their expression, hampered by time-consuming and complex menu interpretation.

If the desired effect is produced on the screen, even this will still have a misleading effect owing to the vibrant life it will have due to the picture being made of light. This will disappear when the picture is printed, however perfectly, and leave an almost dead and flat reproduction. So, from the fine artist's point of view, it is almost a non-starter, but for the commercial or graphic artist it is a good tool.

On the plus side, the artist likes the easy facility it gives them for experimentation, with colour relationships and spacial shape effects, and in general to play with structures of all kinds. It is a good tool for this type of activity because of the speed at which experiments can be carried out. For the artist who operates commercially, the computer is a god-send, but for the serious artist it is a mixed blessing.

The area where CAD is used with great success is in draughtsmanship. The computer takes the place of the draughting board, and all the tools that are associated with it are available in the CAD program. Couple this to a suitable plotter, and the resultant drawings are as good or better than the manual equivalent. These programs provide a wide range of facilities and tools are easily applied, once the program has been learned. Since the criteria here concerns line drawing and accuracy, then the computer medium is ideal and gives a real advantage in speed and flexibility in the same way that the word processor works for the writer. The main obstacle is, as always, the inertia and resistance of the person to making the effort of learning a new process. It means that the designer must forget designing for a while and buckle down to mastering the system. After this painful process is over, life becomes even easier than before for the draughtsman and the writer.

In the case of the dress designer, the picture tends to be a little different. These designers tend to be of a different type to architects, draughtsmen and secretaries or writers. In general, they don't take easily to computers, and consider them more a hindrance than a help; and being, as they say, creative with emotional responses to life, they find the chore of mastering a computer out of the question. This, of course, is a generalization, but valid none the less. Designers also lead very pressurized lives, and would find difficulty in setting the necessary time aside to learn the system. The usual way round this is to allow the designer to continue as usual and to make the pattern technicians carry the load of learning and operating the computer system. This is a pity, because designers who are willing and able to master a CAD system have a powerful tool in their hands. It means that they can sketch their designs in the computer and build their sketch book in it. This ties up all the relevant specifications to the sketch and gives easy access to the resultant style library for generating new styles from old. It also provides the opportunity to learn how to access the production cost system which, in any good set-up, will be interfaced with the designer's terminal. Unfortunately, at the present time, this is a rare phenomenon.

The design process

Before describing CAD systems, it would be helpful to try to define or to formulate what, in general, is meant when the word 'design' is used. This will help to make clear the advantages and disadvantages of computers. It will show what, when and where to use computers to advantage, and when to stay clear of them.

'Designing', everybody would agree, is a process. But what takes place in this process? And what are the ingredients of the process?

First, it would appear that the word 'design' describes something that is regarded by all as the pinnacle, or a most desirable occupation.

The designer is a most highly regarded person in whatever field they operate. They are the initiators, the shapers, the image-makers, the people everyone else relies on for the beginning of something. It carries the implication of 'creation', which then brings the word 'create' into question.

One aspect of creation implies making something out of nothing, but the meaning usually ascribed to it is 'the mixing of known ingredients in a different way producing a new effect'. Is it possible to create anything absolutely new? Or is designing a process of collecting all available data and arranging it in an unusual way? Can anyone, for example, create an entirely new animal? If asked to do this, the response will be to select from the memory bits of different animals and mix them together in a new way. Everybody will recognize it as an animal, because it is comprised of bits of already created animals. This will produce a strange contradictory feeling in the observer, and then will be stored in memory as a 'new animal', but one not expected to be found in the environment as no one has ever seen one in the flesh before. (Unless, that is, one is a young child with incomplete data and experience, in which case he or she may expect to see one around.) Although this animal could be called 'new' or 'a creation', it is none the less a mixing of the known in a new way to produce a new image, unreal and a product of the faculty of imagination, a faculty which the human being has – in contrast to other animals. This facility of imagination can be used to manipulate data in a lawful way, as when designing an aeroplane, or in an unlawful way by mixing data which is incompatible, such as the new animal. It is comparatively easy to design something new by mixing unlikely bits of life and producing something that shocks the senses; it is usually done to attract attention, and the products of this activity are usually grotesque and what is broadly called 'Mickey Mouse' designs. They usually end up outside the laws of proportion and harmony.

So it appears that nothing can be new, only a rearrangement of the existing, and if a researcher or scientist digs up something 'new' from the surrounding phenomena, this will be new to us because it was, hitherto, hidden from our senses. This new piece of data can then be manipulated by a designer, and mixed with the already known to produce a new image or product. There are other words that describe processes or activities which are allied to designing, and sometimes it is difficult to distinguish where one begins and the other ends. They are 'research' and 'invent'. The word 'research' implies 'explore' and search (why there is a 're' at the front is puzzling). How the process of inventing differs from designing is also a question to be considered. The image of the 'inventor' is not as impressive as 'designer'. An inventor is usually associated with creating new ideas and devices for making life easier, or the invention of 'likely stories', etc.

Designing also includes the creation of style and taste, which are the components of what we call 'fashion'. Fashion is in general terms the adoption of a particular image, an activity revolving around outer appearances designed to make a notable impression on others.

To this end, fashion designers strive to produce a look that they hope will be adopted by a section of the population. This, it is hoped, will bring the designer notoriety.

Unfortunately, a lot of contemporary designers resort to shock tactics, producing gaudy disharmonized products which are rapidly becoming the norm. It is perhaps understandable since everything seems to have been done before, and unless it is outside the bounds of acceptability it is not acceptable!

The formula is 'anything as long as it is different'. There seems to be a horror of being associated with the word 'stereotype', even though stereotypes are the results of fashion.

Research

The process of research seems to contain both inventing and designing.

Research arises either from curiosity or a desire and thirst for knowledge, and also a requirement from some sector of society, via a manufacturing concern. The first step in the research process is finding the questions. What, why, where, when, how, and who wants it and how many want it.

Once the question has been accurately formulated, or as accurately as possible (because the question, if accurate, will produce the right answer), the way is open to proceed.

The next step is to invent or design appropriate apparatus to probe and prod the relevant areas, to encourage them to reveal their secrets. Once revealed, they are added to the already known in that area, ready for product development by the designers. So it would appear that the process of 'research' is a response to specific requirements either of the mind or body. The requirement must be broken down, analysed and a detailed specification presented to a designer, who is someone experienced in that field and has access to and can manipulate and arrange data in a lawful way to match the specification. If there is not enough data, then the designer must know how to make a detailed specification which will be handed back to a research team; the latter will start a process to extract from the environment yet more of its secrets. Or there may be the need to collect mass data by means of surveys, and analyse them to extract statistical data, hitherto not realized or known.

It may help to make a small list of design projects, and consider the basic specification for each one to see what is involved. The specification can be very detailed and grow in the form of a tree. The main concept is the trunk, which splits off into branches, and so on.

Any design project can be divided into two basic concepts. The first is function and the second is decoration. In this instance, the word 'function' will apply only to physical phenomenon, and the word 'decoration' to psychological phenomenon, in the role of affecting the human being through the sense of sight. It is also possible to apply the word 'function' to psychology, as in the case of most art forms. For example, the function of some paintings is to have an effect on the emotions or feelings of people.

It will be interesting to make a small list of design projects and divide them into these two categories in order to clarify things a little. These will only be approximate and the reader may not necessarily agree with the reasoning.

1. *Aeroplanes.* The outside of a plane must be 100 per cent functional, and the inside about 80 per cent function and 20 per cent decoration.
2. *Sailing boats.* Below the water line and up to the deck, the boat must be 100 per cent functional, the deck approximately 80 per cent function and 20 per cent styling; and the interior design should be 70 per cent function and 30 per cent decor.
3. *A meal.* This should be 80 per cent function, and 20 per cent decoration.
4. *An advertisement.* This is an exception, where the function can only be applied to psychology. The function of an advert is to influence people.
5. *A building.* This cannot be divided into function and decor until the basic specification is known. A factory, for example, is 100 per cent functional. A block of flats can also be purely functional, and consist of rectangles to maximize the use of the space available. But a cathedral probably comes under the heading of 'art', and its function is to influence the psyche or spirit.
6. *Textiles.* This area of design has quite a few functional aspects, such as warmth and protection, which can be broken down further; the decoration aspect is also vast.
7. *Clothing.* This is the same as textiles, and will be taken as a separate subject.
8. *Nick-nacks.* These are purely decoration and need not have any function, although they are quite often based on functional objects.

It will be interesting to take the aeroplane and elaborate a little on its mechanical specification.

The concept of making a flying machine entered man's head many eons ago. It came directly from watching birds; if there had been no flying objects around, then it is debatable that man would ever have had the notion of 'getting off the ground'. After many attempts at making flying machines, man gradually collected data derived directly from trial and error. Today, there exists a vast bank of tested knowledge and data for aircraft designers to draw on.

The first line in the specification will be one of the following:

1   Passenger
2   Freight
3   Pleasure
4   Bomber
5   Fighter

Whichever one is chosen, the next line will contain a little more of the requirement. If it is 'pleasure', then there will be options of:

1   Glider
2   Aerobatics
3   Microlight
4   Hang-glider
5   Light joy-rider
6   Helicopter

If 'glider' is chosen, then after deciding on single- or twin-seater, the rest of the specification will be of flight characteristics. Weight, wing span, wing area, lift forces, wind-resistance forces, centre of lift, centre of gravity, lateral resistance, etc. All of this can be calculated from an existing pool of data and will produce a flying machine, the efficiency of which will depend on the designer's depth of understanding and skill in finely relating the data.

The designer will be constrained by the laws of aeronautics and have relatively little choice in the overall shape of the craft. There will be small details that can be played with to make the appearance stylish and generally desirable, and it can be decorated in colour with pretty patterns if required, but this is usually done by another designer, expert in that particular field. So designing an aeroplane is controlled by physical laws, and is therefore basically a functional product with overtones of decoration and styling.

This applies to all functional products, with the ratio of function/decoration varying accordingly.

A fighter aircraft's shape will be totally determined by function, and its colour by its background. The skill will be in the designer's mastery of the available data and the ability to assess accurately the quantities and measurements in mixing the ingredients to match the specification – and in discovering better relationships between the known data. If an exploration is carried out then a 'discovery' happens, or if an experiment is done then also a discovery can be the result. These are other words describing parts of the same processes.

It would be a good exercise for anyone to take an item, imagine a specific set of circumstances for its requirement, and write a full specification for it.

For example:

A fighter aircraft

1. Attack or defence or attack/defence
2. Altitude of operation, low, high, both
3. Subsonic, supersonic
4. Vertical take-off, short take-off, optional
5. Number of crew
6. Stability at all speeds; wing shape and area
7. Maximum speed, minimum speed (stall speed)
8. A scale of minimum turning radii for given speeds
9. Rates of climb related to engine output and angle of climb
10. Load carrying requirements (re/armourments)
11. Fuel capacity
12. A scale of operational ranges related to fuel consumption and speed
13. Unladen weight and full-up weight
14. Maximum speed and fuel consumption at sea level and at maximum height
15. Costs and market

These are the main areas which can in turn be expanded; this gives some idea of the process of designing a fully functional product.

Computer-aided design in clothing

Designing clothing also consists of a mixture of function and decoration. But in this instance these words need to be related in a different way.

If the question – What is the function of clothing? – is put, then the two main answer categories will be:

1. Physical or body requirements
2. Requirements of the psyche, mind and emotions

Computer-aided design (CAD)

The 'physical' can be subdivided into movement, comfort, temperature and protection. To achieve these properties, a garment can have various degrees of fit and be made of a variety of different fabrics – from the extremely close fitting such as the corset and the swimming costume, to the loosest garment such as the sari.

The requirements of the psyche can be described by two words: appearance and decoration. This gives rise to the phenomenon that is called 'fashion'. Many people have tried to define and analyse fashion and there has been much written about it by psychologists. However, the bottom line is always 'the desire for attention', which takes the form of 'to be the same as everybody else' (acceptable), or the opposite. Most wish to be 'the same' but excel in their choice or taste.

These two functions of clothing (to satisfy both body and mind) become mixed in every kind of way. Some garments are designed exclusively for the body but because of some quirk of imagery, the need to be different or to ape, this garment can become fashionable, something that must be worn. Some garments are designed purely as decoration, and some a mixture of both. They all end up with their own image, depending on who is associated with that type of garment. It depends on what type of influence a person is prone to that determines their dress.

There are four main areas of design in the sphere of clothing manufacture:

1. Textiles
2. Shoes
3. Garments
4. Embroidery

Each of these have their own dedicated computer systems, which will be described in turn.

1 Textiles

This area consists of five categories:

1. Fibres
2. Dyes
3. Prints
4. Weaving
5. Knitting

Fibres

The designing of man-made fibres is carried out by chemists, and they no doubt use computers of various kinds to measure, evaluate and store data, but probably not dedicated to fibres only. Alongside the fibre chemist will be the dye chemist, who will be designing dyes to suit the various fibres.

The fibre chemist is a relative newcomer to the scene, since only natural fibres were used until recent times. These were dyed with natural dyes, extracted from either vegetables or minerals that were available in the area. Techniques for getting the dye to enter the fibres, and remain there without damaging them, have been perfected over the centuries.

Many of the vegetable dyes are still regarded as the most beautiful and subtle, and with time and sun-resisting characteristics that are almost impossible to copy.

There are several requirements to aim at when either designing or selecting a natural fibre.

The length of the fibre is critical to the stability of the cloth that is woven from it. In nature, fibres vary a lot in length; wool, cotton, silk and flax are a few examples. In contrast, a man-made fibre will be a continuous filament.

The length of the fibre determines the strength of the yarn when it has been spun together. Spinning produces a continuous thread, being made possible by the friction of fibres against each other, so the longer the fibre the more friction there will be. When this is coupled to the twisting of the fibres round each other, which when pulled tightens the fibres on to each other, the friction and strength increases.

Cloth woven from short-fibred yarn is unstable; in other words, it will stretch and 'bag' or loose its shape when pressured or wetted. 'Shoddy' was a name given to reprocessed cloth, which was torn and returned to fibres again; but the fibres were shortened in the process and thus the cloth made from it was very unstable and also cheap.

Man-made fibres are called 'continuous filaments', and can be produced in required thicknesses. They can also be spun together to give texture and heat-retaining or heat-repelling characteristics. Also, each filament can be dyed a different colour and then spun together to produce multi-coloured yarns.

There is one other very important property that a fibre must have, and that is crease resistance. Ideally, when a fibre or filament is bent, it must recover its original shape. This property must remain constant throughout normal temperatures, so that a garment will not crease from the heat and pressure of the body, and also be capable of resisting washing and cleaning temperatures. Natural fibres come with their own in-built properties and have to be accepted as such, but man-mades can be designed to remain stable at quite high temperatures to facilitate permanent pleating, where the filament will remain kinked at temperatures lower than the designed 'change heat', and will not be creased or lose a crease at normal temperatures. The permanent pleating is put in to the cloth by steam baking at high temperatures in large ovens capable of coping with mass-production requirements.

Dyes

This area is very specialized and vast. Because of the rapid development in man-made fibres, a means of colouring these new products must be found. It is all a matter of chemistry and designing substances that will penetrate the fibres and stay there regardless of external influences. This is not an easy exercise, having to devise chemicals to penetrate different substances and also to produce a wide range of colours without affecting the properties of the cloth.

Some cloth is woven with different yarns which require their own dying techniques. They are woven this way to produce special characteristics, such as texture, touch or feel and heat retention, and also dye selection – where only certain fibres will pick up a particular colour leaving the others untouched.

Printing, weaving and knitwear

There are dedicated computer systems that have been designed for this area.

At the time of writing, an American company called Computer Design Inc., CDI, a company that specializes in software, has produced a range of programs covering yarn design, printing, weaving and realistic 3D solid-image representation. It also offers a pattern design program in 3D, with 2D conversion, but that will be covered in a separate chapter.

Before going into details, it must be said that these software programs are very powerful and require a very powerful computer to run them. This means that the system is very expensive, and only large companies or combines can afford to acquire them.

The first part of the computer program deals with yarn construction. It enables the designer to choose the number of strands in the yarn and to twist them together, and to colour each fibre differently if required. Then to weave a cloth with the resultant yarn, choosing from various types of weave or to design a stripe or check pattern. This can be achieved very rapidly and the effect assessed accurately owing to the realistic image on screen. Added to this are the vast colour options available which give the designer the facility to view many different colour schemes and effects in minutes.

Once satisfied with the design, the instructions can be passed on to the mill for mass production without having to go through the long process of making sample lengths in order to realize the effect of a design.

There are also programs that will enable the design of knitwear cloth and garment patterns. The facility for designing the knitting yarns also applies here. These programs can be directly linked to an automatic knitting machine which will produce the prototype design very quickly and facilitate rapid adjustments ready for mass production or, if required, a 'one-off' supply where each garment is made for the individual. One of the main producers of this type of program is Shima Seiki who make the Shimatronic systems.

There are techniques for accurately reproducing subtle colour combinations that have been arrived at by using the computer's 16 million colour options, so the designer has access to almost infinite colour choice. But having said all that, considerable difficulty arises when the colour has to be printed out accurately from the computer, to be handed to the dye chemist in order for it to be copied. This, though, is not the designer's problem, and is another story.

There are also software programs that can be coupled to graphic packages that enable the production of silk screens for printed textiles. The system allows the designer to peel off the layers of the colour printing sequence and plot them individually, ready to be converted into the screens. This eliminates the arduous task of manually producing the screens using a light table, which takes a great deal of time.

In order to see the effect of a newly designed cloth, it is possible to dress a computer-generated human image with the fabric design in question.

This can be done in two ways. The first is by scanning into the computer, through a colour scanner, a photograph of a model dressed in the type of garment that will be suitable for the material. Then, by using one of the options in the GA program, blank out the existing material in the photograph and replace it with the new design with just a press of a button. It is then also possible to change the colour combinations in the fabric and to see the effect of them in a realistic setting. This is achieved in a very short time compared with the time it would take to paint each illustration on paper to see the same effects. It also enables the fashion designer to dress various types of garment in different materials and colour, ways that make it easy to vizualize the structure of the range of clothing for the coming show. This technique includes the shadow effects of the original photograph and gives a completely realistic representation.

The same process, using solid 3D imagery, is even more realistic

Computer-aided design (CAD)

and effective. Instead of a photograph being scanned into the computer, a model form (a stand or human dummy shape) is digitized into the memory and, with the use of a powerful 3D program (such as produced by the CDI), a garment can then be designed directly on to the model form on the computer screen. First, this appears in wire-frame form and is then filled in to make a solid realistic form, complete with shading, which can be rotated and looked at from any angle. This garment design can then be dressed in any of the newly designed fabrics that have been generated on the computer and shown to prospective buyers, thus eliminating the long and costly process of producing sample lengths of cloth and making them up into garments in order to show the effect of a cloth to the buyer. This makes the textile manufacturer much more flexible and cuts down development costs dramatically. They can then afford to make smaller quantities of a design to match their customers' requirements, instead of insisting on a minimum production run of a design in order to cover the production costs, which has, in the past, meant several thousand metres of cloth for the one design. If the clothing manufacturer wished to make that cloth exclusive to their company, then they would have had to buy the complete production run of that design. This is a big gamble, since predicting future demand is always a hit and miss affair.

Clothing, shoe and embroidery design

These manufacturing processes are carried out with the help of GA (graphic art) software programs. Basically, they consist of a wide range of drawing and painting options using an electronic pen on a graphic pad that manifests on a colour monitor with the ability to rapidly change part or the whole of a design.

Graphic art programs for computer application are very numerous, and vary considerably in their depth and sophistication. There are paintbox programs that can be bought for as little as £30 which run on 16 bit computers like the Amiga and Atari St and Macintosh, or even cheaper for the Spectrum, Amstrad and Commodore 64, which are 8 bit machines.

The 16 bit machines mostly run medium-resolution packages with up to a 512 colour palette, and even higher when backed by a special graphics processor – up to a 4096 colour palette. These usually run on a medium resolution colour monitor of around 640 × 300 lines. The Amiga and Atari St are both powered by the MC 68000 processor, which is a 32/16 bit/bus configuration and, for the price of about £350, gives a powerful machine of exceptionally good value. Add to this another £250 for a colour monitor, and the total of £600 gives the basis for a very wide range of applications, including a graphics capability that has considerable potential. This category of machine is used by the home operator and amateur artist, but it cannot be compared to the professional systems; however, at those kind of prices it is good value, and can be used successfully in a commercial role.

The Macintosh computers are also very good, and run on the same processors as the Atari St and Amiga; Macintosh offers a wide range of software but it is a little more expensive. The Macintosh also has a full range of CAD/CAM software written for it, which includes pattern construction, grading and layplanning. IBM-compatible PC-type models also run various CAD/CAM programs. The Ormus system by Concept 11 is one example.

The Ormus system is basically a designer's package which links a graphic program, called 'Pluto', with a PDS and grading program, and the whole lot is run by a Tandon computer or, in theory, any IBM clone.

Most of the major clothing-systems manufacturers now have CAD software running on IBM-type machines, using either the intel 80286 or the 80386 processors using VAG resolution screens. These give a very acceptable performance and are being improved continuously.

An example of this is the Pluto graphics program by IO Research Ltd, which runs on an IBM-type machine, and will cost around £2000. It gives 16 million colours and supports high-resolution graphics, provided that the high-resolution monitor is used (this will cost an extra £2000). Added to this will be a thermal colour printer, for another £4000.

A typical IBM system will consist of:

1. IBM clone plus a hard disk, from £1500/£3000 ($2000/$3000)
2. Graphics card and software from £2000 ($2500)
3. Colour scanner from £2000 ($2500)
4. Colour printer 'ink jet' or 'thermal' from £2000 ($2500)
5. High-resolution monitor from £400/£4000 ($600/$6000)
6. Digitizer and pen, £200 ($300)
7. Plotter for line drawings from £2000/£7000 ($3000/$8000)
8. Polaroid camera system up to £2000 ($3000)
9. Optional 3D and animation software from £1000/£4000 ($1500/$6000)
10. Buffer to free program while printing is being done, £800 ($1000)
11. Optional laser or standard printer, from £1200/£4000 ($1500/$6000)for the laser and £300/£600 ($450/$900) for standard 24 pin or daisy wheel

The total can be from £14 500 to £25 000 ($20 000/$35 000). All of these prices are for the year 1990.

These prices represent the cheaper professional packages. If a dedicated system is envisaged, such as in the CDI software, then the hardware will be similar to that just mentioned, except for the computer, which would be an 80386 type and a suitable memory. This means a 32 bit machine with at least 8 mega/bytes of RAM and a 60 meg hard disk. One of the companies that produce this type of hardware is Silicon Computers. It is the Silicon computer that CDI uses to run their software. A complete system by CDI, which includes 2D and 3D, graphics plus the pattern-construction program, can cost over £100 000 ($150 000).

There are other companies producing similar software but, at the present, CDI are the pioneers in the field of realistic solid 3D graphics and the software to convert 3D to 2D. It looks as though they will continue to be so in the foreseeable future. The main factor that will determine graphic development is the improvement of memory capacity and the speed of access to the data. Work is being done on CD (compact disk) to adapt it as a memory device which will have very large capacity and fast access. Also in development is the waferscale integration (WFI), which combines a massive memory and processor on to a single disk of about 6 inches in diameter, having the capacity of at least 5 times greater than hard disks and an access time 1000 times faster than present access times. This type of development will open up many new areas involving solid modelling and animation.

There is also development in transputers and new forms of memory that can match the fast new processors. If this development is matched by advances in the direction of super/high resolution monitors, then it will open the doors to yet more commercial applications, particularly in the realm of entertainment.

After the design of the woven or knitted fabric, the next stage is to design the garments or shoes and any embellishments that may go on to the finished article in the form of embroidery or other similar application.

It is with the help of the graphic art programs that the design of clothing is carried out where the silhouette and design details are devised and recorded in sketch form ready for the pattern technologists to create a garment as true to the sketch as possible. This also applies to the designing of shoes but, whereas the garments are usually designed in 2D (that is 'flat'), the shoe designs are nearly always designed in 3D (solid imagary), where the style lines and details are drawn over a basic shoe shape (a last) which has been put into the memory on a 3D digitizer. More of this will follow in later chapters.

It must also be added at this point that there are embroidery software programs that enable the embroidery designer to create designs and feed them directly into a computer-driven embroidery sewing machine which will then carry out the design automatically, so saving a great deal of time and making for greater flexibility.

Software programs for designing knitting patterns are also available to run in conjunction with sophisticated computerized knitting machines.

The means of application is with a stylus (electronic pen) on an electromagnetic board called a digitizer or graph pad, which has a matrix of very fine wires in a longtitude and latitude configuration which, when touched by the stylus, light up the corresponding pixels on the screen.

Displayed on the screen are menus of options such as the choice of thickness of the brush, pen or pencil, also a colour palette from which to choose the required colour to draw or paint. Added to this are many other options, including various geometric shapes such as circles, rectangles and straight lines to facilitate decorative pattern designing, plus an option to mix the basic colours to get any shade or tone needed, up to 16 000 000 degrees. It is also possible to capture small areas of a design and increase or decrease the scale and then repeat that piece covering the screen, thus producing an allover repeat effect.

The GA part of a system is used by dress, shoe and embroidery designers to make their working sketches and colour specification for submission to a selection process by sales and production managers and also retail buyers. Once the design has been accepted for sampling and showing, the next process can begin; this is the construction and design of the garment patterns from which the design will be cut out and made. This is also a form of designing and, because of that, the software programs are called a PDS program, or 'pattern-design systems'. This will be examined in Chapter 6.

Computer-aided design (CAD)

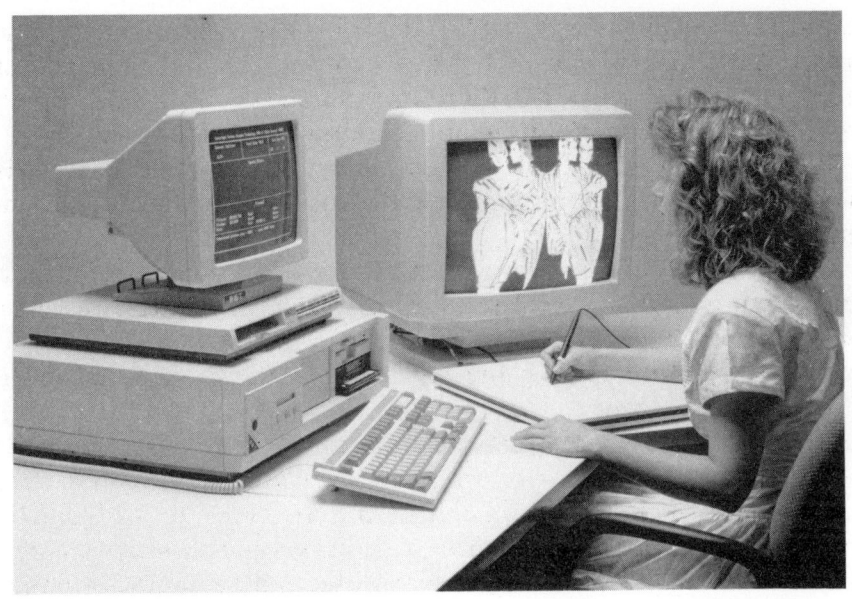

Creative Designer 150 features a fast 32-bit CPU computer, 16 million colour capability and over 200 powerful functions
(Courtesy Gerber Garment Technology, Inc.)

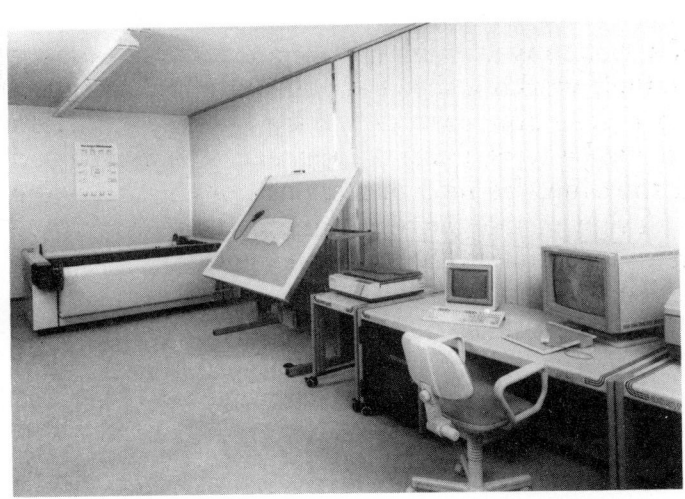

Assyst Designer and Assygraph graphic art systems
(Courtesy Assyst GmbH)

84   Computers in the fashion industry

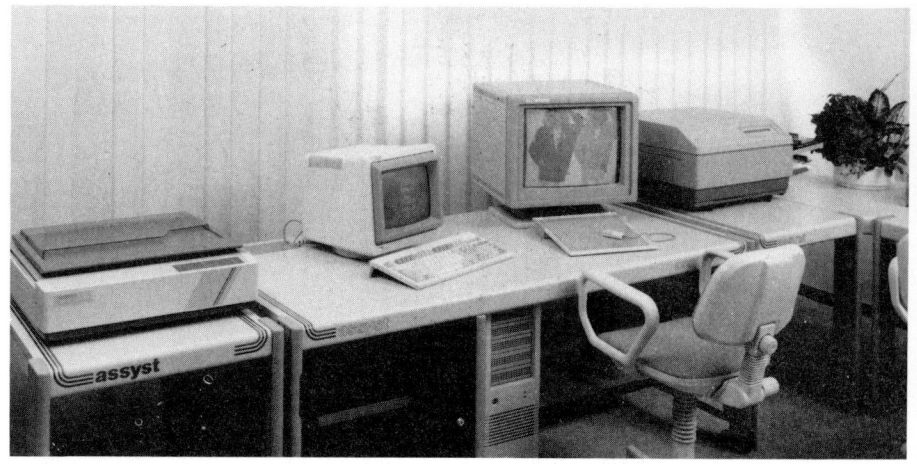

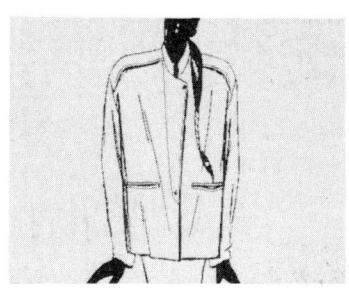

In the beginning: the sketch

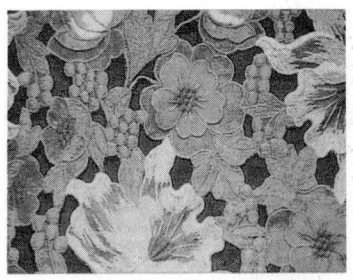

Material pattern, taken by video camera (photograph from screen)

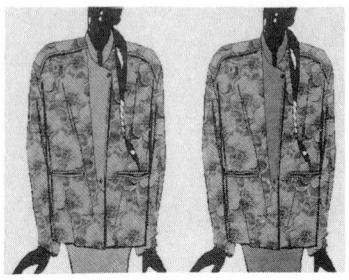

The finished style in two colour variations

(Courtesy Assyst GmbH)

Computer-aided design (CAD) 85

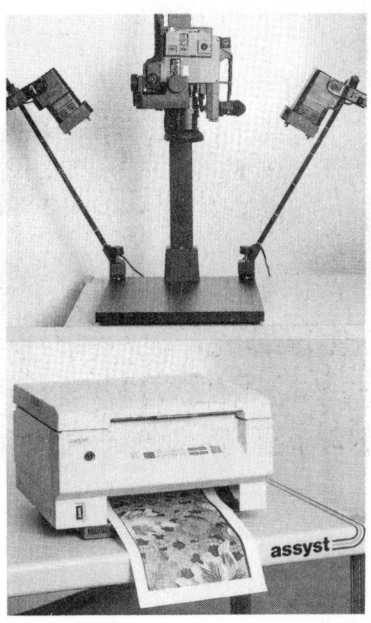

*Assyst video thermal and colour printer
(Courtesy Assyst GmbH)*

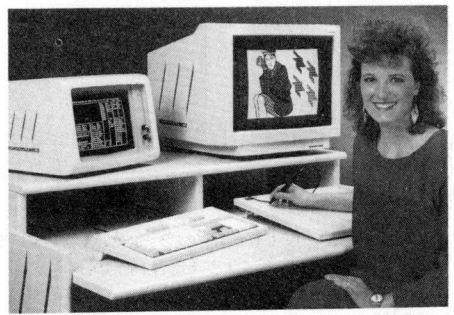

*GA system for CAD
(Courtesy CIM Microdynamics Ltd)*

86 Computers in the fashion industry

Examples of two-dimensional fabric superimposition (Courtesy CIM Microdynamics Ltd)

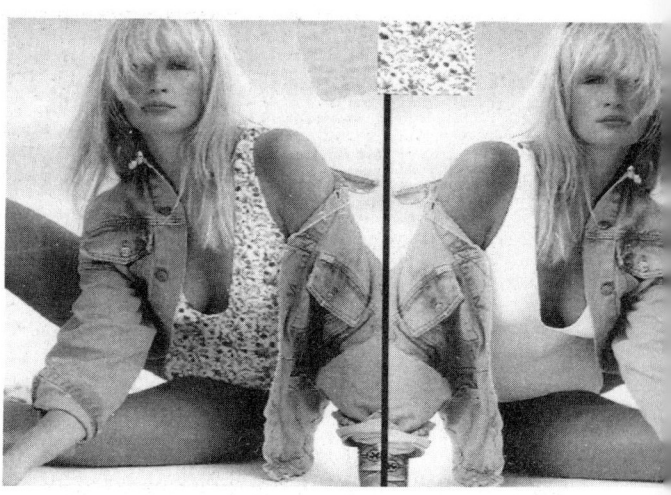

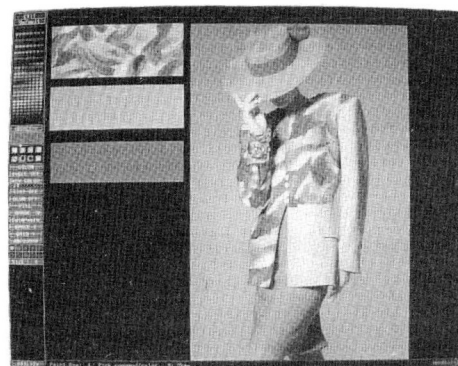

Screens of fabric overlays on photograph input and check design process (Courtesy CDI Technologies Ltd)

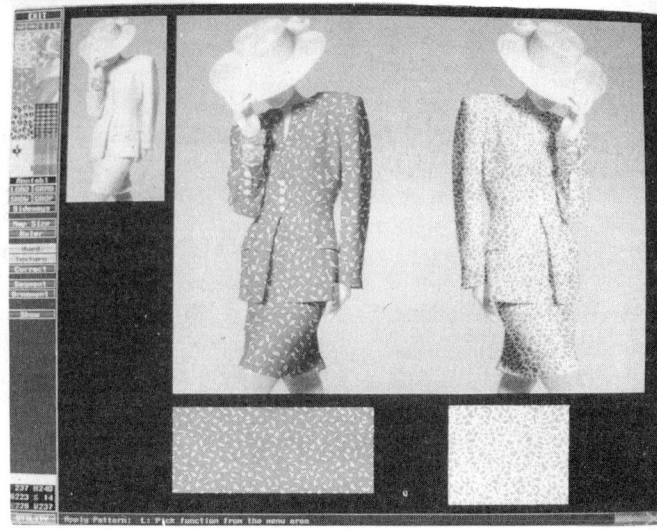

Computer-aided design (CAD) 87

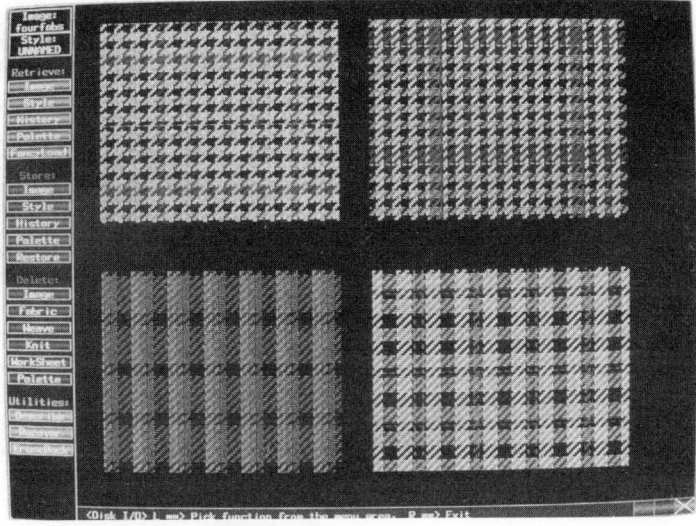

Textile design menu
 (Courtesy CDI Technologies Ltd)

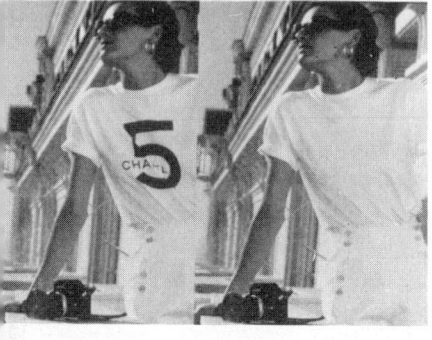

Two-dimensional
 graphic system.
  (Courtesy CDI
 Technologies Ltd)

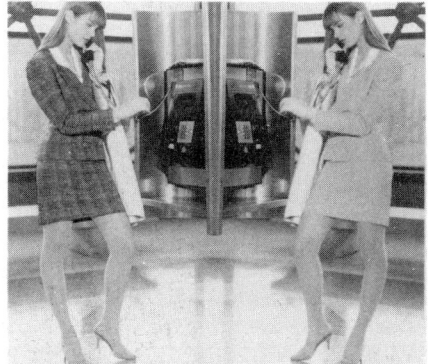

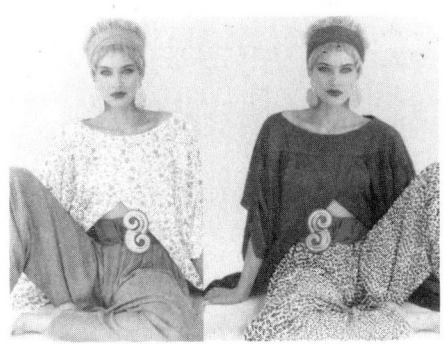
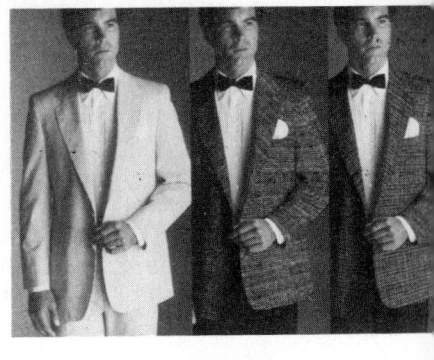
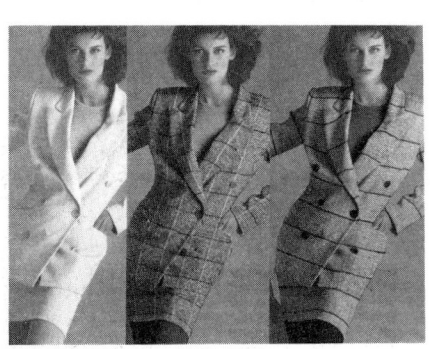
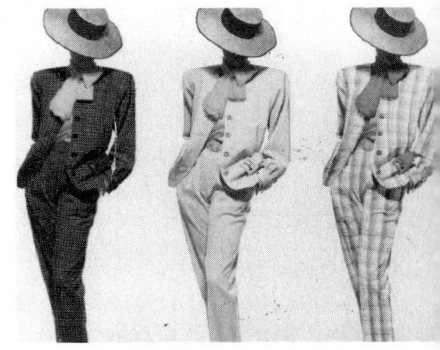
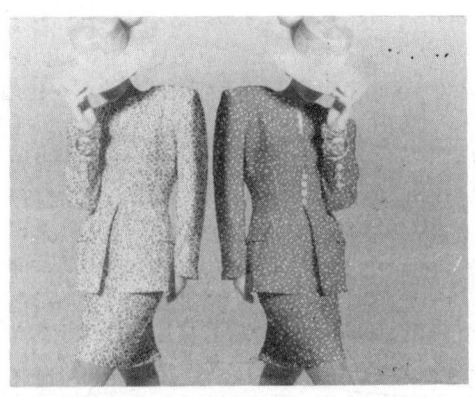
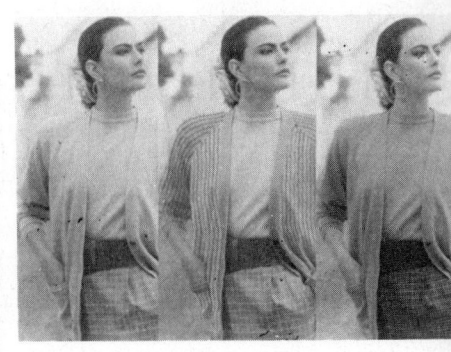

Scanned photographs are dressed in different fabrics.
  (Courtesy CDI Technologies Ltd)

Chapter 6

Pattern-design systems (PDS)

The PDS software program is the last part of the system that comes under the heading of CAD. The programs that follow are CAM (computer-aided manufacture).

At the time of writing, PDS systems are not all that popular with designers and pattern cutters. The process of designing patterns is difficult enough without the added burden of a complex program to learn and manipulate. At the present time, all PDS programs are 2D; this means that the technique of pattern cutting is, by definition, what is called 'flat pattern cutting', as opposed to modelling, which is the technique of making patterns by applying the material directly to the model form in order to arrive at the pattern shapes. It would take too long to describe the two methods in detail, but the essence of the situation is that flat pattern cutting is a kind of shorthand technique based on the feedback from modelling.

At one time, all patterns were arrived at by modelling in cloth on a stand or model form of the human shape, and the resulting shapes were the patterns from which further garments would be cut and made up. Modelling is the only way to extract balanced 2D patterns from a 3D shape, and to arrive at a true understanding of a very complex shape: the human body. Somebody then hit on the idea of taking a basic pattern shape from a body and, by a cleverly worked-out system of manipulations, altering the basic pattern 'on the flat' to any desired style without (in theory) having to use the model form or a live human body. These 'flat manipulations' have been elaborated over the years, and have proved very useful in speeding up the process of pattern construction and helping to standardize a company's fit and sizing. This technique takes a long time to master, but it cannot be used alone; that is, it must be used in parallel with the technique of modelling, otherwise patterns can go badly out of balance in the hands of a pattern cutter with insufficient experience.

For this reason, the PDS computer system is a dangerous tool. It is purely a flat medium and resists the use of modelling, plus there is the difficulty of mastering the PDS program and the illusion the computer gives of infallibility. Also, there is the fact that the pattern technician is working at reduced scale. All of these factors tend to encourage ill-fitting and badly proportioned garments. For these reasons, the PDS systems tend not to be used and, until they are improved and made easier, there will be continued resistance to them.

Having said all that, in the hands of an experienced pattern designer and one that has taken the trouble and effort to learn a PDS system thoroughly, it can be an excellent tool when used correctly.

In order to make it work to advantage, there would have to be a long period of integrating the PDS by means of gradually feeding its memory with every conceivable kind of verified pattern shape and style. Patterns that have been modelled and also flat cut and made up, have been tested and sold as successful items. Once there is a library of tested material in memory, as data for further design manipulation, then the PDS really starts to achieve results; the experienced pattern cutter can do wonders with all of this easily accessed and proven material. Prior to computers, if the designer wanted to redesign a style based on a previous good seller, a laborious search through miles of hanging card pattern styles had to be made and, more often than not, the one that was wanted had been thrown away. Added to this, the PDS system can be made to remember previous pattern-construction processes and automatically carry out small parts of the pattern-design process; this could save time, but it presupposes a very thorough understanding of the software and a depth of pattern-cutting experience. All 2D PDS programs are menu driven, either the menu is on the screen or on a data pad (digitizer board), and either a mouse or, more often, a stylus is used to select the item from the menu.

A PDS system menu consists of several basic functions. They are:

1   Change outline of pattern
2   Draw lines, straight, curved or freehand
3   Erase, cancel, annul
4   Measure
5   Call up one or more pieces
6   Move patterns on screen

7   Join patterns, fuse together
8   Copy patterns
9   Pairing and mirroring
10 Scaling
11 Arcs and circles
12 Pivot darts
13 Add and subtract seams
14 Manipulate points using x and y coordinates
15 Text

These can then be expanded as required.

The main difficulty arises when the menus get so large that they require a long learning period; this is made worse by the fact that each part of the menu has its own procedure, and has to be adhered to exactly to give the desired result. Sometimes the menu item has a sub-menu, and the sub-menu also has a sub-menu and it can go on to another sub-menu, each of which must be studied and practised before a perfect outcome is achieved.

Having spent time and effort to master this PDS program and become proficient in it, it would be good to think that the operator could sit down at another similar system of another make and be fluent on it at once. Unfortunately, this is never the case. All the various makers of systems devise their own menus, and they are all different in wording and operation. Some are longer and more complex than others, but all are formidable. They are formidable because pattern construction is a complex affair. But a lot of the items included on most pattern systems are not used on a regular basis, and tend to complicate matters rather than help.

If there was some standardization of menus and their means of application, then it would make things so much easier and PDS programs would be used much more readily.

Also, the constant use of the keyboard instead of just the mouse and screen menu makes most programs 'user unfriendly'. Having to remember numbers and letter codes to work a program is rapidly becoming old-fashioned and cumbersome. The new programs that are just emerging are all 'point and fire'-type procedures that do not require a lot of tedious memorizing of unrelated codes.

Digitizer

Before anything can be done it is necessary to enter patterns into the system, either finished style patterns or block patterns, which are basic patterns with no styling, used for manipulating into styles by means of 2D flat-pattern techniques. This is done using either a digitizer or a scanner. Digitizing and scanning are the means of inputting shapes into the computer memory. These can be 2D and 3D.

The digitizer is a large adjustable table area, like a draughtsman's table, under its surface is a very fine electrified matrix in a longitude and latitude configuration of x and y coordinates. The pattern is fixed to the surface with tape and a hand-held stylus with cross hairs, like a rifle sight, is used to outline the pattern by registering points round the pattern contour into the computer memory and at the same time giving each pattern piece a style number and size using the keyboard. Only half the pattern needs to be digitized as the opposite side can be generated by the computer.

There is a certain amount of skill in digitizing, and it takes time to learn how many points to digitize in order to get accurate curves. This is a fairly time-consuming activity, and accuracy will depend on the operator placing the cursor precisely over the edge of the pattern. The accuracy of the digitizer is to within one-tenth of a millimetre, so there is no lack of precision in the hardware, but most operators cannot get more than within a half a millimetre accuracy due to visual limitations.

The other method of putting patterns into the computer is by using a scanner. This is rather like an outsized photocopier, but is designed to register just the outline rather than the inner contents of the pattern. The scanner is very much faster than the digitizer and, in some cases, can match its accuracy.

Pattern manipulation

Once the patterns are in the system, they can be manipulated to the next stage. This is either pattern styling directly from the block patterns or style alteration from existing styled patterns. Other functions, such as layplanning and grading, will be outlined in subsequent chapters.

As mentioned before, the menus of the pattern program are quite large, and each item on the menu must be studied and mastered in order to be able to link all the required processes together. This takes time and practice. The computer manufacturer will imply that it is easy and automatic, but it is not.

Manipulations of patterns, at first, can take longer than doing them manually. This is because for a long time mistakes are made that often entail starting again, and spending much time studying the manual and particular menu item, or inadvertently wiping out the last half-hour's work.

There are help explanations with each menu item, which are often not very explicit, or written in pigeon English, owing to translation from another language. Some menu titles are also inexplicable, and have to be learned the hard way. If the pattern cutter is not very experienced, then there is no predicting what will come out at the other end.

There is not much point in outlining the menus here; suffice to say that they are divided into three parts 1 pattern manipulation; 2 pattern finishing (such as seam allowances, notches etc.); and 3 grading.

As was said earlier, in the right hands the PDS program is very useful but, in the wrong hands, a tool for turning out rubbish.

3D PDS

Three-dimensional pattern-design systems are the latest innovation. They are the dream of the boss who sees a semi-automatic pattern-cutting program that can be operated by any idiot, without having to rely on good and well-paid (in some cases) pattern technicians. It is a strange irony that it has created the opposite effect.

First, it is necessary to outline and explain the essence of the system.

It first requires a 3D digitizer, which is one that enables the placing of an object that takes up space into computer memory. This is similar to the 2D digitizer, but instead, if using a flat surface, the cursor has to pass over a model form (stand). Instead of taking two measurements (x and y coordinates), it takes three (x, y and z) and produces a wire-frame image of the model which can, if required, be filled in to make a solid form. This 3D representation can be viewed from any angle by rotation. Then the idea is to build or model the garment, with computer-generated cloth, on the model form, as if it were the actual full-size stand.

This requires a high level of skill, even when modelling normally, but to model with a stylus and a set of instructions through a computer and on a screen is even more difficult.

To model in this way is possible only if the program is sophisticated enough to permit accurate handling of the material.

The next stage is to remove the material from the stand, having first accurately marked the seams, pockets and suppression areas, plus manipulating the amount of flare needed in the various places and then to make good all the lines and check for accuracy before copying off on to card and adding the seam allowances. At the present time, the suppression areas are only represented in the form of degrees of stress within the flattened pattern. What is then required is for the pattern technician to select the correct places to release the tension.

This will open up the darts, pleats or whatever is representing the suppression. The amount of tension in the flattened pattern shape is gauged by a matrix of lines within the flattened pattern, and also a graduated colour which is darkest at the point of greatest stretch and gradually lightens as the stress decreases. When the pattern is split to the centre of the deepest tonal shade and where the matrix of lines converge most and then open until the colour is the same everywhere and the lines are parallel, that will be the point of correct suppression and will mean that the surface is completely relaxed. Then seam allowances must be added and parts numbered and sized, and the information saved in memory.

If all of this can be accomplished satisfactorily, then this system will be very useful, but it will require a pattern technician of even greater skills to operate the program than would otherwise be necessary.

Thus an idea that set out to automate the pattern-construction process has had the opposite effect: instead of doing away with pattern cutters, it has made them even more essential. Whether or not some AI (artificial intelligence) can be applied here in the future is a big question mark. It may be that high-tension areas in the pattern can be recognized by the program and an automatic splitting process included, in which case it would make the life of the pattern cutters a little easier, but that is all.

Building pattern libraries
Pattern cutting is probably one of the most infinitely variable occupations that exist. It has three aspects, which are variable between two opposites. They are:

1 Fashion
2 Material characteristics
3 Size and shape of body

Each one of these can send a sane pattern cutter 'two sheets to the wind' – Let alone all three together! In this trade, pattern cutters and designers spend their whole life learning, and quite often relearning, techniques that have evaporated owing to the fashion pendulum swinging slowly back again to the same set of problems, but different in degree, to the ones of ten years ago. Purely as a matter of interest, and to be able to assess what needs to be put into a good pattern-cutting library, it may be helpful to analyse the designing of garments in general and to categorize the parts.

The first definition is the function/decoration ratio. Every garment is a mixture of the two, and it is necessary to list some of the functional properties.

First, there is the issue of comfort versus appearance. These two can be incompatible in a close-fitting garment. When the fashion dictates skin-tight fitting then comfort can be ignored at the wearer's expense.

The pattern designer has to find the right balance in the degree of fit that will allow a reasonable amount of movement, even to breathe. This can be a difficult problem in many types of fashion garment, as opposed to the purely functional garment. There are many aspects of function in clothing. The area of sport shows a few:

Swimming costumes.	Tight-fitting elastic, smooth and slippery.
Ski outfits.	Speed or pleasure. For speed, the same as swimwear. For pleasure, warm and stylish, and with plenty of room for movement and comfort.
Sailing.	Warmth and ease of movement. Waterproof qualities; some styling.
Underwater diving.	Waterproofing and warmth.
Horse riding.	Comfort astride the horse, and much traditional styling.
Tennis.	Comfort and freedom of movement and dispersion of heat.
Motor racing	Comfort, protection from fire, and styling.
Working clothes	Comfort, places to store things, protection from heat, cold, abrasion or wet. Bright colours to warn of presence. Some styling.

There are more, but these give an idea of the functional properties involved. Patterns including all of these properties need to be stored in the computer for manipulation into future designs.

The next set of factors entail degree of fit or silhouette. There must be examples of garment patterns with every degree of fit, that have been proved and previously sold, stored in memory.

Other details, such as collar styles, pockets, sleeves, and seam styling, all need to be available in memory ready for slight or major alteration in order to establish new styles based on previous good sellers. If enough material is collected, then designing new ranges can be achieved much quicker and more cheaply.

The storage of designs can be expanded in all directions. Libraries of patterns covering outerwear, underwear, daywear, eveningwear, sportswear, and work clothing can be built up, and could cover both sexes, plus infants, children and teenage groups. All of these areas could be broken down into price and age categories and, to complete the picture, segregated into image or fashion trends linked to a data base detailing the size of the different markets associated with each type of fashion imagery, and the age groups and price ranges appropriate to the area. To support this 'design bank', there needs to be a data base of survey statistics detailing potential market numbers related to age, girth and height in both male and female adult sectors and also growth areas from birth to full maturity.

If this were established and was seen to be of good quality, it would be a very valuable commodity. But, as with everything else, pattern libraries will spring up filled with rubbish.

As with all computer data, it will have to be 'backed up', that is, stored on a separate disk and kept in a safe place in case of fire or theft.

Pattern-design systems (PDS) 97

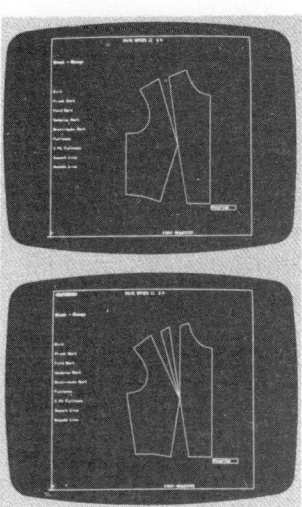

Darts can be manipulated, relocated, split, combined, or eliminated

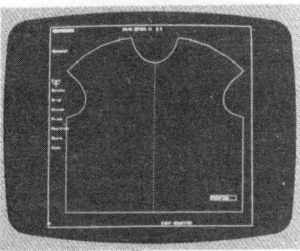

Mirror piece so that you can see how it will actually appear as a pattern

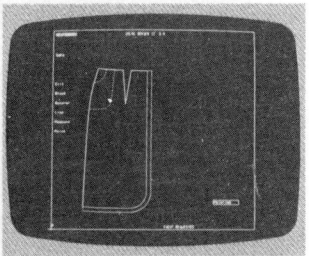

Add seam allowances, measure and add grade rules

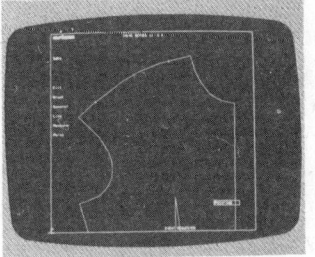

Notches, punch holes, etc. can be added where desired

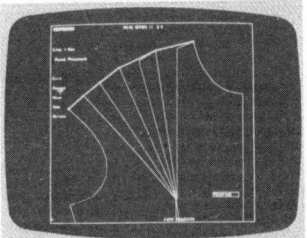

By adding points, the computer can be instructed to draw a line for shirring, as shown here across the shoulder seam

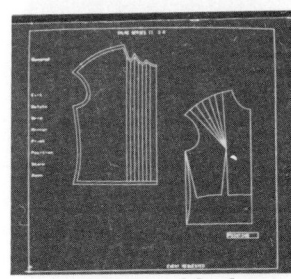

Any proven block or production pattern stored in the system can be used as the base pattern for a new one. Therefore, the sound control procedures for such centralized base patterns will yield a more consistent fit with less trial and error pattern making

PDS screen shot of pattern manipulation   (Courtesy Gerber Garment Technology, Inc.)

98 Computers in the fashion industry

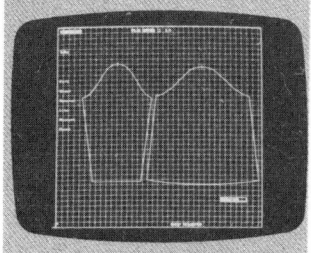

Create a grid for measuring and orientating pieces

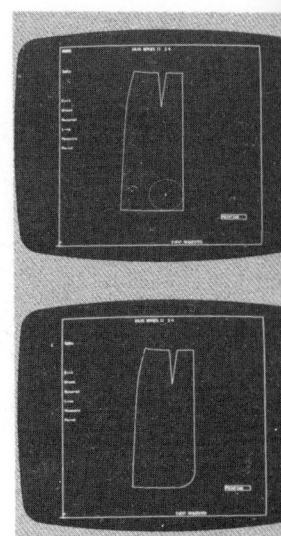

Change shapes

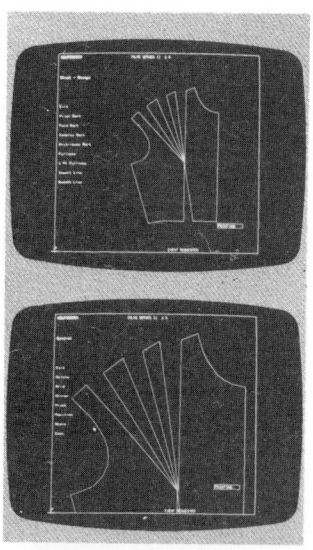

The ability to change scale on the display. Here a shoulder seem has been magnified

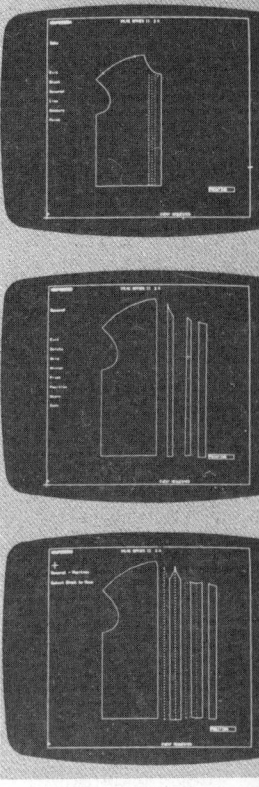

Tucks, underlays, et can be created from newly created block (Courtesy Gerber Garment Technology, Inc.)

EDS program examples

Pattern-design systems (PDS)   99

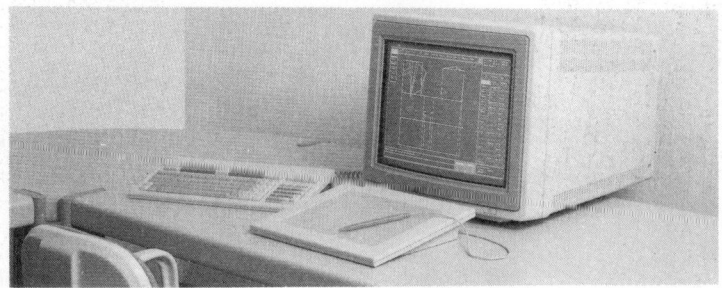

The Assycad design system for constructing and editing garment patterns
 (Courtesy Assyst GmbH)

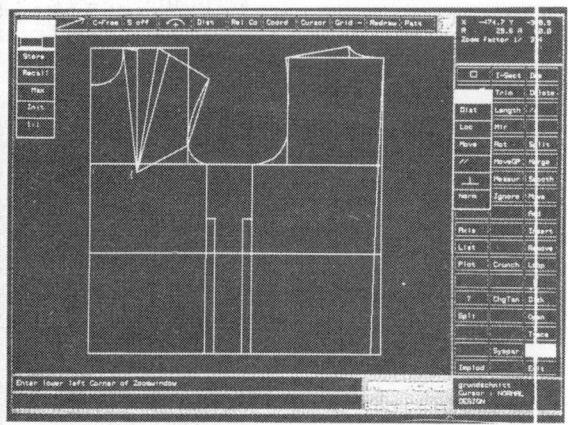

Construction of a base pattern

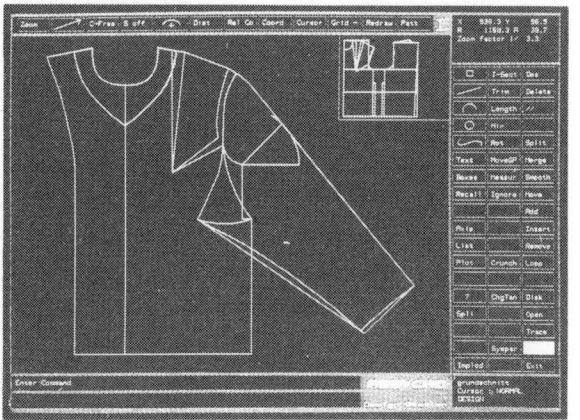

Construction of a collar and sleeve

PDS screen
 (Courtesy Assyst GmbH)

Definition of pattern parts

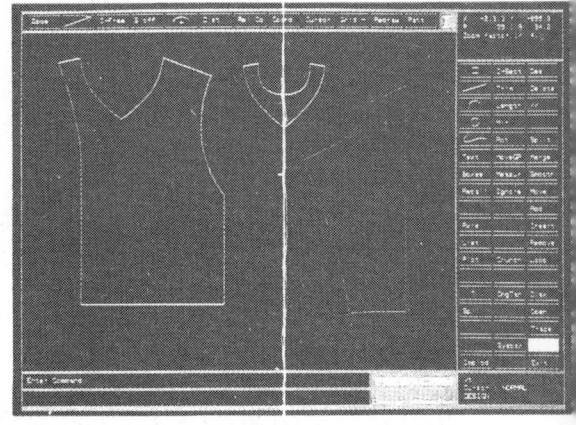

Rapid pattern grading

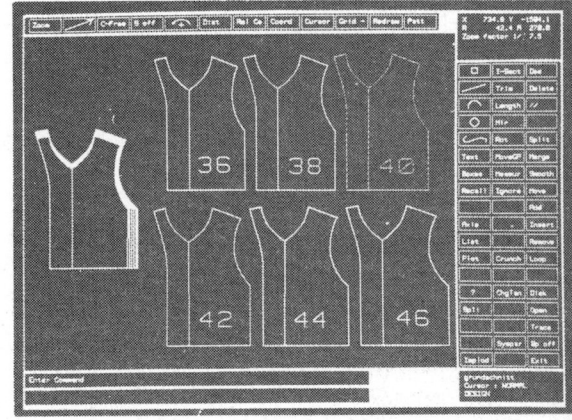

*Nested draft grade
(Courtesy Assyst GmbH)*

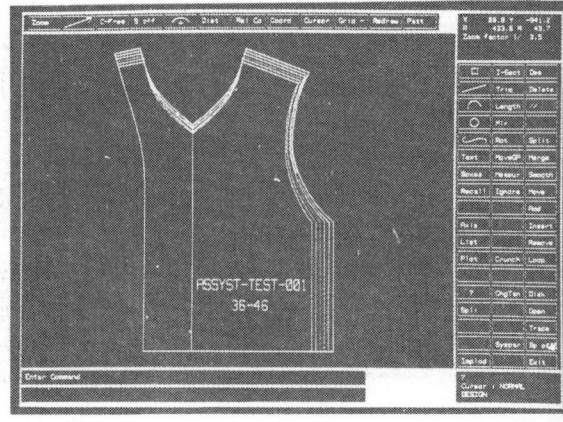

*PDS screens
(Courtesy Assyst GmbH)*

Pattern-design systems (PDS) 101

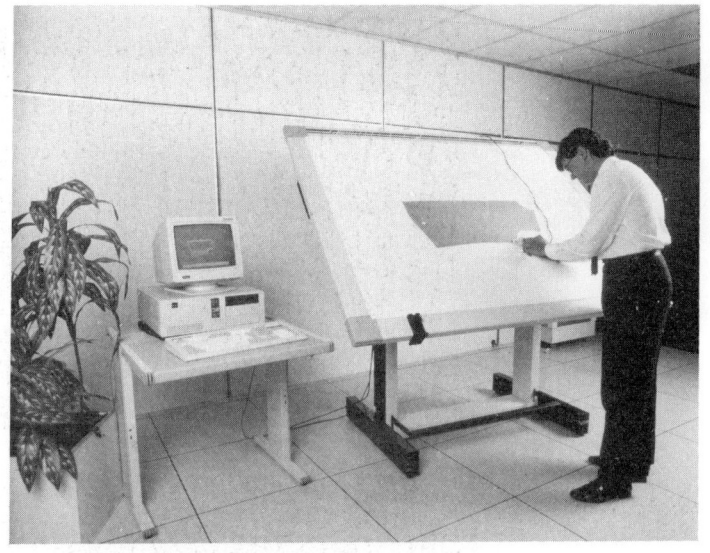

*Digitizing a pattern into the system
(Courtesy Investronica UK)*

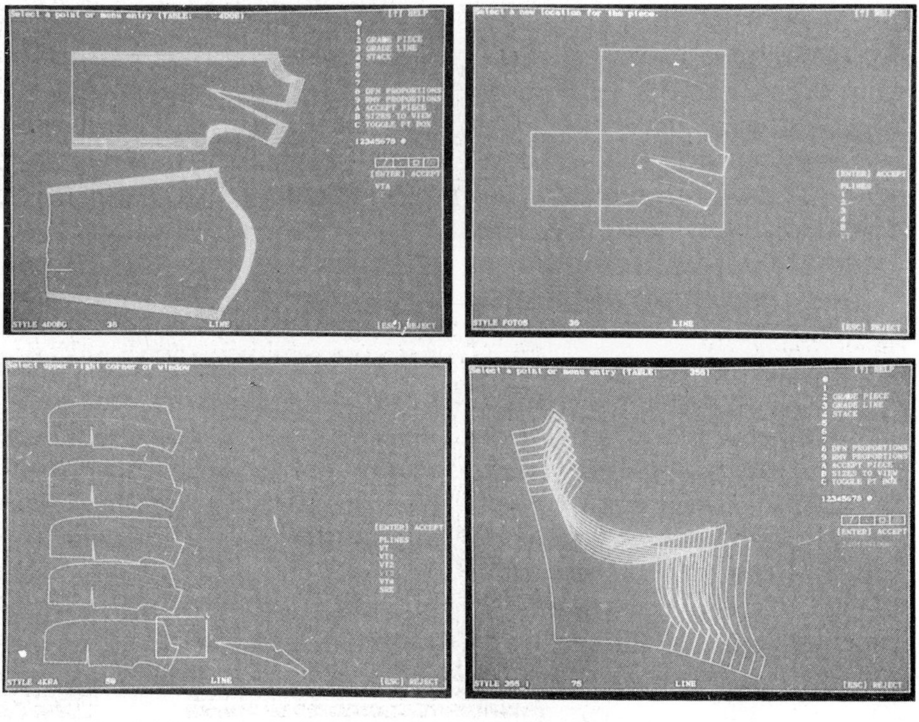

*PDS screen shots of pattern construction and grading
(Courtesy of CIM Microdynamics Ltd)*

102 Computers in the fashion industry

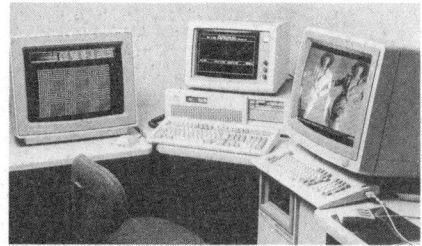

Hardware for cheaper design systems based on the PC MS-DOS
(Courtesy CDI Technologies Ltd)

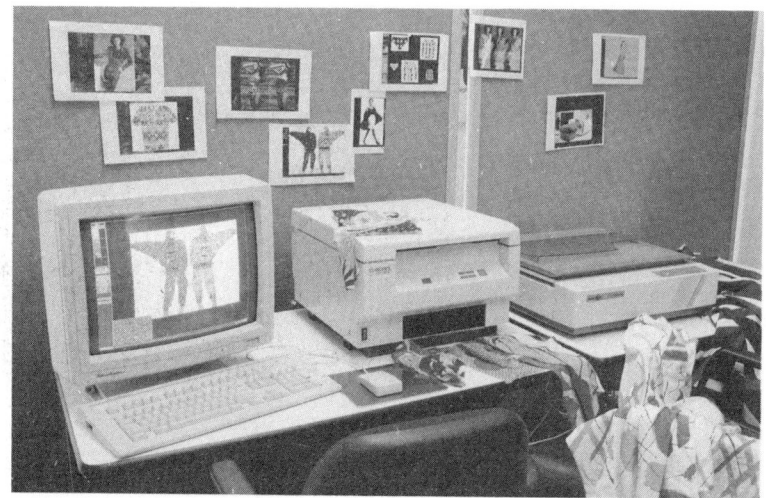

Complete two-dimensional system
(Courtesy CDI Technologies Ltd)

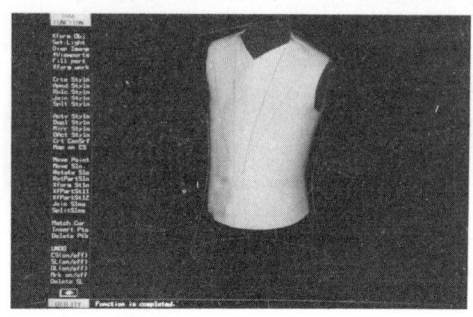

Solid three-dimensional modelling with man's suit outlined ready for conversion to a two-dimensional pattern
(Courtesy CDI Technologies Ltd)

Stages of three-dimensional solid modelling PDS system (Courtesy CDI Technologies Ltd)

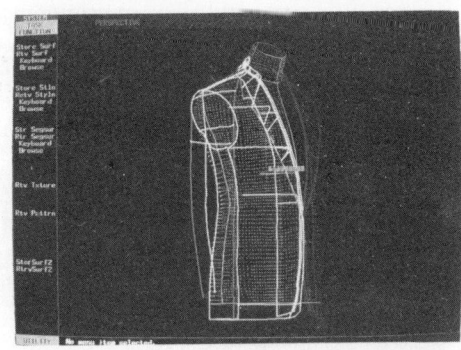

Solid three-dimensional suit completed (Courtesy CDI Technologies Ltd)

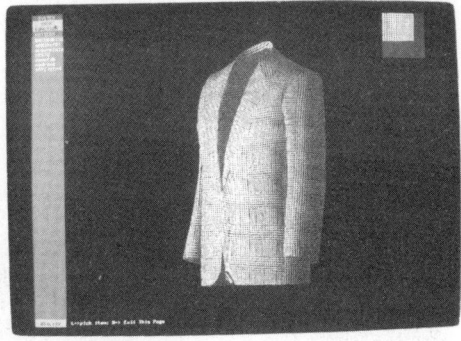

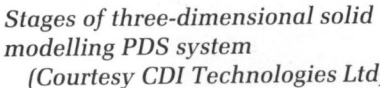

Three-dimensional pattern system. A sleeve flattened from three to two dimensions ready for completion by pattern technician (Courtesy CDI Technologies Ltd)

104 *Computers in the fashion industry*

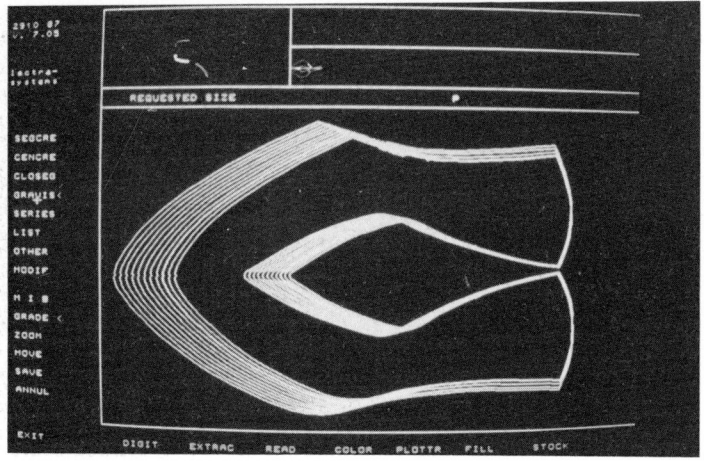

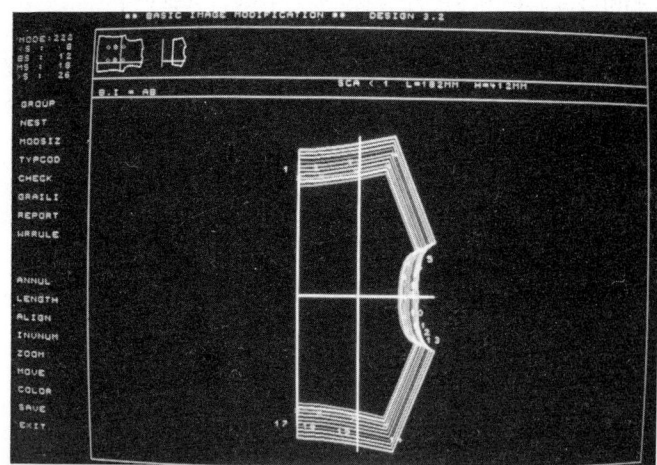

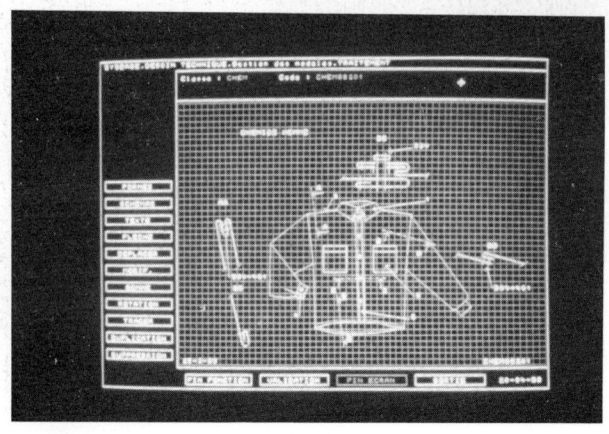

Pattern-design systems (PDS)

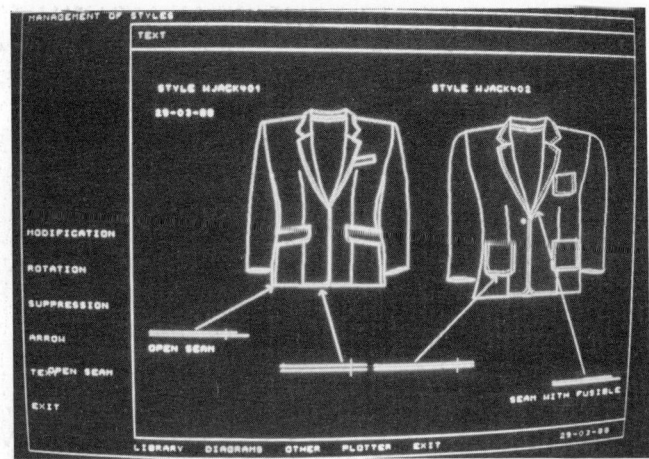

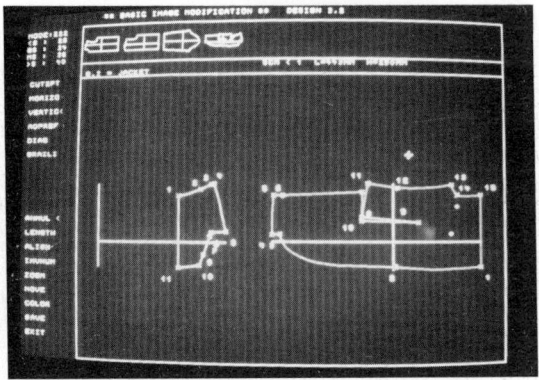

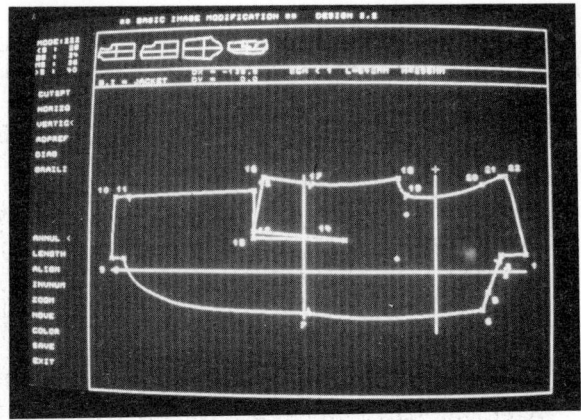

Screen shots
(Courtesy Lectra Systems)

Chapter 7

Computer grading with CAM

The first part of the manufacturing or mass-production process is making a set of patterns of all sizes from the perfected production pattern, which is usually a size 12 for women's clothing and 92.0 cm chest for men. This is called 'grading'. The production pattern is based on the sample pattern that the first garment is made from for showing to the retail buyers. The production pattern is a very accurate derivative of the first pattern, and may differ in detail owing to the fact that it has to be engineered to conform to mass-production techniques, but the final styling will be indistinguishable from the original sample. If done manually (without a computer), the process of grading is a long, and often monotonous, procedure. It entails the use of a set of instructions, which are a list of the increments that have to be applied to the various parts of the pattern pieces in order to enlarge or reduce the dimensions. These grading increments (or rules) are the quantities that change the pattern from one size to another. When done manually, this entails each size being accurately drawn round and increased, then carefully cut out, and all the information that is on the pattern, such as size, style number, number of pieces, and grain line, must be clearly printed on each pattern piece. If there are six sizes to be made, then this process can take a whole day just for one style, and maybe even longer depending on the complexity of the style and how many pieces there are in it. The quality of the final result depends on the accuracy and diligence of the grader. Sometimes a mistake in the increments can go unseen until the last piece of pattern has been graded and cut out and they are stacked on top of each other in order to check the even increase of the various parts. Sometimes these mistakes take a long time to rectify. It is possible that mistakes can go undetected and only show up in the finished garments, or while they are being machined. In which case, some people are destined for the 'chop', including the grader. The obvious solution to this problem was to use a computer and devise some kind of program that a computer could run that would take some of the labour, time and expense out of the process by automating it as much as possible.

It is not possible to make grading completely automatic, because there are very large variations in grading increments depending on style and other factors. Where a style changes very little, such as in shirt manufacture, then it is possible to make the grading almost automatic.

When the term 'automatic' is used, it means that the process is done by the computer without the use of a human brain or the moving parts of the body. In other words, the operator can press a few buttons and then walk away from the computer and do something else. 'Semi-automatic' means that the brain is still required, but the body is not. This is the case with computer grading. The initial instructions for increasing the pattern's 'one size' has to be given to the computer, and then it can generate all the other sizes automatically. All the resultant sizes can then either be plotted out on to paper or fed directly into the layplanning process (which is described in Chapter 8). It follows from this that knowledge and understanding of the principles that govern size increases still need to be learned and applied by an experienced pattern technician. The savings come from the acceleration of the process, which also means that less staff will be needed to accomplish the work. Most comprehensive computer systems that are dedicated to clothing, such as Gerber, Lectra, Investronica and others, give a program that offers three grading options. That is, three ways to apply size increments using the computer.

The first is 'manual/digitizer' input. The second is 'grade rule/digitizer', and the third is 'keyboard/monitor' direct grade on screen. The first, manual/digitizer, entails making a nested grade on the pattern draft by hand before going to the computer. This produces an 'increment path' along which the cardinal point moves. The increment path is then divided up into the number of sizes required. The complete pattern draft, with its grading points, is then fixed to the digitizer surface and the separate pattern pieces, one by one, are digitized and, at the same time, the increment path is input with instructions to divide it into as many sizes as the style requires. This means that the computer is fed with the pattern shape

Computer grading with CAM 109

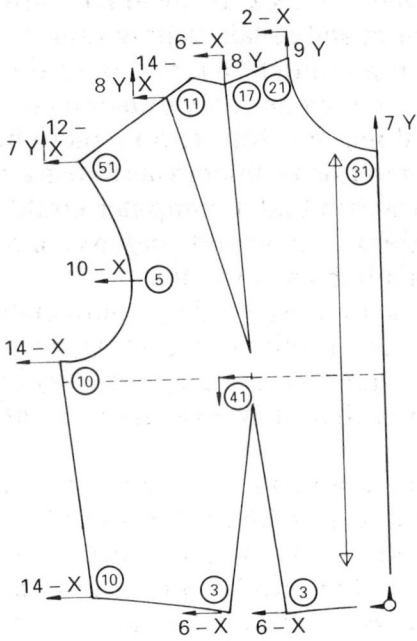

Figure 9 This is a women's basic front block pattern which has been prepared for digitizing with grade rules allocated to each of the cardinal points that control the change of size. These grade rules can be extracted from a grade-rule library which will be a matrix from 1.0 mm to approximately 15.0 mm in all of the x and y coordinates. This will give 15 × 15 × 4 = 900 grade rules to choose from. This matrix will be printed out and hung in a convenient place for reference.

Grade rules can also be written for individual styles without having to use the grade-rule library.

As the outline of the pattern is being digitized, the rules are entered as and when the cardinal points are arrived at

110 Computers in the fashion industry

and the size instructions at the same time, plus all the other related information on the pattern – such as style, grain, punch holes, notches, darts and number of pieces, etc. The computer can now generate all the sizes ready for layplanning.

The second method of grading on the computer is the grade rule/digitizer mode. This requires the grader to allocate a grade rule number to each cardinal point on the pattern where an increase is required, and writing that number at the cardinal point. After going through the whole pattern doing this, a list of the rules is entered on a 'source file' and the x and y grading coordinates listed alongside the appropriate rule number. The complete grade-rule list is then entered, via the keyboard, into the computer memory with the designated style name or number. The next stage is to commence digitizing each pattern piece into the computer and, at each cardinal point, the grade rule number is entered, thus linking it to the x and y coordinate for the size change at that place. When this is completed, the graded patterns are ready for application to layplanning.

The third method used for computer grading is the keyboard/monitor direct mode. This method is simply grading manually through the computer; the patterns have already been entered, via the digitizer or scanner, into memory and are selected in turn for grading, using the keyboard and grading menu on screen. The cursor is accurately centred on the cardinal point to be graded and

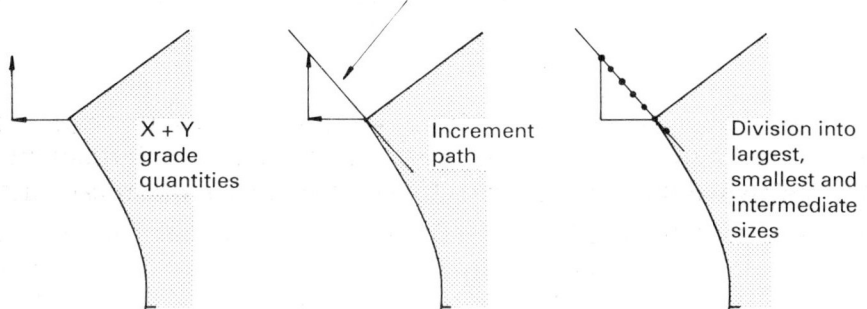

Figure 10 *When using the computer to digitize a pregraded pattern draft, it is necessary to establish, beforehand, all the increment paths that the cardinal points follow; and on arriving at one of these points in the process of digitizing, the largest and the smallest sizes on this line are digitized as well as the base pattern point. The computer will then automatically establish the other sizes by dividing the increment path into equal or unequal segments according to the size code being used.*

This diagram illustrates the creation of an increment path along which the cardinal grade point, on a pattern, moves

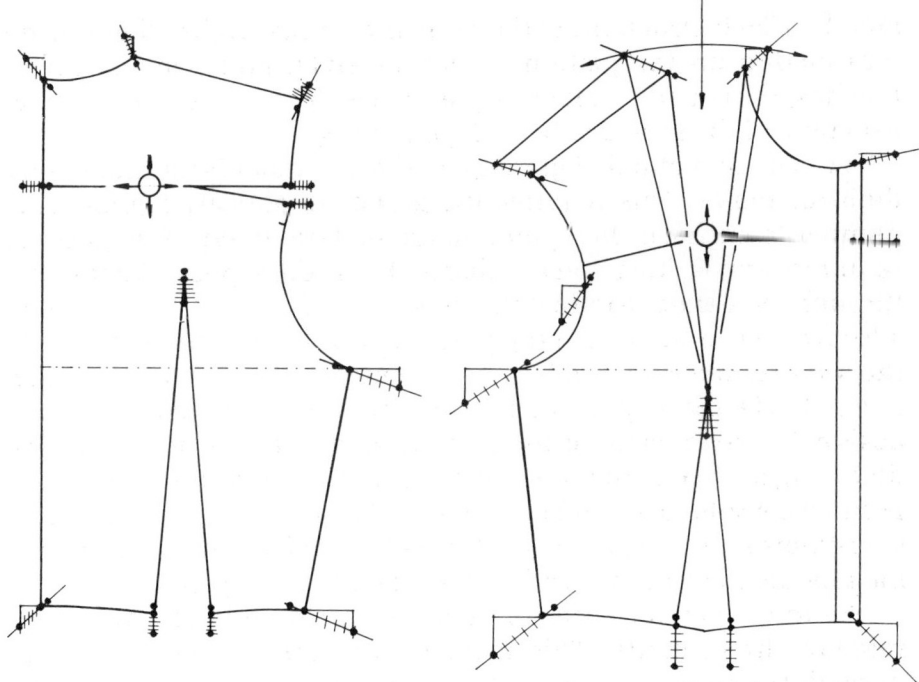

Figure 11 *This is an example of a pregraded bodice pattern, showing the increment paths. It is not necessary to divide up the path, as is shown in the diagram; the computer will do this automatically. The only points required are the three, on each cardinal point, marked by dots*

the x and y quantities entered. This is done for all the pattern pieces, and a nested grade is requested on screen to check the increments. When satisfied that all is correct, the grade data can be entered into permanent memory for future use.

Grade-rule library

Instead of creating grade rules for a specific style at source, it is possible to build a reference library of all the grade rules that are likely to be needed. So, you could have a library starting at rule number one and continuing perhaps up to one hundred or more. When preparing a source file for a style, the rule number is selected to match the requirement for the point in question and, when asked, the computer will extract it from the library and apply it at the place selected.

There is the question of whether the use of a library is quicker

Grade-rule table   Date: 16-7-89   Library Metric Imperial
                                                                     Main

Mode Rule	Sizes: Code	10 X.Y	12 X.Y	14 X.Y	16 X.Y	18 X.Y	20 X.Y	22 X.Y	X.Y	X.Y
121		00,80	00,–80			00,–240		00,–400		
122		00,40	00,–40			00,–120		00,–200		
123		50,–20	–50,20			–150,60		–250,100		
124		00,–50	00,50			00,150		00,250		
125		00,–100	00,100			00,300		00,500		
126		–40,–100	40,100			120,300		200,500		
127		–60,50	60,–50			180,–150		300,–250		
128		–40,00	40,00			120,00		200,00		
129		–40,40	40,–40			120,–120		200,–200		
130		40,80	–40,–80			–120,–240		–200,–400		
131		70,00	–70,00			–210,00		–350,00		
132		–30,20	30,–20			90,–60		150,–100		
133		–60,00	60,00			180,00		300,00		
134		50,30	–50,–30			–150,–90		–250,–150		
135		70,20	–70,–20			–210,–60		–350,–100		
136		80,–30	–80,30			–240,–90		–400,150		
137		–10,30	10,–30			30,–90		50,–150		

Conversion from metric to imperial

0.3 cm = ⅛ in
0.6 cm = ¼ in
0.9 cm = ⅜ in
1.2 cm = ½ in
1.5 cm = ⅝ in
1.8 cm = ¾ in
2.1 cm = ⅞ in
2.5 cm = 1 in

Figure 12 This is a grade-rule source file. A sheet similar to this has to be filled out before using the computer to grade via grade rules.

The column on the left is the number allocated to the rule and the x and y coordinates are given for the smallest and largest. Each computer manufacturer has their own procedures, which vary only in detail

than making individual source files. This will depend on the variety of styling passing through the company and the familiarity of the technician with the library rule numbers. In any case, the process of grading is not automatic, and requires an experienced pattern technician to program the computer with the appropriate instructions.

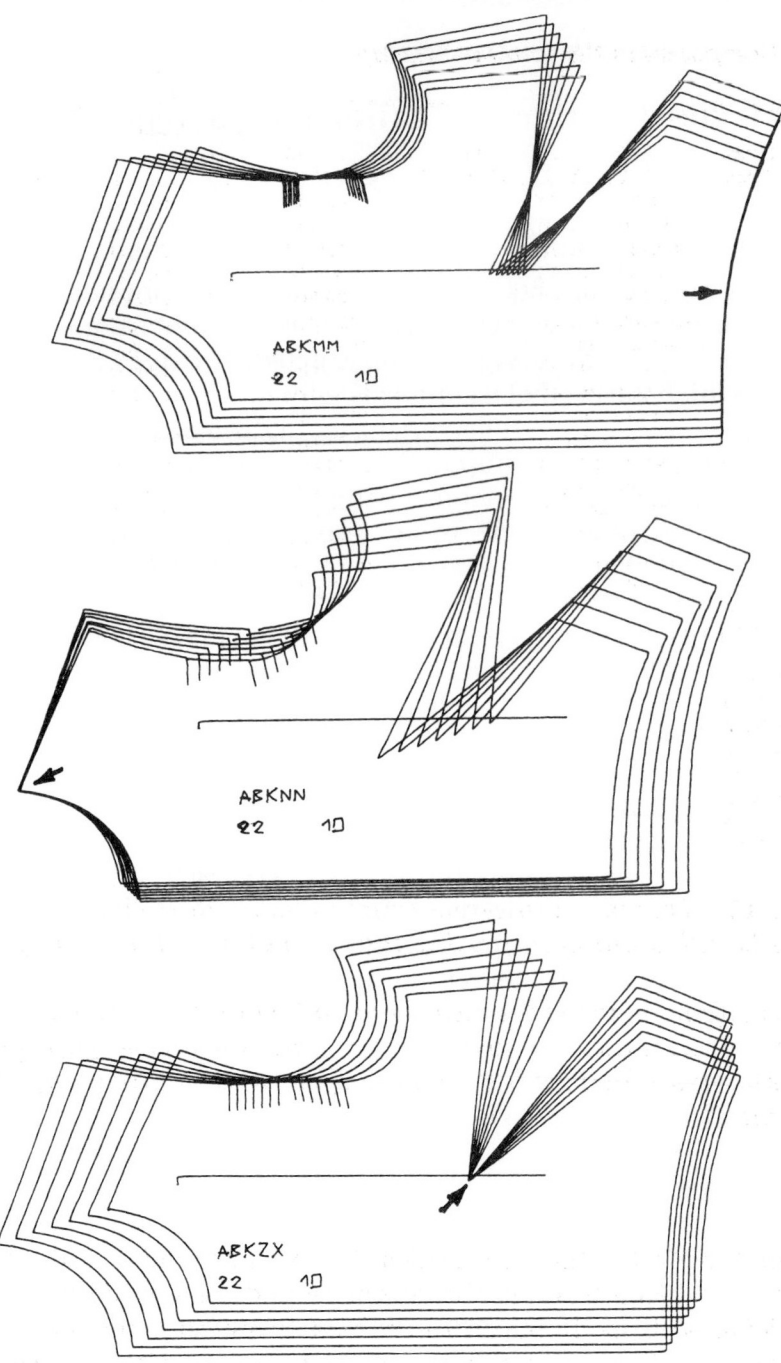

Figure 13 *Three identical front bodices with identical grades, but with different zero points. They all look different but are in fact the same, having been graded from three different static points – as shown by the arrows. This is just to illustrate the rapid flexibility of a system (in this case Lectra). By selecting a different cardinal point on the screen, all the grading increments are recalculated from the new zero point, and when the pattern is cut into pieces the grading quantities are automatically distributed in the correct way*

Block construction and tailoring systems

There are two other applications that can be programmed into the computer and used to good effect.

The first is the 'block construction' system. A block is a basic styleless pattern that fits the body closely, but is loose enough to allow reasonable movement. It is the starting point from which the pattern of a specific design is constructed. It can be a 'standard block', which means that it conforms with the current sizing code in use at the time and is a reflection of the statistical average size and shape derived from a population size survey. A mathematical system can be set up to enable a pattern technician, or anybody so interested, to take a few basic body measurements from the standard size chart and construct a block pattern of any standard size required, instead of using a grading technique. There is no advantage in using this sytem for standard sizing, as it is quicker to use a grading method. It comes into use when a non-standard block is required; in other words, when the block is for an individual, and not for mass producing 'off the peg' garments. Most block construction systems can produce reasonably well-fitting blocks for individual figures, but if the figure is too far from the norm then trouble is experienced in establishing the correct balance and suppression areas. It is possible to make a system flexible enough to encompass a wider variety of figure types, but becomes very complicated when trying to integrate all the possible body changes. With the use of a computer it is more possible to achieve a workable system, provided that the pattern technicians who devise it know their stuff. It is then possible to offer a service enabling anyone to pay for a block pattern of their own figure, from which they can construct their own designs. When the 3D body scanners are perfected, then these will take the place of block construction systems, and a direct record of the figure shape can be put into computer memory and the block pattern generated from it by a 2D translation, which already exists in embryo, as described in Chapter 5.

The second application is 'tailoring systems'. The classical suit, jacket and overcoats that we are all so familiar with have a different background and development to the light-clothing fashion and underwear sector, and this entails using different techniques to arrive at the pattern.

The styling of the tailored garments has changed very little over the years. The so-called designers in this area consider that a new design has been created when they alter the width of a lapel 1 cm, or change from single-breasted to double-breasted jackets, or move the buttons down 2 cm and make the trousers wider or slimmer.

Also, the adjustment of the degree of fit, loose, medium or tight, will be considered a major innovation. Because of this static styling situation, it has been possible to perfect the various aspects of the manufacturing process to a high degree. To start with, the garments are always padded and lined and generally structured, which hides and enhances the human shape that they cover. They were originally designed with a very practical and functional aim in view. They had to be smart, warm and comfortable with lots of semi-hidden pockets to house the paraphernalia that people carry around with them, and, for city use, have a tone of colour that matched the grime of the surroundings. They had to be durable and well padded to hide the wallets and watches, etc., and generally to smooth off the appearance. To this end, seams were placed in the most suitable places, enabling the control of shape without too much fussiness, and pockets designed to be as inconspicuous as possible with a stylish flap. The collar was a masterpiece of design, mainly being the 'collar and revers' type, which was smart, and enhanced the shirt and tie that was designed to go with it.

Once this formula was established and accepted as a part of the status quo, it became the most enduring design of the century. It was essential that this type of garment fitted well and, at the turn of the century when mass production was gaining momentum, the pattern experts of the day saw the need of perfecting a pattern-construction technique that would give reasonable fit when buying an 'off the peg' suit and, where possible, by paying a little more, to acquire a garment made to the customer's measurements.

A lot of work was carried out by the pattern technologists of the day exploring the principles of configuring patterns to various figure types, and eventually a complex set of instructions were perfected that, when applied, would result in pattern drafts of the required style and fit. These drafts had to be committed to memory and practised by the apprentice cutters until they achieved an acceptable standard of proficiency, which was and is measured by examination. This method of application has its limits in that the drafts are not understood in depth, only memorized, and it was only the originator of the drafts that understood all the principles that were used to arrive at the, as it were, recipe. If cutters were asked to do something that was not covered by a recognized draft, then they were lost; thus there was a loss of essential expertise that was not replaced.

This is happening today in all areas where computers are being used, as the computers are taking the place of direct experience and thus there is no fresh feedback in the way of new knowledge. It is a form of source skill starvation, where no refinement is carried out because of the reliance on the computer data and supporting programs.

Returning to the theme of computer tailoring systems. The complete drafting system that the tailors use for standard and bespoke (individual fitting) had to be encased in a software program that would respond automatically when fed with measurements and figure-type requirements, producing a pattern that would match the customer's shape and size.

The process is quite simple. The customer goes to a tailoring retail outlet (shop) and looks through the styling catalogue and the material swatches, chooses the style and cloth, and then the necessary measurements are taken and fed into a computer modem link (telephone line direct to the central computer). The customer is given a code corresponding to their size and figure type, and the appropriate pattern is generated and relayed to a cutting device that will automatically cut out the shapes ready for assembly by the machinists. The suit will then be sent to the shop, where the customer will have a fitting to determine the exact balance of the garment. Once this is done, the alterations are relayed to the computer where the changes are recorded and applied to the pattern ready for the next order, which will fit the customer perfectly and can be processed without any more fittings. All the customer has to do is to walk in the shop and choose the style and cloth; this will then be fed to the system with the customer's code, and the garment cut, made and delivered. This way of operating does not limit the manufacturing of the garment to the country of the customer, as the retail outlet can be linked to various manufacturers in the world who may have a particular speciality which can be made available to anyone, perhaps at a slightly increased cost.

This, unfortunately, makes the tailoring cutters redundant, but it makes for greater speed and flexibility in supply. Whether this economy will have any effect on the price the customer pays, is yet to be seen.

It only remains to be said that grading on a computer is far more effective both in accuracy and in speed.

There are grading services offered by various bureaux around the world. This is usually coupled to a layplanning facility and sometimes pattern cutting. Smaller companies who do not find it feasible to have their own computer systems may find these an economic proposition, but there is always the inconvenience of not having access to these functions on the premises.

A system that smaller companies may be able to afford is the Cybrid, which offers a unique package of scanner, automatic layplanning and grading linked together in one unit. This is also very easy to use, and the 'idiot' keyboard makes the learning time quite short.

The other large companies such as Gerber and Lectra also offer cheap easy-to-use systems for the smaller company.

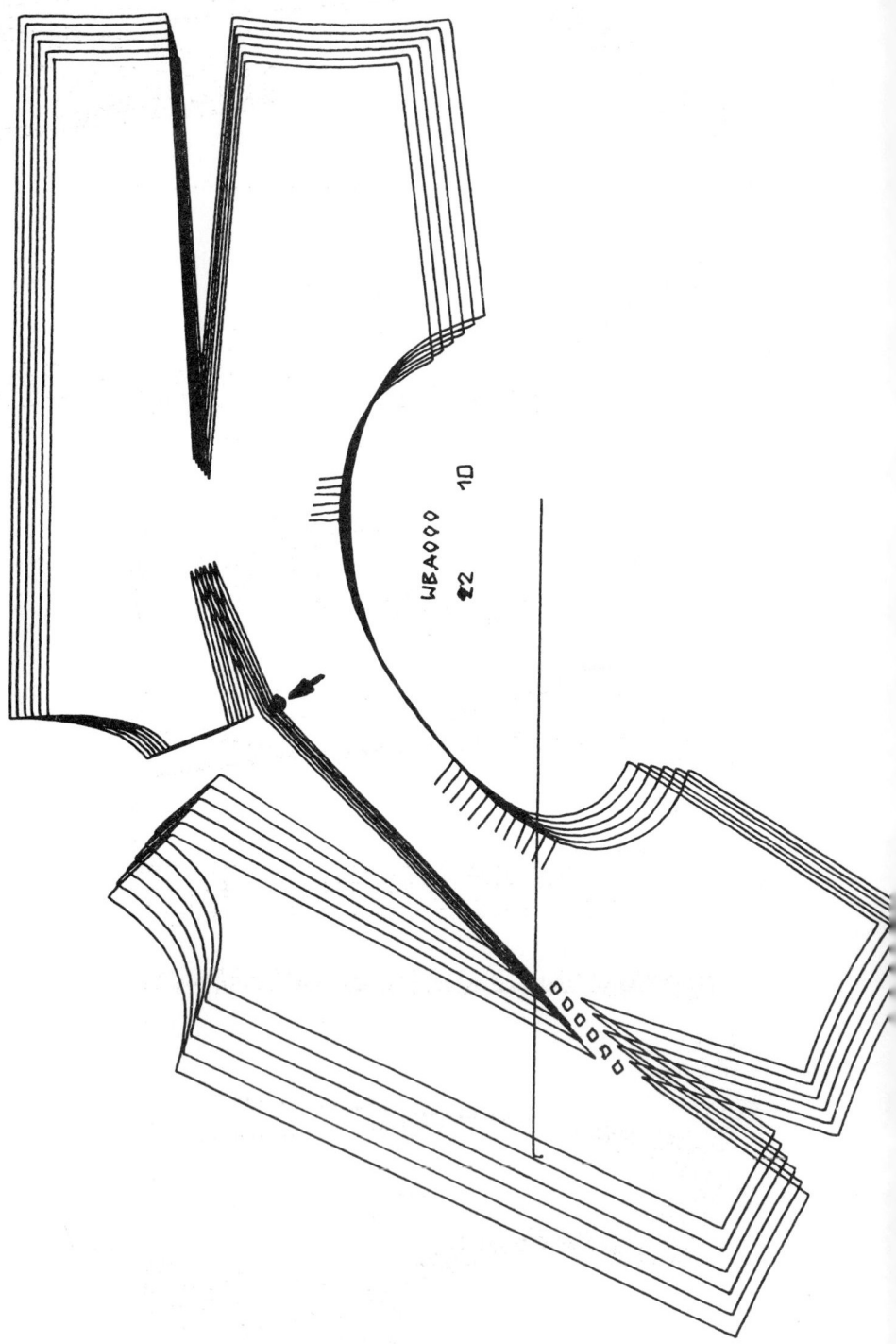

Figure 14 *An example of the redistribution of grade increments when patterns are joined or cut. The zero point is indicated by an arrow*

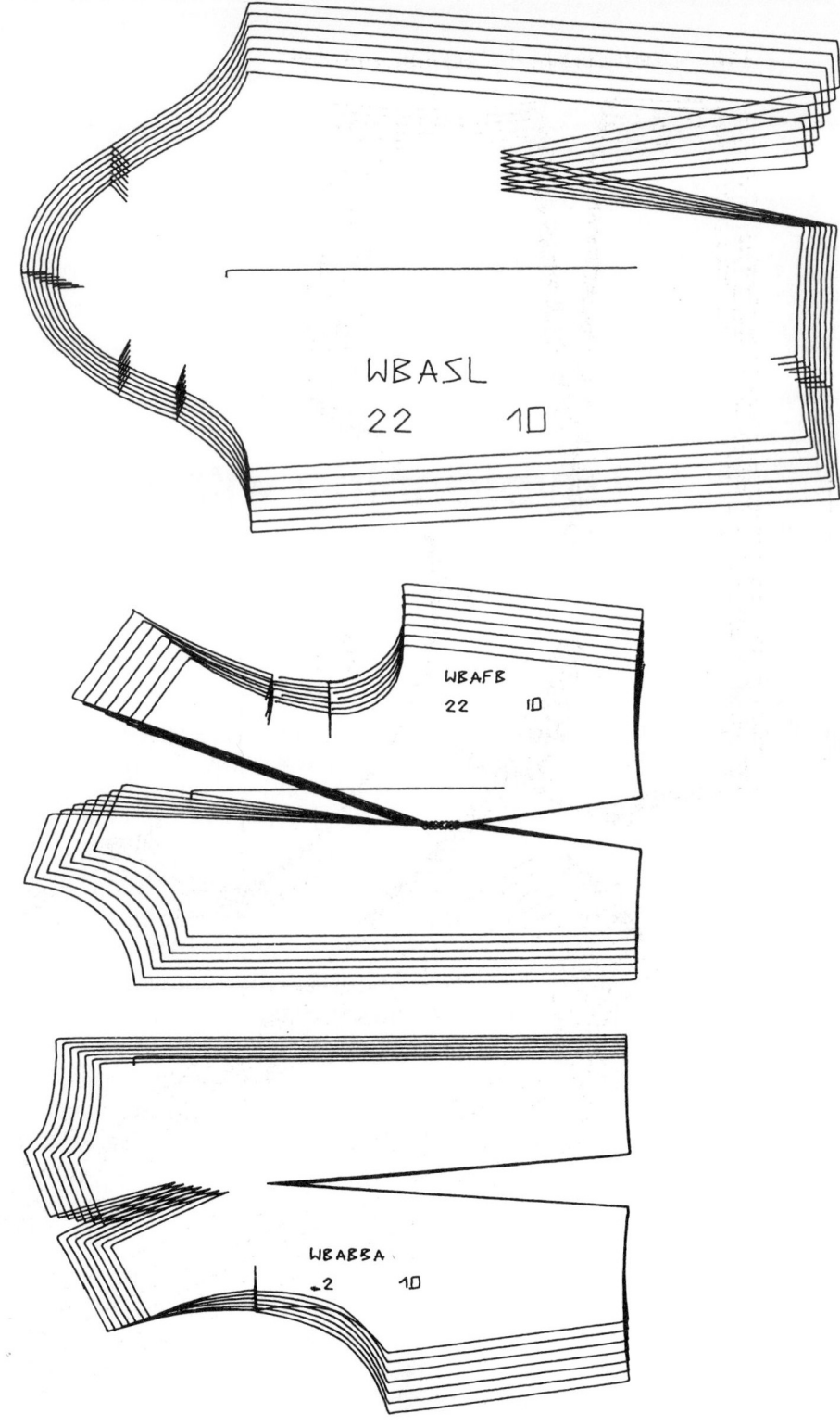

Figure 15 *A miniature print-out of a women's block bodice over seven sizes. This is a nested grade and can be plotted in any scale up to full size, or each size can be plotted separately. This was done on a Lectra flat-bed plotter*

Chapter 8

Layplanning with CAM

Before describing computer layplanning, it is necessary to explain and outline the terminology and procedures. 'Layplanning' and 'marker making' are two terms meaning the same thing. The 'lay' is the resultant column of cloth that is produced when layer after layer of fabric has been placed on top of each other to a height of up to 20 cm or 8 ins. The cloth is said to have been 'laid up' and the length of the 'lay' is determined by the marker: this in turn is the 'plan' of the pattern pieces interlocked as closely as possible within the width of the cloth being used, and marked on to paper which will then be placed on top of the lay, secured, ready to be cut out with a power knife by the stock cutter. The 'layplanner' or 'marker maker' is the technician who is expert at arranging the pattern pieces on to a continuous sheet of white paper and drawing accurately round each pattern piece so that the minimum of material is wasted. The length of the layplan or marker is the 'costing', or the amount of material that a garment uses. This sheet of paper, which is the same width as the fabric to be cut, is the length that the lay is made to; the paper is then secured to the surface of the lay with pins, weights or adhesive, and cut out. Each pattern piece in the layplan is marked with its size, plus any notches, indicating seam allowances and punch hole points for dart or pleat indications plus the style number. The whole 'marker' or 'layplan' is then rolled up and the style and size clearly marked on the outside ready to be passed on to the cutting department with the appropriate cutting order. There it will be allocated to a cutting team, one of whom will be in charge of the 'laying up', and the other will do the cutting; sometimes, one person does both.

A marker can contain several garments of mixed sizes or the same size, and therefore can be of considerable length. In general, the more garments in a layplan the more economical the costing. For example, there may be five garments: two size 12, one size 10, one 14 and one 16. These ratios will be determined by the number of garments sold in each size for that style. In this case, there were four sizes sold in this style and twice as many 12s as the other sizes. Which means that for every layer of cloth in the 'lay', there will be five garments – one 10, two 12s, a 14 and a 16. The cutting docket will also specify the colours to be cut in each size.

This will involve many pieces of pattern, and all have to be accounted for in the correct number and paired to the left and right sides. From this it is clear that it may take a long time to arrange all the pieces, trying many different permutations until a satisfactory compactness of costing is arrived at. It is then necessary to check that all the pieces are in fact there and none are duplicated, or that, for example, there are two sleeves for the same side, or three size 10 sleeves and only one size 14, etc. This activity requires a lot of skill and patience, and a strong sense of striving to improve on the costing that has been achieved so far; at the same time, there is not an unlimited amount of time available. If the marker maker is too slow, he or she may lose out to a faster person who can achieve economic costings more quickly; as with everything aimed at making a profit, 'time is money'.

The layplanner is given the original sample costing to go by. This was done in the design department by the sample cutter, and the wholesale price was based on it plus the profit margin, and the style was offered and sold at that price.

If the original costing can now be improved on, then the profit margin will increase as every centimetre or inch saved is a bonus. From this it is clear that the marker maker is an important part of the overall process, and in some instances can be of utmost value. This is true in the USA, where manufacturers of jeans operate on a very large scale and every centimetre or quarter of an inch saved can mean thousands of dollars extra profit, or the undercutting of a competitor's price – thus leading to more orders. In this situation, the 'super' layplanner is much sought after. There are psychological tests designed to select the ideal person capable of this kind of lonely, persistent work; he or she needs a facility to visualize combinations, and to retain and remix previous permutations.

The introduction of computers into this field has meant that big changes have had to be made.

The first change is to do away with the layplanning room, which is of considerable size, and the second is to train the existing

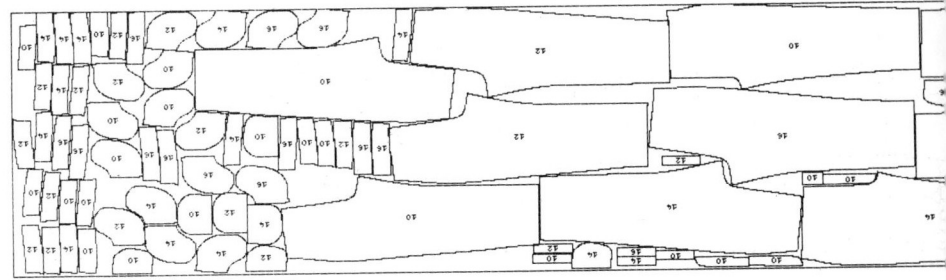

Figure 16 *A miniature layplan printout from the Cybrid automatic layplanner. This shows an efficiency of 85.2 per cent in a mixed marker of a single garment in sizes 10, 12, 14 and 16. It also shows the time it took to arrive at the costing of 7.81 m on a fabric 1200 mm wide.*

The miniature marker can be filed as a record, or sent to a contractor with the garment patterns as a guide to the layplan layplanners to operate the computer layplan software program. The program enables the technician to bring up on the screen, by typing in the style number, the required graded patterns which are displayed in miniature at the top of the screen, and separated into their sizes — which sometimes is reinforced by being in different colours.

The next stage is to tell the system the width of the cloth to be worked on. The fabric width will then be displayed on the screen as two parallel lines, with the left-hand side representing the start of the marker; it will be on the same scale as the pattern pieces. A hand-held stylus is used, which is a pen with a wire at the top end leading into the computer. The stylus is moved over a small graph tablet in front of the operator on the table, and this moves a point of light on the screen; this is usually called the 'cursor', which acts as the selector and the means of moving and manipulating the pattern pieces.

The operator moves the cursor inside a pattern piece and then

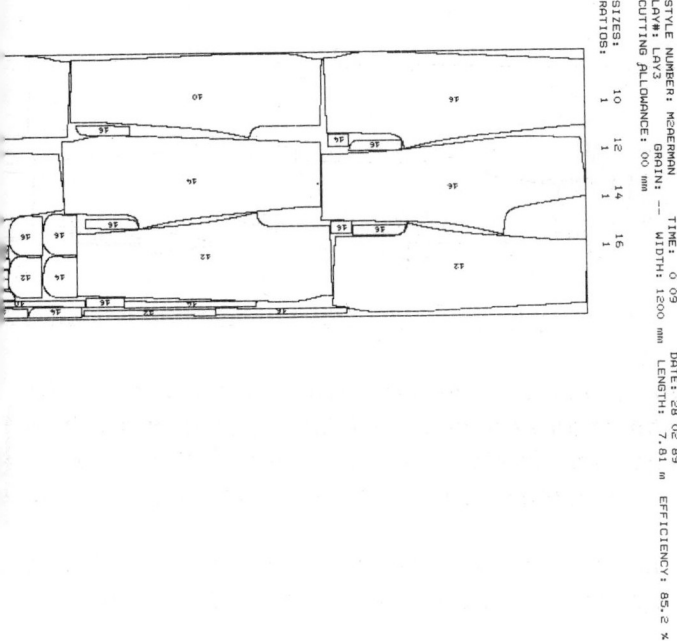

presses down on the stylus and captures the pattern which can then be moved across the screen into the cloth width and positioned close to the edge or wherever. By pressing the stylus again, the pattern is released ready to pick up the next piece, and placed into the cloth width. By operating function buttons on the keyboard, various things can be done to control the movement of the pattern piece. All patterns are configured to lay along the grain of the cloth, as designated by the pattern cutter when constructing the pattern. These grain-line instructions can be overridden; the pattern can be put slightly off grain where it is judged to do no harm, and where it will facilitate a saving of cloth. Also, patterns can be flipped round 180 degrees to face the other way in order to lock in closely with another piece. In fact, any pattern piece can be rotated any number of degrees as required. There are facilities to prevent a layplanner from rotating pieces when a one-way cloth is being planned for, such as cloths with piles going in one direction or a textile design facing one way. In this case, the patterns are directed at the start to face in the same direction and a constraint put on to keep them that way. The marker maker will, however, be able to tilt the pieces a few degrees off grain to help interlock the patterns where necessary. However, the pattern pieces may not be flipped over on to their other side; this is prevented by the program to make sure, for example, that there are not two sleeves for the left side. Added to this, there is a facility for matching stripes and checks. The striped pattern design can be represented, in scale, on the layplan width and the pattern pieces can then be marked for matching; when placed into the lay area, they will automatically align themselves on to the stripe or check in the correct position, which will result in the stripes or checks matching in the final assembly of the garment.

Another option is the insertion of splicing points which indicate the places on the layplan where odd lengths of cloth can be laid in order to cover whole garments in a multi-garment marker, and also shows where to cut the cloth inside the marker length when the end of a roll of cloth is reached. The layplanning software interacts with the PDS grading and cutting software programs, which means that at any stage the other programs can be accessed to change any part that needs adjusting, such as grain lines or punch holes, etc. This is useful when last-minute changes are made to styles, or any details need refining. It means that the system gives much greater flexibility and speed when adjustment is needed, and does not mean a long process of scrapping a whole marker just to alter some small details.

It is not possible to leave a piece of pattern out of the layplan, because all the patterns are displayed at the top of the screen; it is clear when all the pieces have been used as there are none left in any of the size columns above the marker. Also, in more recent systems, a colour monitor is used and each size is in a different colour; this makes the task of multi-size layplanning much easier.

In the process of making the layplan, the percentage of cloth utilization is continually displayed. This indicates the amount of wastage at all times. If a layplan can be made with a 90 per cent efficiency, it means that there is only 10 per cent wastage, which is very good; in fact, anywhere between 80 per cent and 90 per cent is considered a good costing, but it will depend on the size of the pattern pieces and whether there are many small pattern pieces that can fit into the small spaces.

In past ages when all the cloth was woven by hand and was therefore a very valuable commodity, garments were designed to be cut in such a way that no cloth was wasted. The pattern pieces were all constructed from rectangular and triangular shapes and locked into each other exactly. The garments were cleverly designed to accommodate movement, and were of a semi-draped form; this also meant that the same pattern would fit various shapes and sizes, and thus there was no acute sizing problem.

It is only where a culture has a taste for close-fitting clothes that problems of size and cloth wastage arise. These two contrasts of garment design give rise to different pattern-construction techniques. One has simple geometric shapes that lock into each other and requires a very clever mind to anticipate the design related to the layplan. The other requires complex pattern shapes that conform to the body contours and are very difficult to arrive at; when finished, they do not lock into one another, which produces cloth wastage and also the need for more skill in assembly.

Many styles these days, owing to large cumbersome pattern pieces, cannot attain such high-percentage costings and therefore involve high wastage.

Another useful program facility is one that measures round all the patterns and indicates the amount of thread required to sew up the garment.

When the marker is finished and deemed efficient enough, it is accepted and put into the computer layplan file in permanent memory on the hard disk, along with any other markers of the same style but with different size configurations and varied cloth widths. So a collection of options is made relating to the one style and stored ready for access. The computer offers output for the markers in full size, which is drawn out on either a flat-bed plotter or a drum plotter. These two types differ only in that the flat-bed plotting area is horizontal to the ground, and the drum plotter is upright.

The plotters have a continuous paper supply in the form of a roll, which usually is of the maximum width available in order to cover the various cloth widths encountered. This is a wasteful way of operating if the layplan only uses a half or third of the paper width, but it may be more wasteful spending time changing the paper width each time, as this can be rather involved on some plotters. In the case of the flat-bed plotter, the pen moves and the paper stays still, but with the drum plotter, the paper moves in the x axis and the pen moves in the y axis. Both types can plot a layplan much faster than a person can draw round the pattern pieces; and the operator can rapidly plot as many markers as are needed and without having to leave his seat. The flat-bed plotter first draws one section of the layplan. This is called 'a window'. It moves the paper on to draw the next window which must join up exactly with where it left off in the last window. This accuracy depends on the efficiency of the paper-moving device; if the paper slips on its rollers then the line will not match where it left off. The operator has to keep an eye on the plotter all the time in case the paper tears or the roll jams or the ink runs out – or any other mishap that may arise. Although these machines are in general reliable, they are complex; and because they are purely mechanical devices, they are liable to failure at any time owing to stress or age. The last thing the management wants is for the plotter to break down, as it can rapidly bring the whole production to a halt.

The layplans can be relayed to outlying production units any-where in the world. This is done by modem (telephone link) or by putting them on to a tape or disk and sending them to their location, where there is a computer system to feed it on to. They can also be plotted out in miniature and sent with the patterns to an outworker unit where the plan can be copied and drawn manually. If the company is a 'cut, make and trim' (CMT) outfit, it will be small and not have a computer facility.

The final option is to feed the layplan straight into an automatic bulk- cutting machine, but more of that in Chapter 9. The following is a list of features open to the layplan operator:

1. Style identification on both marker and each pattern piece
2. Piece identification on each pattern part
3. Bundle or separation details for parting off the cut work before it goes for assembly
4. Size identification on marker and pattern pieces
5. Area calculation of all pattern pieces in layplan
6. Perimeter calculation of total pieces in layplan
7. Report on number of notches in the layplan
8. Report of number of punch holes in the layplan
9. Calculate number of corners in the marker
10. Scale layplan to any size
11. Put messages on marker and/or pattern pieces
12. Laying up messages on the marker
13. Cutting messages on marker heading
14. Markers put in work schedule and assigned to specific plotters

The final option offered by some systems is 'automatic layplanning'. This is an ingenious program that literally does all of the interlocking manipulations of pattern pieces to produce a layplan.

The style that is required for planning is called up and the parameters are fed in, stating the size or sizes required, and the number of garments to be included in the marker. For example, one of size 10, two of size 12, two of size 14, and one of size 16. This gives a total of six garments in the layplan or marker. If there is a matching requirement, then it is stated; the pattern will have been previously marked for matching points that the computer can recognize and place in accordance with the stripe or check. The width of the material to be used is also stated, and any restrictions relating to one-way materials, etc., just the same as if it were being done manually.

In some programs a time limit can be put in and a minimum efficiency percentage requested. This is only used when time is at a premium, otherwise the program is allowed to run until it reaches an acceptable costing. Some computers are more powerful than others and can work faster and with more apparent intelligence, having the ability to remember parts of patterns that fit together snugly and use that as a block instead of going through every conceivable option, which takes much more time and may never result in the optimum costing.

It is apparent that some computers are slower than others and less efficient, but in general the less efficient ones are cheaper and the old saying 'you gets what you pays for' holds good.

Although the automatic layplanner will usually produce a good percentage efficiency, it is known that an experienced marker maker can usually improve on the computer costing. So when the computer has produced a plan, the technician will spend a little time looking at it to see where, if at all, it can be improved, and then to go into manual mode and alter it with stylus and function keys.

Some automatic system can be given a set of markers to work on overnight without any supervision, and in the morning they can all be plotted off ready for the cutting department. This can save a great deal of time and money. Another advantage is that in very little time the system can arrive at the most efficient width of cloth for any particular style and, if the demand for that style is large enough, then the cloth can be specially woven or knitted to that width.

Most of the large computer systems have a form of automatic layplanning, some of which are better than others. One of the pioneers in this field is the British company Cybrid. Cybrid was the first to design a scanner linked to an automatic layplanning program. This machine uses 'infra red' light, and can scan fifteen pattern pieces into the system in separate scans of two minutes. Then the machine can be set to auto plan the style while the technician gets on with something else. This system is relatively cheap and has been sold world-wide, particularly in Japan.

To sum up the situation, it can be said that the computerized layplanning systems offer very much improved flexibility and speed. This is mostly reflected by the fact that markers can be printed off quickly as repeats when required, instead of the messy and time-consuming process of copying machines and carbon copying, which was the plague of every layplanning department, However, some companies still find it economical to use a copying device alongside their layplanning system.

The advantages in this area are quite spectacular, and demonstrates one of the more successful examples of computer application.

Layplanning with CAM

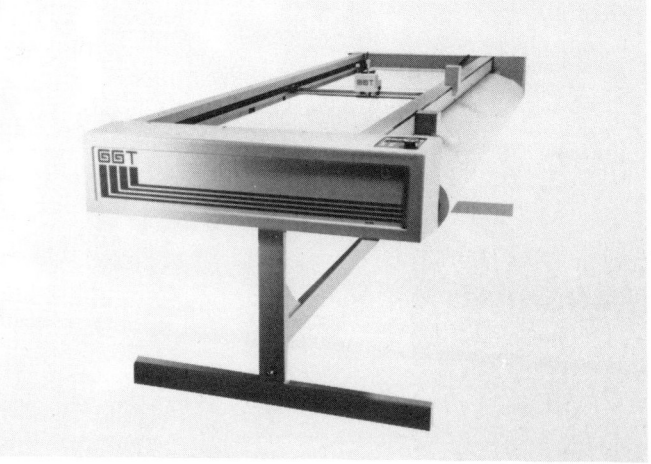

AccuPlot 300 plotter is a space-saving, high-speed pen plotter offering plotting at speeds up to 2300 mm per second
  (Courtesy Gerber Garment Technology, Inc.)

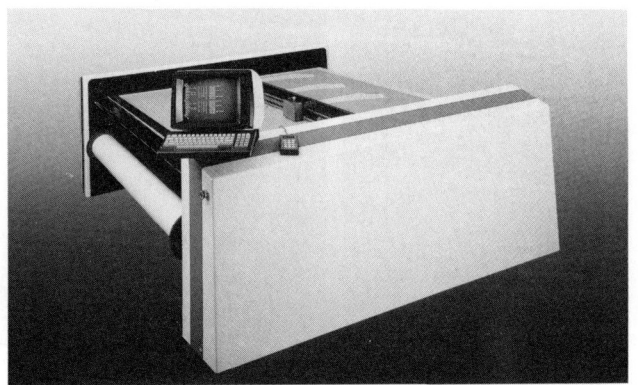

GGT plotter for markers and patterns
  (Courtesy Gerber Garment Technology, Inc.)

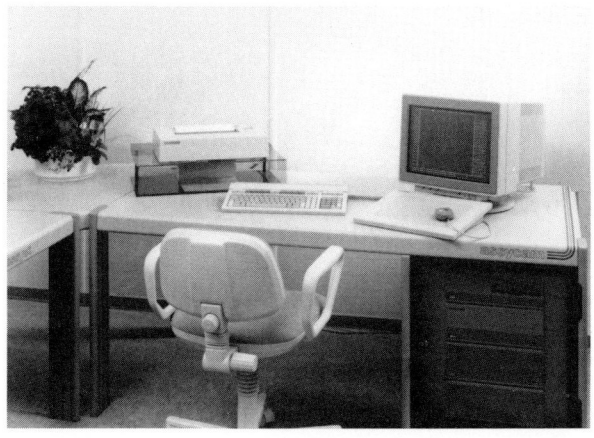

Assyst layplan system
  (Courtesy Assyst GmbH)

130 Computers in the fashion industry

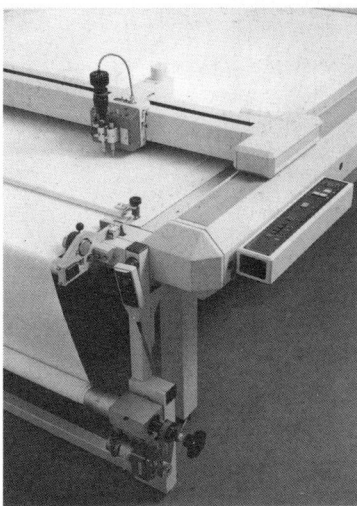

*Assyst plotter/cardboard cutter
(Courtesy Assyst GmbH)*

*Layplan screens and menus
(Courtesy Assyst GmbH)*

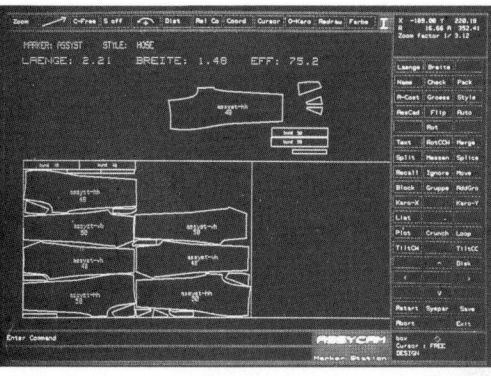
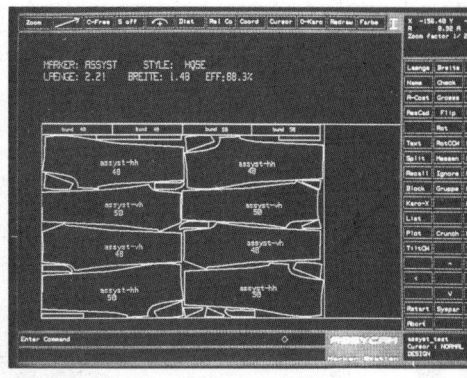

High resolution color display

Finished marker

*Automatic layplanner
(Courtesy Cybrid Ltd)*

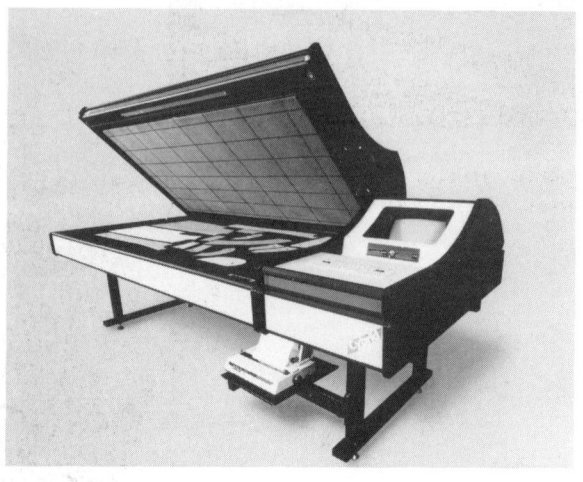

Layplanning with CAM 131

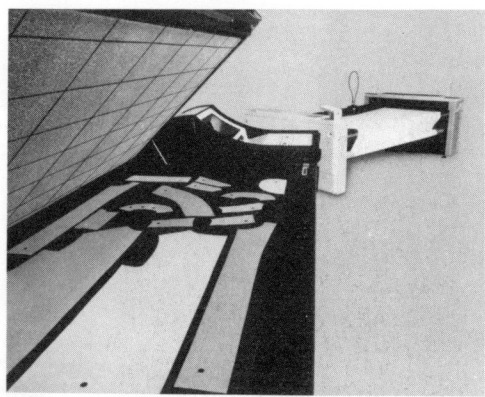

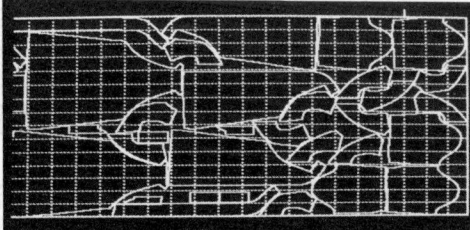

Automatic lay planning system using infra-red scanner for inputs
(Courtesy Cybrid Ltd)

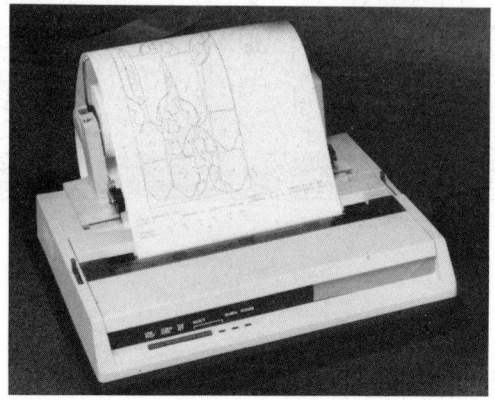

Cybrid mini print out
(Courtesy Cybrid Ltd)

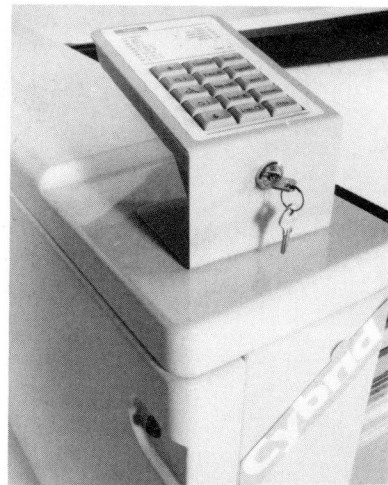

Cybrid plotter controls
(Courtesy Cybrid Ltd)

132 Computers in the fashion industry

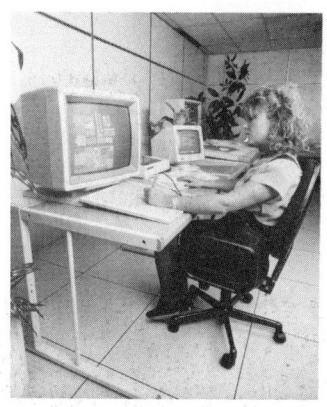

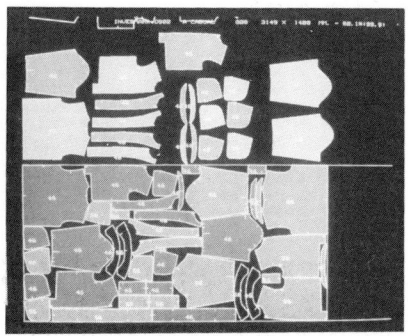

*CAD system with layplan screen
(Courtesy Investronica UK)*

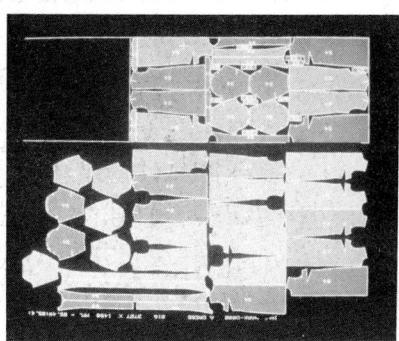

*A layplan done on an automark system
(Courtesy Investronica UK)*

*A high-speed flat bed plotter
for markers and patterns
(Courtesy Investronica UK)*

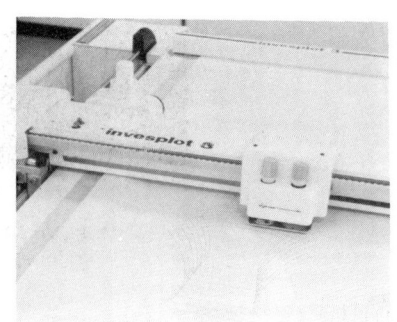

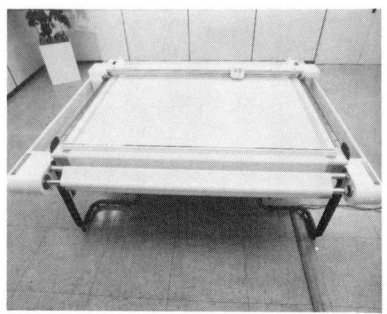

Drum plotter
(Courtesy CIM Microdynamics)

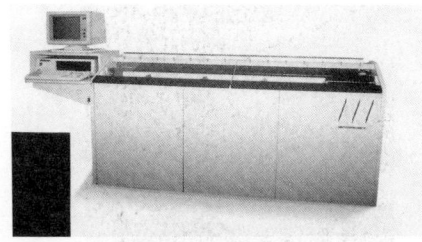

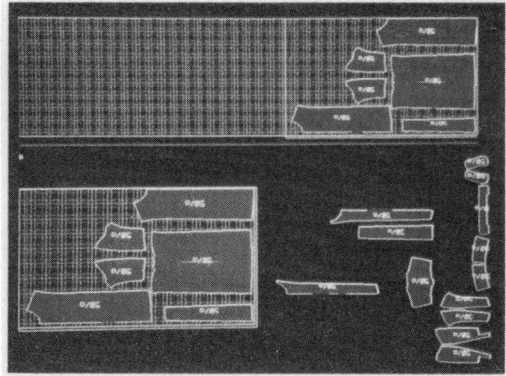

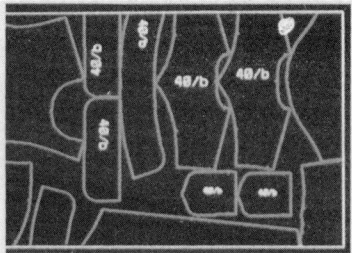

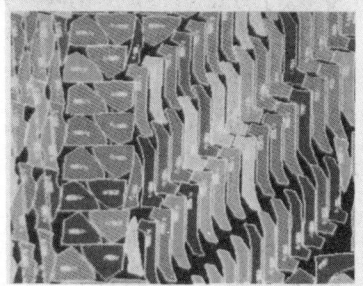

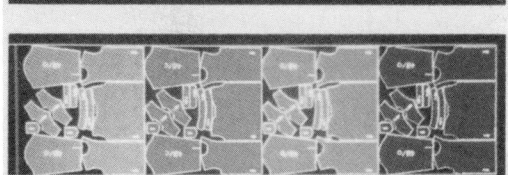

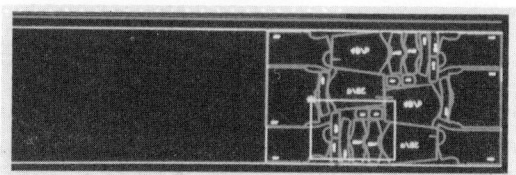

Layplanning
(Courtesy CIM Microdynamics)

134 *Computers in the fashion industry*

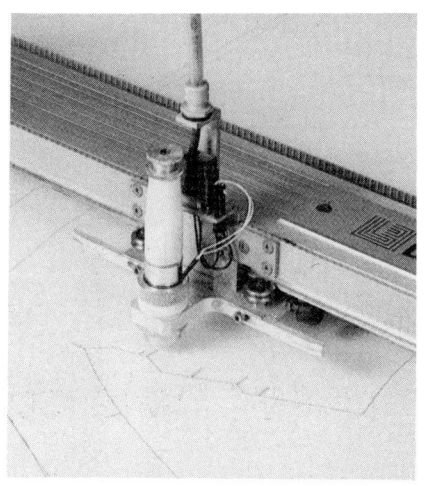

*Flat bed plotter
(Courtesy Lectra Systems)*

Chapter 9

Computer bulk cutting

Fabric inspection

The first area to be considered in this sector is fabric inspection and control. The cloth manufacturers have not kept pace with the automation in garment production, where quality is improving owing to computerization, and where cost per unit is falling. The quality control exercised by the textile manufacturer falls a long way short of the requirements of the garment manufacturer.

The task of the cutting department is made extremely difficult if the fabric is:

1. Badly rolled
2. Stretched
3. Off grain
4. Flawed
5. Inconsistently dyed
6. Shaded
7. Of varying widths

Added to this is the tendency of the cloth manufacturer to under-measure the piece. It is not uncommon for a 100-metre piece to be 2 metres under length and this, if multiplied over a year's production, can mount up to a considerable loss for the garment manufacturer.

This is usually blamed on to the measuring machine, saying that it stretches the cloth and when it is released it is shorter. The situation can be easily remedied, but the reluctance to spend more time and money on cloth quality control is the main obstacle.

It means that the garment manufacturers have to do it themselves. If the company has computerized bulk cutting, it is essential that the quality and efficiency of the cutting is not cancelled out by sub-quality fabric. To overcome this, fabric-inspection machines have to be purchased. These machines vary in the sophistication of their functions.

They all feed the material over a flat area where it is inspected by the operator who controls the speed of the feed and marks any flaws. If the inspection machine is computerized, it is possible to register the flaws in a precise location on the piece which can then be recognized by a computerized spreading machine. The computer will print a report for each roll and summarize all the rolls in a batch report, plus indicating the variations in cloth widths, which is another factor that requires close control. The machine will also re-measure the fabric having relaxed it, and will re-roll it unstretched. The problem of stretching is more pronounced on knitted fabrics than woven, and needs to be controlled carefully. Another type of machine is capable of shrinking the fabric with steam and resetting the weave on grain, drying it and so making it stable and in the correct condition for spreading and cutting. This means that the cut pieces will also be stable and accurate and easy to sew, and will not distort the final garment shape.

Manual laying up and cutting

The laying up of cloth was, until recently, always done by hand, and in all the smaller companies it still is. The lay maker unrolls the cloth on the cutting table and then dumps it all on a sheet of paper on the floor at the foot of the table. Alternatively, there may be available a cloth roll holder which the roll of cloth can spin on.

A plain sheet of marker paper is then cut off to the length of the layplan and laid on the table. The cloth is laid ply upon ply on to this until all the fabric of that roll is finished. The next roll, usually a different colour, is then laid up and so on until there are as many layers as judged suitable for cutting with the straight knife. The lay can be as high as 20 cm or 8 ins if the cloth is thick and loosely woven. If the fabric is thin and closely woven, then a greater number of plies can be laid up. However, they cannot be laid to such a height as the lay will become like a solid plank of wood which the knife cannot cope with, and all the pushing of the knife will only result in smoke rising from the lay and the plies of cloth becoming fused together making it impossible to separate them. This kind of mistake is only made by inexperienced cutters being pressurized by the boss to get through the work quickly. But it illustrates the judgement that needs to be used regarding lay heights and cloth characteristics. When the lay has been completed, the layplan, or marker, is laid on top and secured with clips, weights or long pins. The lay is now ready to be cut out.

The knife that is mainly used is called a 'straight knife', and is comprised of a thin platform on runners with a long narrow straight blade, sharp on one side, driven up and down in a grooved flat shank by an electric motor at the top and guided with the help of a handle. This type of knife can be turned very sharply and manipulate complex shapes with comparative ease. It has a semi-automatic sharpening device attached permanently above the blade (which has a guard for safety). The 'servocutter' uses the same knife and is supported on an overhead gantry; the base is very small and thin and does not take any weight as the knife is suspended on a geometrically jointed arm that maintains it upright and pivoting around an axis while the base slides under the lay, making very little disturbance. The advantage in this method is that the knife is always maintained upright and there is less resistance as the base takes no weight.

One of the latest improvements to the straight knife is the use of air flotation instead of runners on the base, and therefore a thinner base is possible enabling the knife to slide very smoothly with no resistance, the thin base making very little disturbance to the bottom plies of the lay.

The other hand-held knife used is called a 'round knife', which has the same configuration but with a circular blade rotating at high speed. This is only suitable for cutting straight lines, which it does quicker and more effectively than a straight knife.

A third type of cutter is the 'band knife'. This is not hand-held, but a large device anchored to the floor. It has a table work surface through which passes a continuously rotating band knife, sharp on one side. Instead of moving the knife, the fabric lay sections are accurately manipulated through the blade, thus cutting the pattern shapes out. These chunks of the lay are first roughly cut out with the straight knife and moved on to the band knife worktop where very accurate cutting is possible. The 'stock cutters', as they are known, are all very skilled and will have had long training, usually starting as a laying-up partner to an experienced cutter, and gradually being allowed to cut simple parts of the lay, such as belts and facings, which are straight pieces.

The cutters need to keep their attention firmly on the job, as any slip can be very costly in terms of fingers. A lot of cutters now wear mail gloves made of metal to minimize any slip of the hand.

The aim of the cutter is to follow the drawn lines of the pattern layplan as accurately as possible, and not to tilt the knife; this ensures that the bottom layers are the same shape as the top plies.

Another tool used in the cutting room is the power drill, used for indicating various parts of the pattern by making small holes in the cloth that the machinist can see and use as a guide.

Computerized bulk cutting

Only the large company can, at present, afford to run a computerized cutting room. Any manufacturer with a turnover of less than 3 million pounds (5 million dollars) a year will not be advised to buy one, since the pay-back time would be too long and the advantages not sufficient to warrant such a large capital outlay.

But for the large concerns, computer cutting is becoming almost obligatory. It gives greater flexibility and turnround times, which means that small runs of a style can be entertained – whereas before they were uneconomic and completely out of the question. This means that a company can respond to market demands quickly and catch them before they evaporate or change. They need no longer be the slow-moving dinosaurs that they previously were. They can also save on staff levels, needing perhaps only one stock cutter for emergency and special cutting requirements, and less lay makers because of automated 'laying-up machinery'. Laying-up machines are usually called 'spreading machines'. These vary in their complexity from manual to fully automatic. The cloth is loaded on to the machine in either roll form or lapped pieces (concertina folds).

With the manual type, the operator puts the fabric on the conveyor and pushes the device along rails, up the table and the cloth is unrolled and laid along the table behind it; it is then cut off at the end of the lay by hand, and the conveyor is pushed back again to the other end and so on until the lay is complete. The same machine, for a little more money, can be motorized, and it will then travel up and down under its own steam.

The ultimate spreader can carry multiple rolls of fabric and be programmed to select different pieces and lay up the required number; all the operator has to do is watch over it while he/she sits on a comfortable seat that travels up and down with the spreader. It will also be sensitive to the flaws that have been located by the computerized cloth inspection system, and tell the operator when and where to make the necessary adjustments. The spreader also will lay the fabric up without any internal stresses; this means that the cloth is fully relaxed, with the help of a vibrator, when it is placed on top of the previous ply. This ensures that the cut pieces are accurate and do not change their shape after cutting, thus making sure that the finished garment is perfectly balanced.

In the most advanced cutting rooms, the tables will have air-flotation surfaces which, when switched on, enable the operator to easily slide the complete lay on to a cutting unit with a computer-driven cutting head. This immediately releases the laying-up area and spreading machine for further use.

Computer-linked controlled cutting heads are used on a wide range of products, not only fashion wear. They can be used where any two-dimensional shape is required. This will include products such as sail making for yachts; car-seat covers; carpets and interior linings; shoe manufacturing; all engineering products that entail flat metal shapes that can be cut with gas torch heads and electric arc cutters; anything from ship construction to small car components.

Its application to fashion enables the choice of single- or multi-ply cutting. The first multi-ply cutter was produced by Gerber in the mid-1970s and was used to cut car fabrics and carpets. Gerber gradually improved the speed and flexibility of the cutter, which made it suitable for fashion production where thinner materials are used.

The cutting head is controlled and moves along an arm that bridges the cutting area in the x coordinate, and the whole bridge and cutting head is moved bodily along the cutting area in the y coordinate direction; at the same time, the knife, which is a 'needle' straight blade, sharp on one side, is rotated in the direction of the cutting line. It moves up and down at great speed and the automatic sharpening device can be programmed to work according to the characteristics of the fabric, only sharpening when required. It is capable of cutting both low- and high-ply lays with a computer-linked blade temperature monitor which controls the speed of cutting, ensuring that no overheating and burning and fusing of fabric occurs. The head on some cutters also incorporates a drill for marking dart lengths, etc.

The blade of the cutter must travel below the level of the lay in order to cut the bottom ply; in order that the table is not cut to pieces, the surface is covered with a layer of closely packed bristles which the lay sits on and through which the blade passes harmlessly.

The lay is made on top of perforated paper, using the automatic spreading machine or by hand. It is then conveyed on special tables which have air-flotation surfaces, enabling one or two persons to push the lay on to the computer cutting area, where it is mechanically pulled on to the bristle cutting surface. Once in place it is covered by a sheet of polythene and a vacuum is switched on, which operates through the bristles on the undercutting surface and sucks all the air from the fabric lay, thus making it compact, rendering it solid and in a stable condition for cutting.

The maximum height of the compacted lay should not exceed 8 cm; in some cases, where the cloth is difficult, it is usual to play safe and have less plies, because the computer will slow the cutting down if too much heat is generated. Judgement has to be used as to the lay height, speed and material characteristics. The correct relationship of these three is very important. It may be better to make smaller lays and cut faster than the reverse. When the lay is ready for cutting, the layplan for the 'cut' is selected on the computer control board and loaded on to the system. The start button is pushed and away it goes following the plan on the disk and cutting straight through the polythene and cloth lay. The cutter works at great speed and accuracy. It can cut at least eight times faster than a human and twice as accurately. The only drawback is that the shapes that are cut out have no identity, in that there is no paper pattern on the top indicating the style size and number of pieces, etc. Each company will have its own solution to this problem. Some may plot a full-sized marker and lay it on top of the lay as it is being cut, and some will have a miniature layplan printed out as a guide for the sorting team to go by. But, however it is done, there must be no mistakes and each piece must be clearly identified. When all the lay is cut out, the parts are moved to the sorting area where the work is prepared for production (machining and finishing).

Some companies will incorporate a whole day's cutting on one disk; this means that all the layplans for that day are recorded in order of cut on the same disk, and the lays made in that sequence and fed to the system as required. The cutting room of a large company will almost certainly have a conveyor system where the computer cutter is fed by mobile air-flotation tables, or the computer cutter itself is mobile and will move from one table to the next.

There are three main layouts for computer cutting. The first is where there are several rows of static laying-up tables, each with spreading machines and air flotation. Along the end of these tables is a transverse track on which is a single mobile air-flotation table than can move to abut the ends of each of the other tables so that the lays can be transferred from the static tables, where the lays are made, to the mobile one which will convey the lay to a single static computer cutting head, which will drag the lay from the mobile table on to the bristle surface for cutting. The second layout will

Computer bulk cutting

comprise of a set of static tables, as in the first system, and a mobile computer cutting head that transverses along tracks that butt on to the ends of the laying-up tables and then drags the lays on to the bristle surface for cutting.

The third layout will be in the form of an 'H', with a mobile cutting head transversing between banks of tables either end of the computer cutting unit (see illustrations at the end of this chapter).

The substances that can be cut by these systems are not limited to garment fabrics. Any knife-cuttable material can be handled, but the thickness of the cut will be determined by the hardness and resistance of the material. Some examples are fibreglass, foam, rubber sheet, plywood, carpet, vinyls, aluminium composites, and other soft metals.

The speed of cutting will depend on the resistance in the lay, but on average the knife can cut at approximately 7.0 m (23 ft) per minute. If daily cutting scheduling is required, then layplan pattern perimeters can be quickly measured by the computer and a total cutting time calculated for each lay and the day divided up accordingly, slotting in the cuts as and where needed.

The reciprocating straight-needle knife is the only way, at present, of cutting high multi-ply lays; but other means are available for cutting low-ply and single-ply lays.

The most used single-ply cutter is the laser. The great advantage of the laser is that it has no degradable cutting edge. The laser beam can cut in all directions and does not need to be sharpened and rotated as does a knife. The disadvantage is that the cutting is achieved by heat; this limits the cutting to one layer because it fuses multi lays together. It is ideal for cutting leather and is used almost exclusively in the shoe industry. Although only one ply at a time can be cut, the speed at which it achieves this makes it ideal for mass production. The leather previously was cut by hand round metal patterns (and still is in the smaller companies), and great skill, speed and dexterity was achieved by the cutters. However, computer cutting by laser is far quicker and more accurate, giving a greater consistency of quality and increased output.

Another form of cutting, which is very similar to the laser, is the 'plasma' cutter. This uses a pinpoint gas flame and also can cut in all directions and does not need sharpening and, like the laser, can only cut one ply without fusing the layers together.

Computer-controlled lasers are also used in the pattern-cutting department to cut patterns out in card. Where a company has a CAD/CAM computer system, it is not necessary to cut card patterns at any time, but some managers feel more secure if they have the patterns in card and do not have to rely on storing all their patterns on disk or tape. They are fearful that the patterns are either not safe or that they are not entirely trustworthy on disk, but most are now convinced of the reliability of computer systems and trust them implicitly.

There is yet one more method of cutting materials. This is by 'water jet'. A company called Durkopp has developed a machine that compresses water to very high pressures and can cut a range of substances with it. The jet of water is approximately one-fifth of a millimetre in diameter and is moving at three times the speed of sound.

To produce this speed, a pressure of 4000 bar is needed and a very ingenious compressor has been designed to achieve it. When the water leaves the cutting nozzle it is converted into kinetic energy and is capable of cutting all types of material. As with the laser and plasma cutters, it can cut in all directions and does not blunt; but it has the advantage that no heat is involved and consequently can cut multi layers of material without fusing them together, and has a minute cutting width which enables very precise and accurate manipulation.

It can start its cut anywhere, even in the middle of a pattern (not needing a run in), and is thus capable of making holes of any size or any interior cut-out shapes of any kind.

There is no dust as the water carries it into the bottom of the cutting space and damps it, preventing it from flying about. The wide range of substances it can cut include all textiles, and rubber-like materials – fibreglass, plywood, foam, polystyrene; in fact, anything than can be cut with a knife. The depth of thickness that can be cut is obviously not very great as the energy in the very thin jet of water is soon absorbed, but nevertheless it can cut several plies of cloth and up to 6mm of plywood and the corresponding in fibreglass. The problem of disposing of the water is overcome by draining it away below the cut surface, and some of it is vaporized. If coupled to a multi-axled robot, it can be used to cut in three dimensions, but this of course is not applicable to the fashion industry.

There is one other company that has produced a water cutter and that is Lectra, the French company who offer all modes of cutting except 'plasma'. Both Durkop and Lectra water cutters are used extensively for the cutting of leather, mainly for shoes.

Matching stripes

Automatic check- and stripe-matching systems are making an appearance. Investronica, a Spanish company, have – along with a wide range of other computer cutters – produced a single-ply plasma cutter that uses a TV camera to scan the material and work out where to cut the pattern pieces so that they match when sewn together.

This is not a very rapid process, as it needs a high level of human input to arrange the cloth accurately on the cutting surface before the camera can scan the cloth prior to cutting out the style which has been pre-prepared regarding the points on the garment to be aligned. This area is still in its infancy, as the weaving and printing of fabrics is not consistent enough to pre-plan markers accurately for bulk cutting and will, for a long time, require labour-intensive input to cope satisfactorily with the problems in this sphere.

This highlights the problem of cutting bulk stripes and checks. The layplans can be made so that the stripes match accurately, basing the stripe or check repeat on average measurements taken from several rolls of cloth; however, the weave and print always vary slightly, which undoes a lot of the accuracy of the marker. The way that this has been overcome in the past is by blocking, but this is wasteful of fabric and time-consuming.

There is now a technique of pinning using plastic pins that can be cut through without harming the blade. This is still in its infancy and does not eliminate all the headaches.

To sum up, the technology of bulk cutting is highly developed and successful. The only calculation that must be done is relating the cost to turnover. With high turnover the hardware will pay for itself in an economic time-span. The other point is that the cutting department will be manned by a different type of technician.

Computer bulk cutting 145

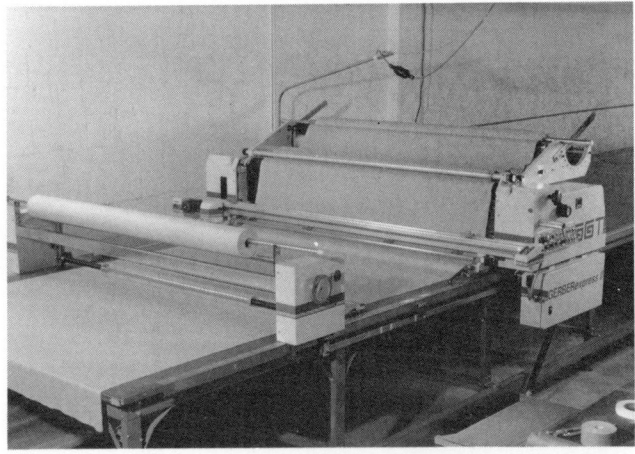

Express II Gerberspreader features a roll winding system, providing optimum tension-controlled, distortion free fabric spreading at speeds up to 73 metres per minute
  (Courtesy Gerber Garment Technology, Inc.)

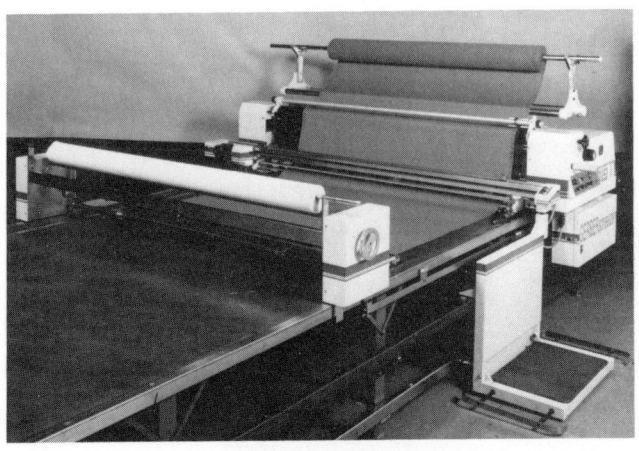

Express I spreading system features a logical control panel and trackless guiding system for precise, tension-controlled, high-speed spreading
  (Courtesy Gerber Garment Technology, Inc.)

146 *Computers in the fashion industry*

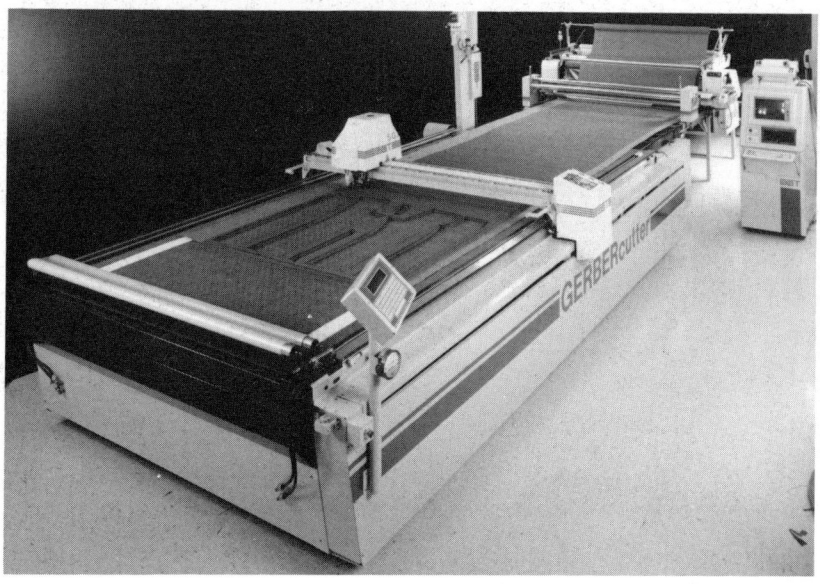

S-93 high-ply Gerbercutter provides speed, flexibility and accuracy while offering fabric labour savings and exceptional cutting performance at speeds up to 8 metres per minute
   (Courtesy Gerber Garment Technology, Inc.)

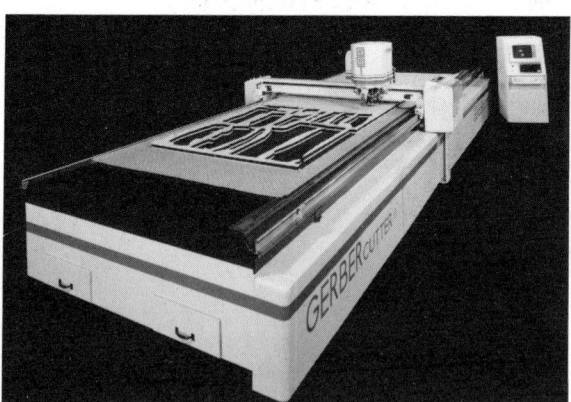

S-91 high-ply Gerbercutter cuts up to 76 mm of compressed fabric utilizing GGT's vacuum hold-down, automatic knife sharpening and knife intelligence
   (Courtesy Gerber Garment Technology, Inc.)

Computer bulk cutting 147

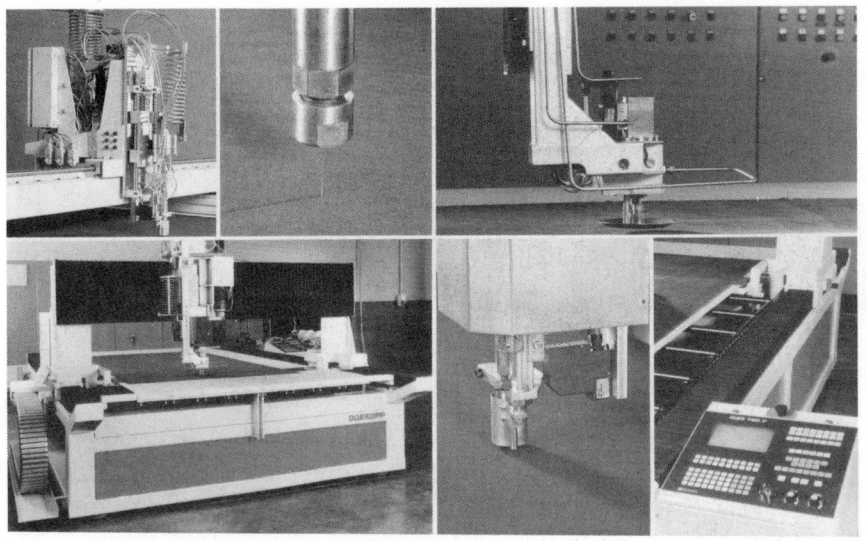

High pressure water cutter used for cutting many categories or substances, from cloth to metal
  (Courtesy Durkoppwerke GmbH)

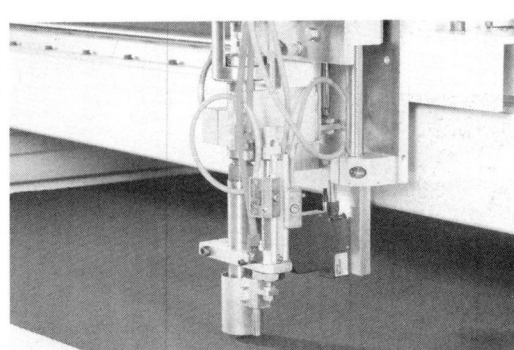

Water cutter head
  (Courtesy Durkoppwerke GmbH)

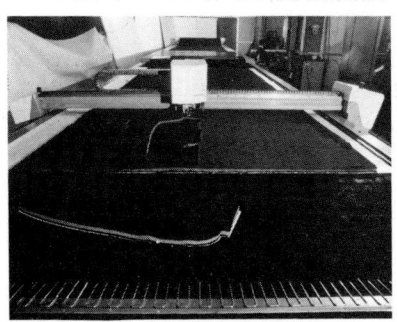

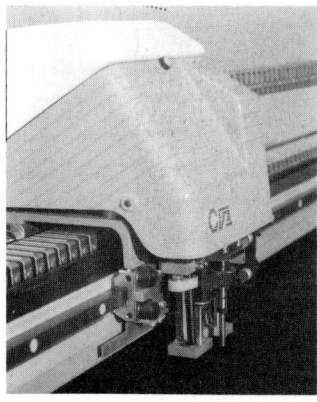

Bulk cutting hardware for medium to high ply lays (Courtesy Investronica UK)

Low-ply automatic cutting machine (Courtesy Investronica UK)

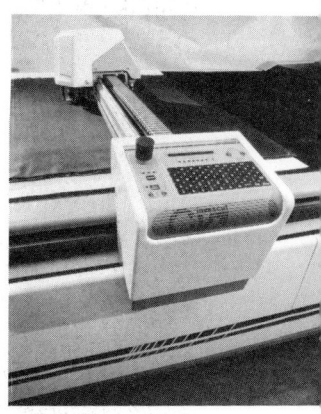

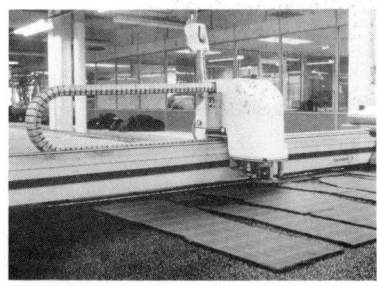

Automatic matching of stripes and checks using plastic pins to control inconsistencies in the weave. These can be cut through without damage to the knife (Courtesy Investronica UK)

Computer bulk cutting 149

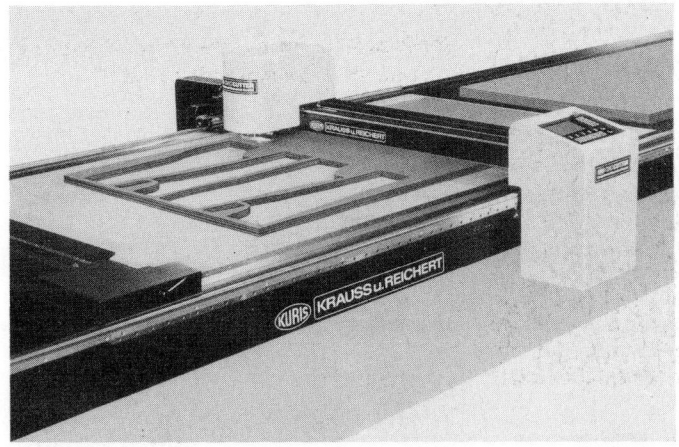

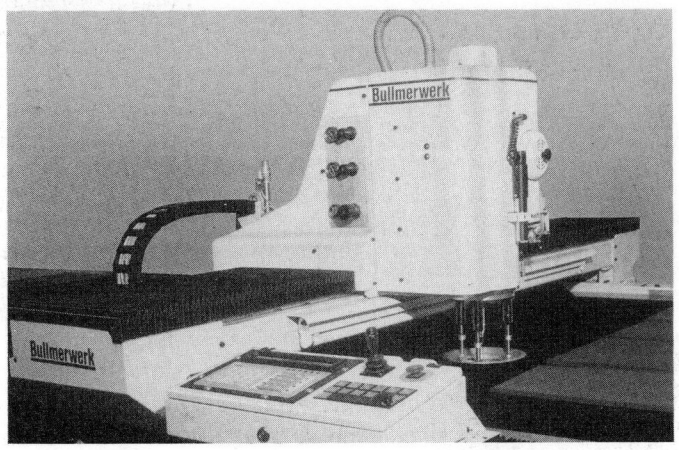

Bullmer and Kurts cutters used by CIM Microdynamics
  (Courtesy CIM Microdynamics)

150 Computers in the fashion industry

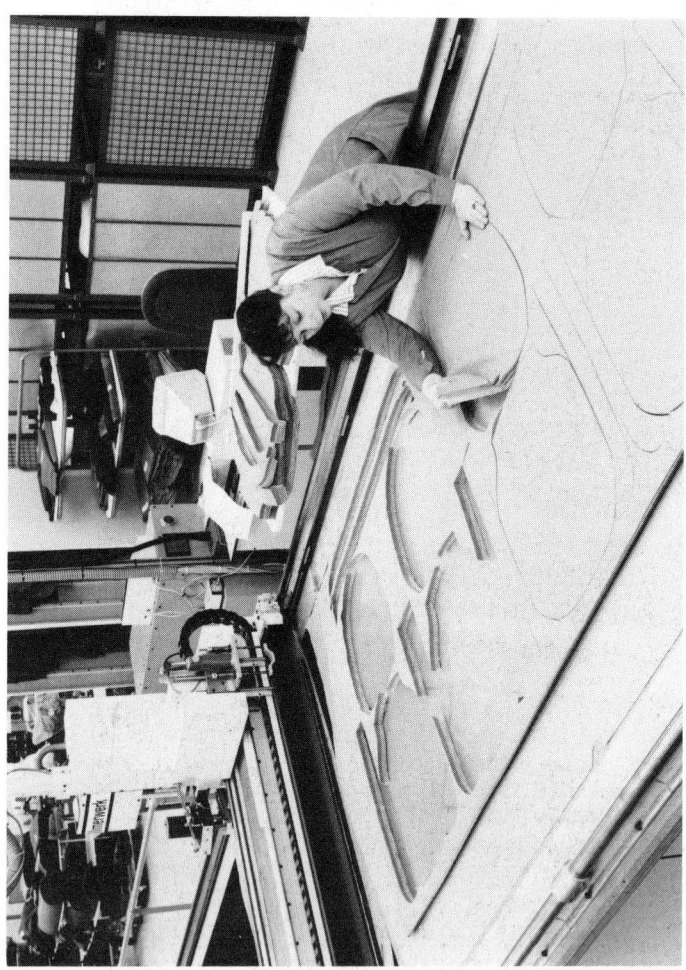

The Bullmerwerk bulk cutter
(Courtesy Bullmer Works Ltd)

Computer bulk cutting

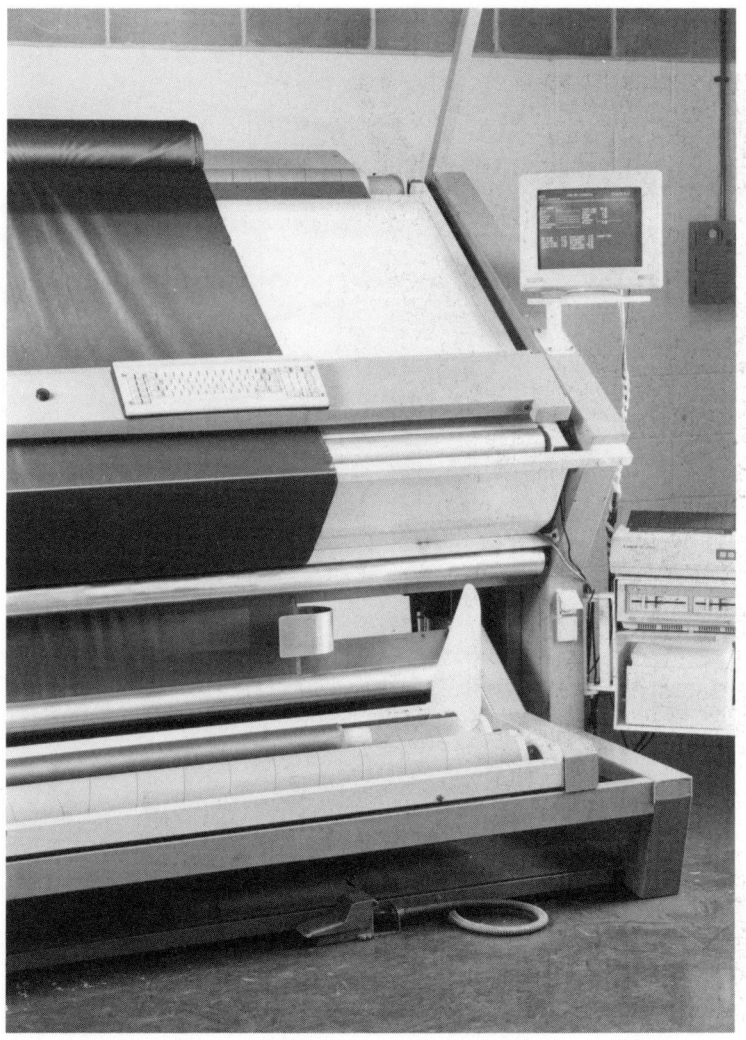

Computerized cloth inspection by Butex. Developed with the help of Bullmer
   (Courtesy Bullmer Works Ltd)

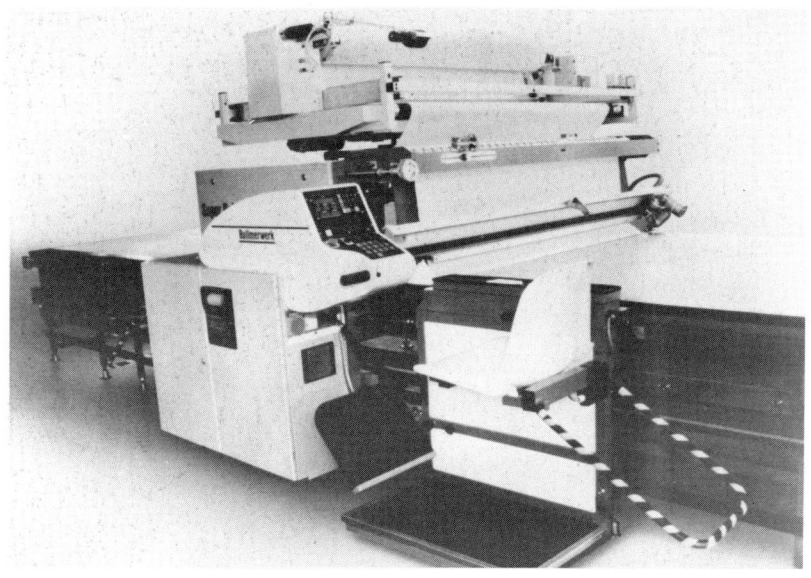

Computer-controlled spreader linked to the cloth inspection and layplanning program
  (Courtesy Bullmer Works Ltd)

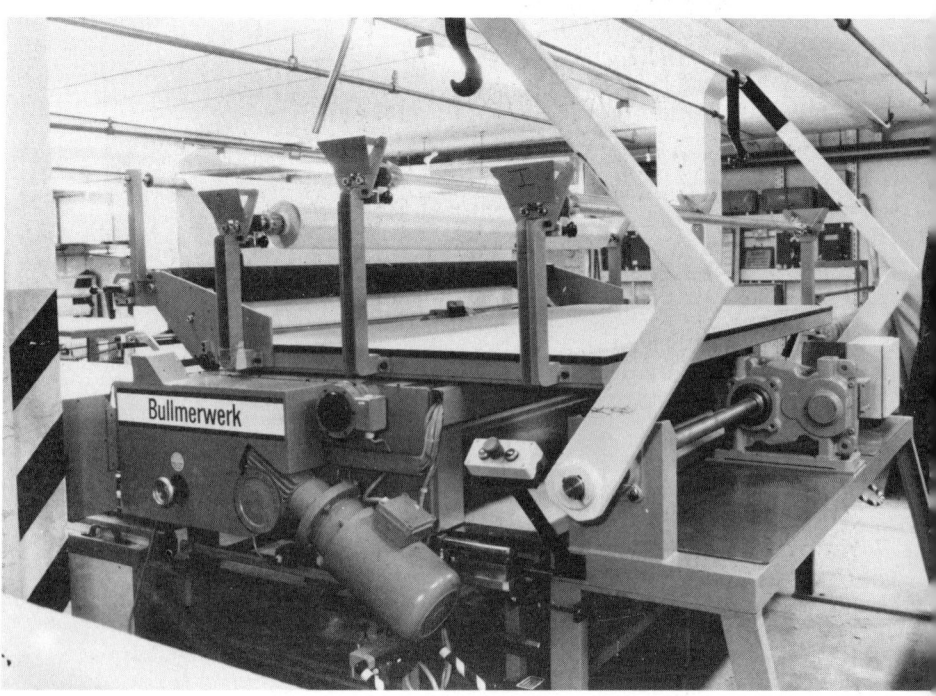

Power cloth loading device to service the laying up machine
  (Courtesy Bullmer Works Ltd)

Computer bulk cutting 153

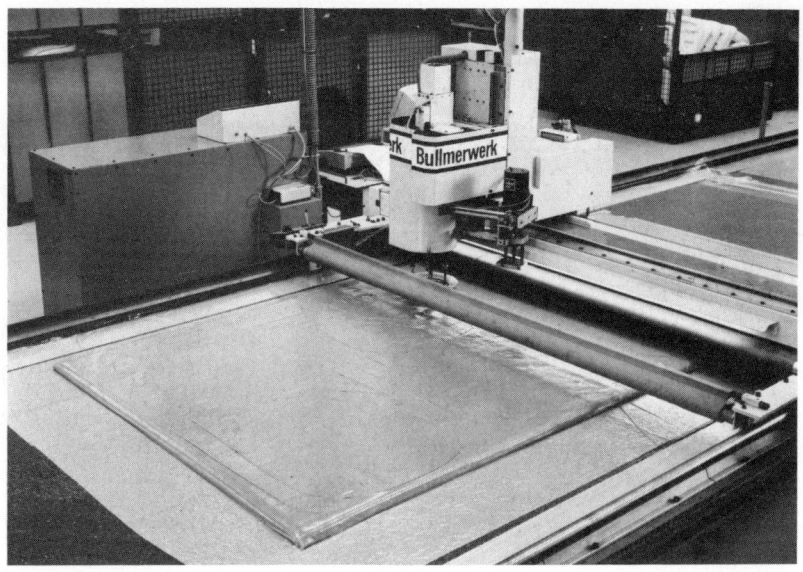

Bullmer bulk cutter
  (Bullmer Works Ltd)

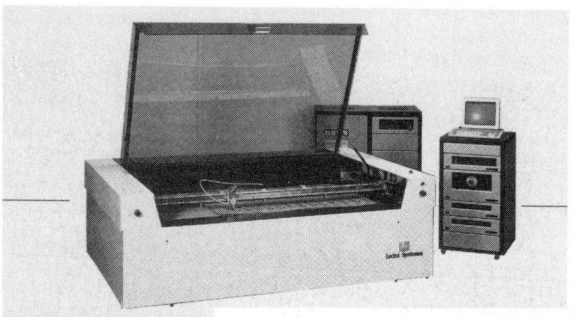

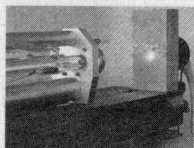

Leather or pattern card laser cutter
  (Courtesy Lectra Systems)

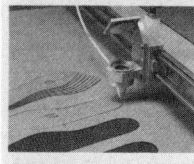

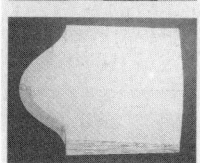

154 *Computers in the fashion industry*

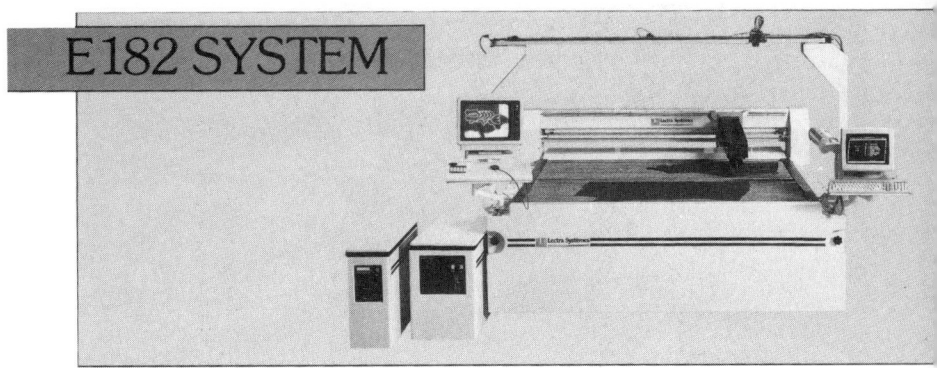

Water jet cutter used for leather and other similar materials (Courtesy Lectra Systems)

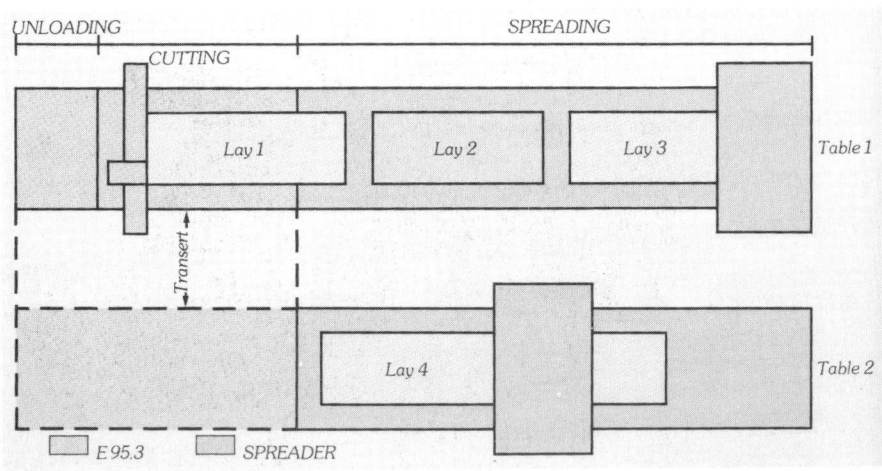

Automatic table conveying system plan for better auto-cutting (Courtesy Lectra Systems)

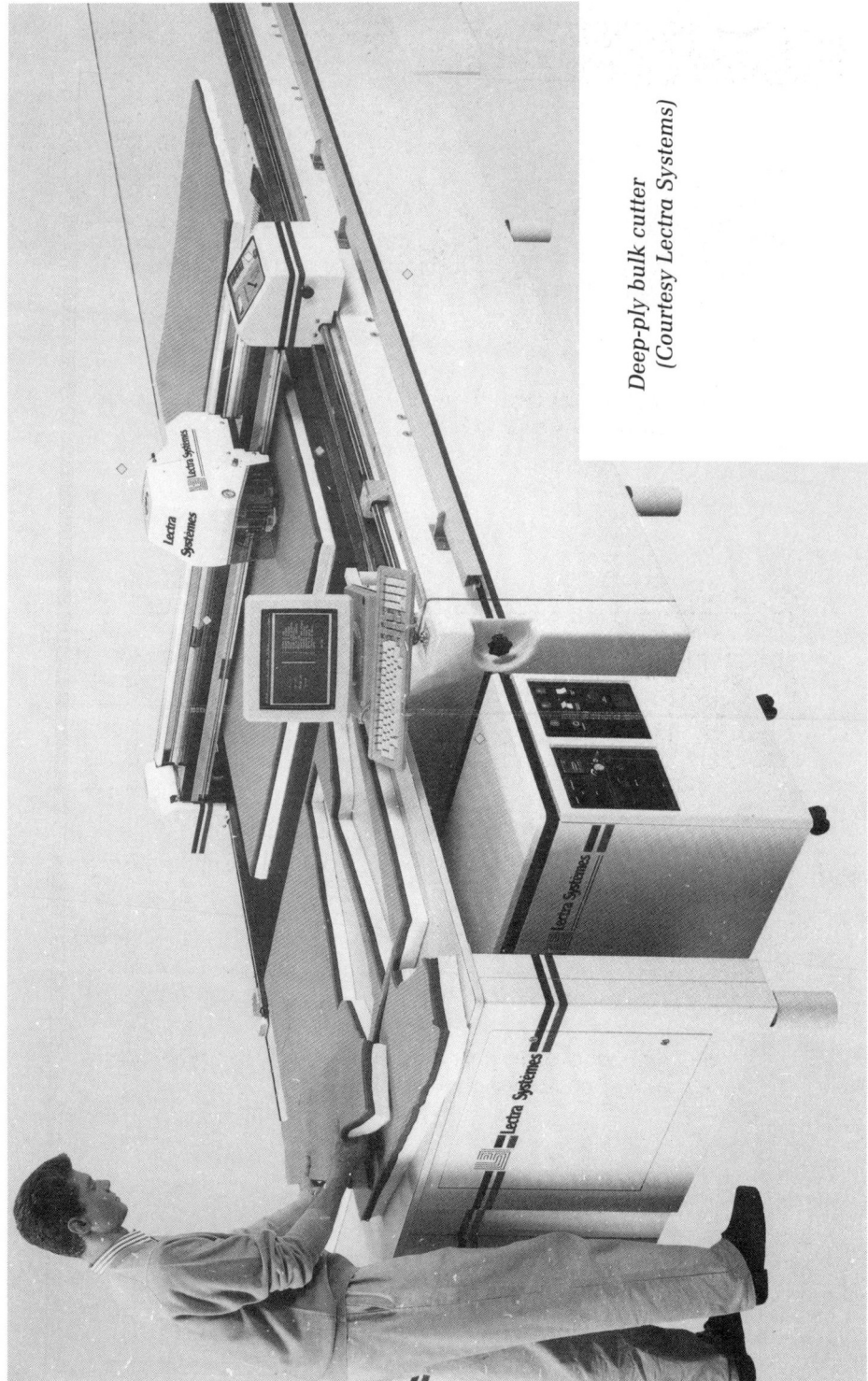

Deep-ply bulk cutter (Courtesy Lectra Systems)

156 *Computers in the fashion industry*

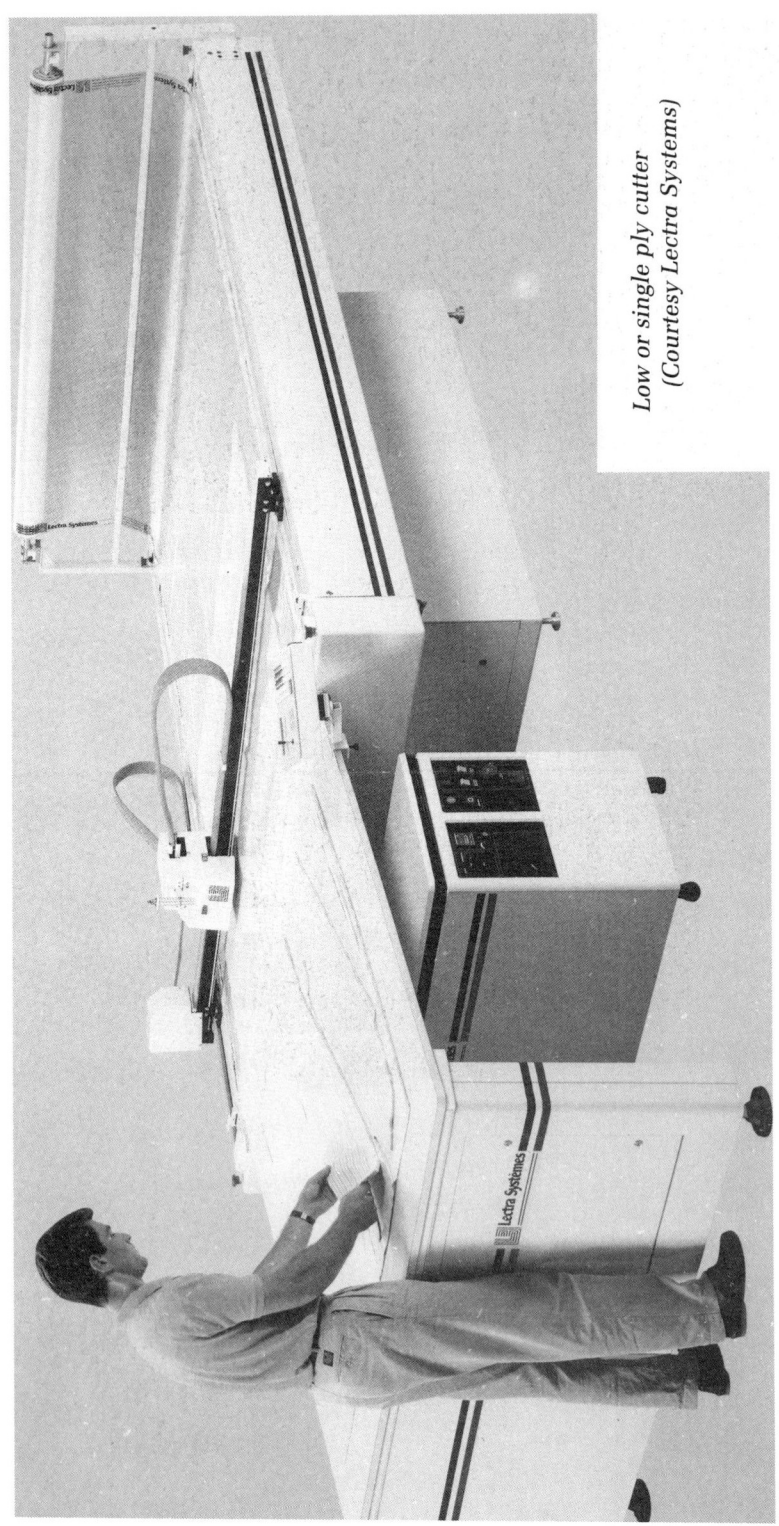

Low or single ply cutter (Courtesy Lectra Systems)

Computer bulk cutting 157

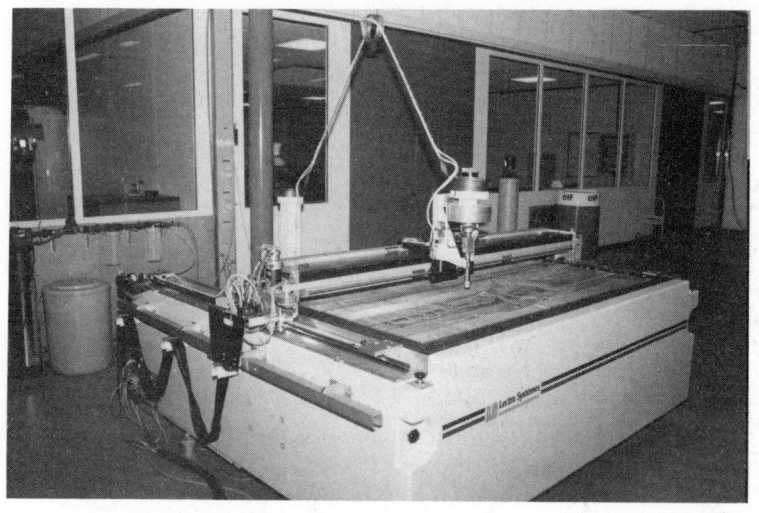

Water jet cutter
(Courtesy Lectra Systems)

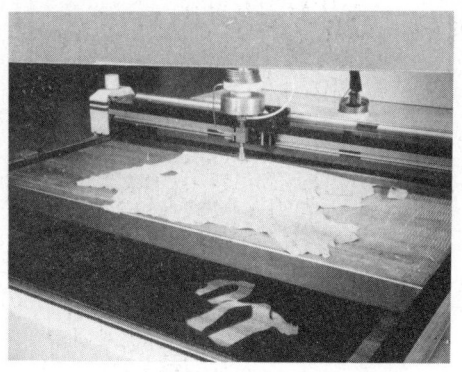

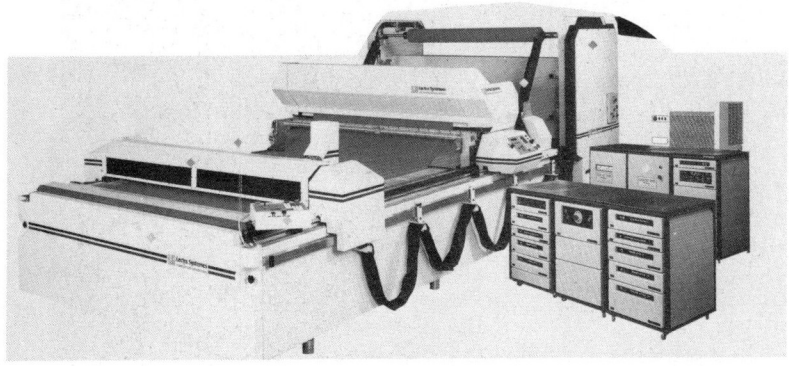

*Laser pattern cut out machine
(Courtesy Lectra Systems)*

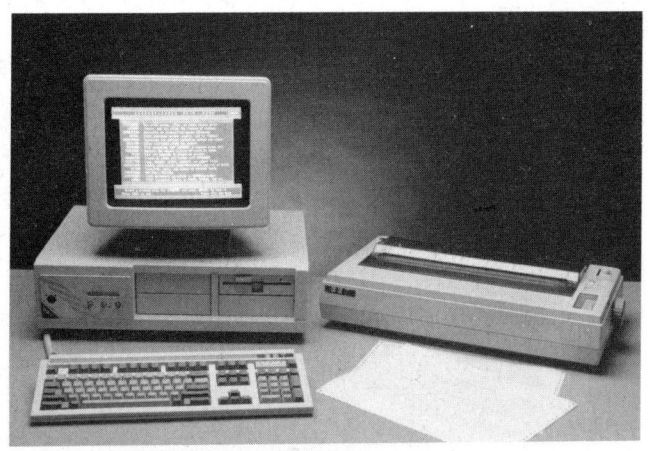

*Gerberplanner instantly analyses cut order planning alternatives and selects those that will best meet the user's specific manufacturing needs
(Courtesy Gerber Garment Technology, Inc.)*

Computer bulk cutting

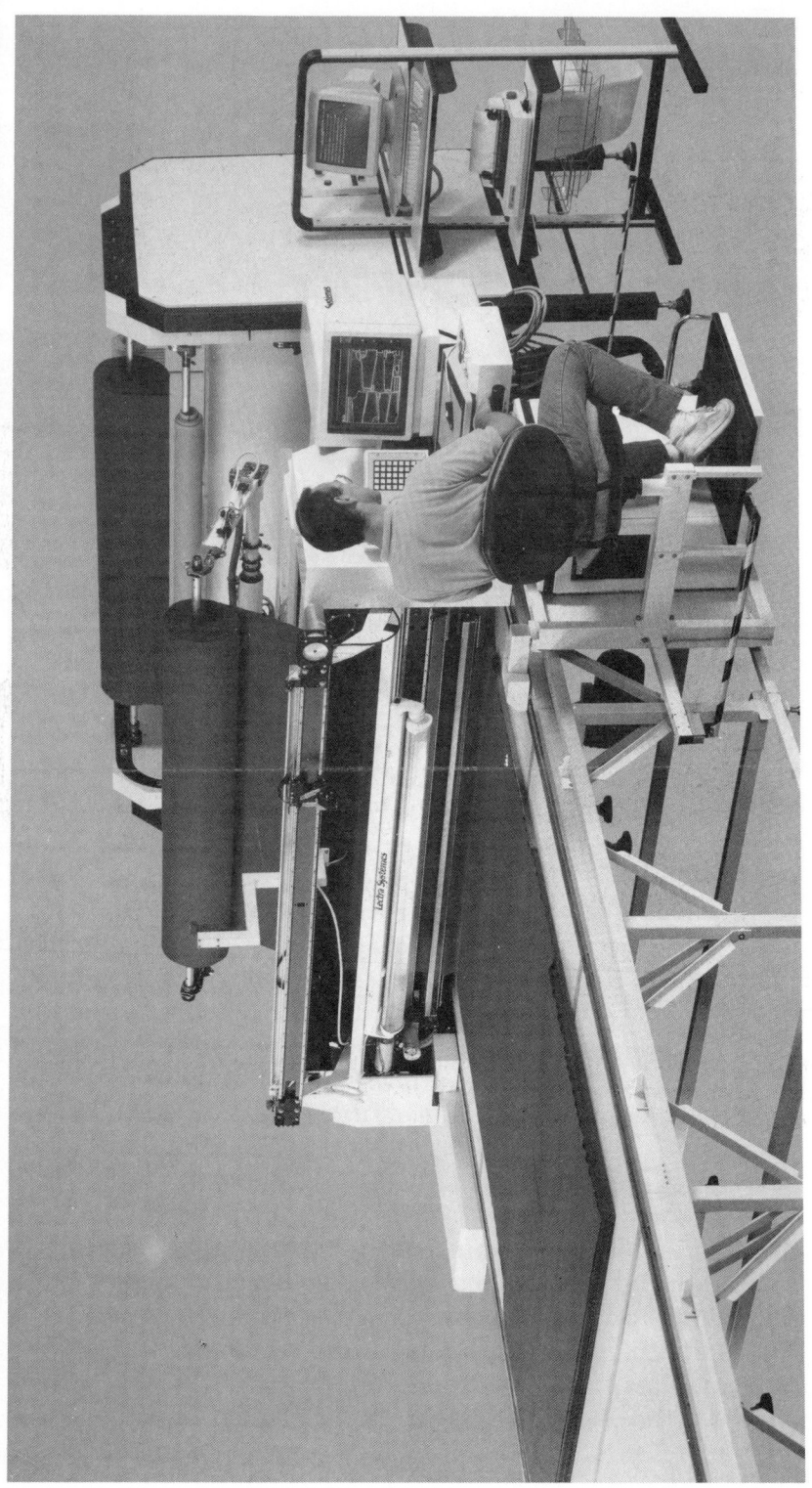

Computer-controlled laying up machine or spreader (Courtesy Lectra Systems)

Chapter 10

Computer-aided production machinery

The application of computer technology to production involves a different set of problems to those of design and cutting. The designing process mainly deals with drawing lines in a two-dimensional plane, and then cutting in two dimensions. It is relatively easy to reproduce these activities using computer-controlled devices.

The picture changes when the main activity involves selecting and picking up pieces of floppy material and carrying out complex spatial manœuvres – in most cases, with more than one piece. When operating with solid materials, such as wood or metal, this can be done very efficiently, as in the car industry where robots carry out very complex three-dimensional processes. But in clothing manufacture the problem is almost insoluble because of the huge variables in surface texture, weight and general handling properties of fabrics. It is therefore virtually impossible to manufacture clothing using robots.

Training a human being to handle and machine these materials is difficult enough; and when this process is analysed to establish the exact movements and positions at each stage, it is soon realized that the problems are colossal. The dexterity of the human hand and the minute calculations and adjustments that have to be made each millisecond by the eye and relayed to the hands and fingers is mind-boggling. The hand alone is a miracle of invention, let alone the complex physical and nerve systems that are required to control it. In addition there are the continuous adjustments needed for the body as a whole to orientate itself in relation to the work area. A floppy piece of cloth defies control at every point on its surface, and the sizes of the pieces of cloth that constitute a garment vary so much that this in itself is an almost insurmountable obstacle. This is mainly because the two parts to be sewn together need to be placed with enormous accuracy in relation to each other. When dealing with finished or part-finished garments and their movement around the factory, the task of automation is made easier because the degree of accuracy needed to locate and move the object is not so critical.

In spite of this, work has been going on for a long time to automate parts of the process that are within the bounds of possibility. The first breakthrough was the invention of the sewing-machine. Two hundred years ago nobody would have thought this possible, but it was achieved, and ever since designers have been honing the sewing-machine to near perfection – so who is to tell what will be accomplished in the future?

At the present time, there are companies experimenting with robotic arms that have the sewing device at the end, endeavouring to sew parts together in a three-dimensional mode rather than flat as with the conventional sewing-machine. How the pieces ready to be sewn will get into place accurately has not been established – by human hand, it must be assumed.

The manufacturing area of a clothing factory will have many human inhabitants for the foreseeable future, unlike many other manufacturing establishments which, even today, are largely deserted. But it poses a question that goes quite deep into the future of human activity and our way of existence. Is it the healthiest path that leads to the deskilling of man through the automation by computers and of his usurpation from activities that can be greatly satisfying?

What has been achieved to date is automatic sewing along preset paths using placement devices to feed the machine, and jig-clamping devices to move the fabric past a static sewing head. Sometimes the fabric is static and the needle has limited mobility, but the piles of fabric are placed accurately by hand to the place where the machine can continue.

The automatic following of a sewing path has been achieved, not by computer or electronic technology, but mainly with the use of mechanical cams that guide fairly complex cog-wheel complexes; these in turn move the fabric that has been placed by hand and held by some form of clamps.

This is purely mechanical, and does not require any electronic input. It is mainly used where there is large-scale repetition of the same operation, such as shirt-collar sewing and shirt cuffs. It is applicable where there are very small variations in the sewing path. In the case of a shirt collar the styling changes are small, and so the mechanisms that operate the sewing path can be designed with small variables that will give enough flexibility to sew all styles of shirt collars without having to have a different machine for each collar design. This type of machine has been in use for a long time and is very efficient and reliable.

Until fairly recently, all lockstitch machines – that is, the machines that are used to close seams – were purely mechanical and controlled by human judgement and skills. The only control was through a foot-operated variable clutch which controlled the power input to the sewing movement, and any overrun in the sewing path was rectified by the operator manually winding the machine forwards or backwards and then having to pick up a pair of scissors and cut the thread in order to continue along the next seam. This wasted a lot of time; a three- or four-second adjustment when repeated a thousand or more times and multiplied by the number of machinists, adds up to a large chunk of production time, which is money lost.

This was probably the first area to which electronics was applied in the form of a sensor that recognized the end of the cloth and stopped the needle in the correct place and cut the thread at the correct length from the stitching line. These devices were not very reliable at first and required a mechanic always to be available to maintain and reset them; now, however, they are very reliable and need very little attention.

A typical specification for a modern lockstitcher would sound like this:

Quiet, high speed, single-needle lockstitcher with automatic thread trimmer
1 Control panel mounted on the machine head on level of eyes, easy access and more leg room.
2 Factile sensor to detect end of cloth, electronic memory of cloth thickness.
3 Adjustable sewing speed from 230 spm (stitch per second) to max speed of 5000 spm steplessly variable (infinitely variable).
4 Auto back tacking, repeat back tacking, half stitch.
5 Thread wiper.
6 Needle stop position selector.
7 Slow start switch.
8 Thread cutter, electronic control.
9 Auto foot lifter, pressure and height.

10 Auto selection of material thickness.
11 Stitch type and length.
12 Seven-day program set memory storage.

Depending on the cost, lockstitch machines will have all or some of these options.

There are many types of special machines for doing various operations. One of the most common is the overlocking machine used for oversewing the raw edge of the cut cloth to stop it fraying, and to improve the appearance of the inside of the garment. These come in various degrees of sophistication. There are single-needle and double-needle overlockers and safety overlockers. Also, there are a range of attachments. The ordinary single- and twin-needle machines are used for the reason stated above, but the safety overlocker is used for closing at the same time as neatening the cut edge; this is used on all kinds of knitted fabrics or any stretch material, as the stitch characteristic is to allow the seam to be stretched without the thread breaking.

The attachments that can be used with the overlocker are:

1 Blind hemming ruler for jersey and knitwear
2 Serging ruler
3 Ruffler
4 Piping ruffler
5 Binding tape guide
6 Tractor foot
7 Serrated angle knife
8 Chain cutter
9 Tape cutter
10 Backtack
11 Cleaner
12 Tape feeder
13 Puller

None of these machines have any electronic input, and are totally manually operated.

Then there are the buttonhole machines and the button sewing-machines, but once again these are operated without electronic devices.

Other types include zigzag machines and blindstitchers for invisible hemming, and double-chain stitchers that are used where there is hard wear and stretching to cope with. These are also purely mechanical.

However, computer technology has been applied in several areas of the sewing operation.

The sewing of inset sleeves has always been a highly skilled operation where the sleeve head has to be prepared by easing it to a predetermined shape, and for this an automatic sleeve-easing machine has been produced that is programmable round sixteen separate segments of the sleeve head and can cope with the change in the grain of the cloth on the sleeve head, easing the fabric different amounts at different parts of the head. The sewing line is controlled by a photo cell that ensures an even seam allowance all around the sleeve head. When this has been done, the sleeve is ready to be sewn straight into the armhole without the need to ease one on to the other.

Another development is the electronically programmable lockstitch. This is a multi-purpose machine that can be programmed to follow a predesigned sewing path. It is ideal for small-area decorative stitching, such as fancy jean pockets and belt decorations, or handbag and shoe decorative top stitching. The parts are placed in a clamp and the design established, tried and approved; then it can be stored on a memory card and used when required. This type of capability is also applied to shirt collars and cuffs, and gives even more flexibility than a straightforward mechanical system.

There are also embroidery machines that are linked to computer programs. The design can be sketched using a graphics program and then the design is fed through a computer-controlled embroidery machine which can be a single unit or a bank of machines, all doing the same pattern where mass production and low price are being catered for.

The profile stitchers that have been described can be of two different types of design. The first is where the sewing head is static and the work is clamped on to a movable platform and controlled by a computer program; or it is the reverse, where the work is clamped down and remains static and the sewing head is mobile and controlled by the computer.

Another useful device that has been successfully developed controls the accurate matching of stripes when sewing two parts together. This is done by placing a light sensor above and below the work piece, so that the position of the stripes above and below can be accurately aligned by a variable speed feed foot that can make fine adjustments between the two plies. It presupposes that the cut pieces are cut accurately to start with and aligned as close to matching as the eye can see, and then the final accurate alignment is done by the machine. Other semi-automatic machines include the zip attacher for skirts, various buttonhole machines and button attachers, and autojig machines that assemble jacket foreparts on men's suits. There are many other specialized machines designed for individual operations, such as:

1. Computer-controlled sewing of darts and pleats.
2. Computer-controlled sewing of piped and welt pocket openings.
3. Computer-controlled patch pocket setter and sewer.
4. Computer-controlled waistband-attaching machine.
5. Computer-controlled automatic profile stitching machine system.
6. Computer-controlled loop attaching machine.
7. Computer-controlled automatic sewing edge track.
8. Computer-controlled continuous elastic attachment in lingerie.
9. Computer-controlled auto lockstitch buttonholer.
10. Computer-controlled pattern sewing-machines, plus pattern input device.
11. Computer-controlled monogramming and embroidery machines.

These are some of the options offered to the manufacturer at the time of writing.

Another facility that is now available is the replaceable and updateable computer-program system. The idea is to make the system a separate unit from the machine, and instead of replacing the whole unit, to update only the brain – thus saving money and time. Singer and Mitsubishi are the companies currently offering this type of technology. The features listed by Singer are:

LCD PROGRAMMABLE SYSTEM

1. Programmable system, operated through stitch count or sensing.
2. Sews up to eight seams in any one pattern.
3. Can sew multiple-pattern programs.
4. Memory for instant recall of programs.
5. Basic memory, ten single programs, ten multiple programs.
6. Any element of a program is easily modified at any stage.
7. Autostop at the end of seams can be by stitch count or sensing.
8. Auto pivot, adjustable pivot delay for all corners.
9. Sensor sensitivity is automatically adjusted by passing the fabric across the sensor.
10. With one actuation of the treadle, the whole program is set in motion, i.e. back tack/stop at the end of seam/needle down/ presser foot up/foot down/needle up/trim, etc.
11. Operation console constantly displays all pattern details.
12. Cursor indicates location of pattern cycle during sewing or while being programmed.

13 Can be programmed for manual sewing on the last seam with no intermediate presser foot lift.
14 The basic ELNP motor can be upgraded to the full LCD programmable system.
15 This applies to all one- and two-needle lockstitch machines, plus zigzag and chainstitch machines.

Although Singer has been mentioned in this instant, it does not mean that they are alone in this field. All the large machine manufacturers are developing products on the same level. Some will take a lead then others will take it back.

It will be useful to have a list of these companies in order to get some idea of the choice available:

1 A.M.F. Clarbro
2 Brother
3 Juki
4 Mitsubishi
5 Necchi
6 Pfaff
7 Reece
8 Singer
9 Rimoldi
10 Union Special
11 Durkopp
12 Eastman

Some of these companies offer a range of machinery designed specifically for the shoe industry. They are basically the same machines, but are geared to the heavy work required for sewing leather. Although the shoe industry has not been spoken of in depth, all the technology mentioned in this book applies equally to this area. They obviously use a lot of machinery that is found only in the shoe sector. In general, it can be said that shoe design and manufacture is very highly developed and, in many respects, ahead of the clothing sector.

Pressing

This area is probably the least computer-aided of all the manufacturing processes.

The programs that are used control the temperature and the timing of steam and vacuum applications. These can be pre-designed for different fabric characteristics, which eliminates the variations in pressing due to inconsistent operators.

The other area where this technology is particularly useful is in the fusing of interlinings of all kinds. This process requires accurate control and the time and temperature input is critical, and differs with every type of fabric.

The design of fusible interlinings for every conceivable type of cloth has meant that exact data for their correct use has been evolved, and to be able to carry this process through successfully the appropriate machinery had to be produced.

This type of machine is now highly developed and computer-driven. One of the leaders in this field is Meyer, who have a very sophisticated piece of hardware to do this job.

There are many manufacturers of pressing machinery but the ones of note are:

1   Macpi
2   Veit
3   Meyer
4   Eurosew
5   Test
6   ESP
7   Orton
8   Kobe

All these machine and pressing companies show their products regularly at the IMB Exhibitions at Colne, Germany, and the Bobbin Exhibition in America, along with all the CAD/CAM computer systems. If an overview of developments is required, then these exhibitions are essential appointments. Other exhibitions of a more local nature are held annually.

Computer-aided production machinery

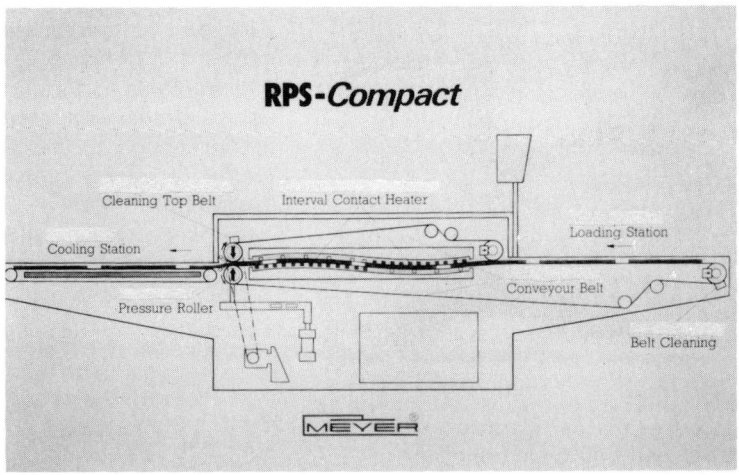

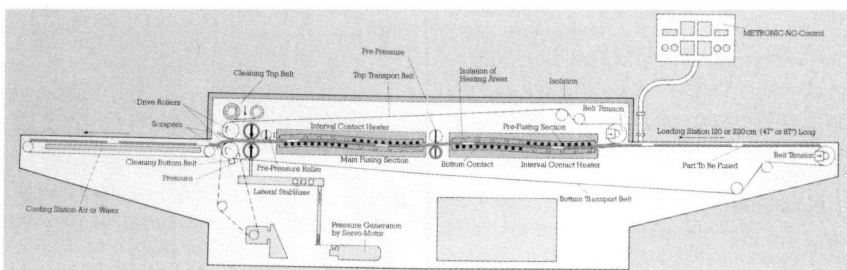

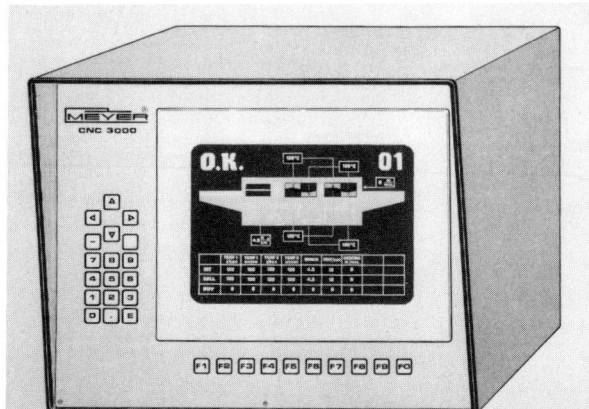

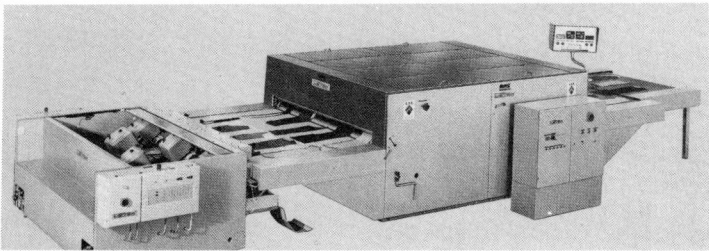

*Meyer's computerized cloth fusing machine
(Courtesy Meyer Machines UK Ltd)*

170 Computers in the fashion industry

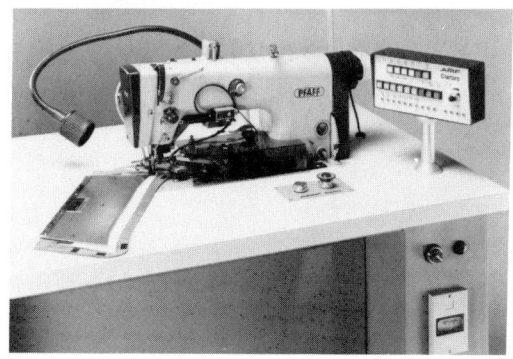

AMF Clarbro autojig assembling garment components up to about 600 mm long, including sharp-pointed components such as shirt collars. Adhesive patches on the jig provide appropriate 'instructions' to the microprocessor control system
  (Courtesy AMF Clarbro)

General view of the AMF Clarbro autojig for assembling large upholstery panels, both domestic and automotive. At the end of the cycle, the jig is automatically moved to the 'parking' position (top left). Then, when the next jig commences sewing, the completed component moves from the park position back to the operator for unloading
  (Courtesy AMF Clarbro)

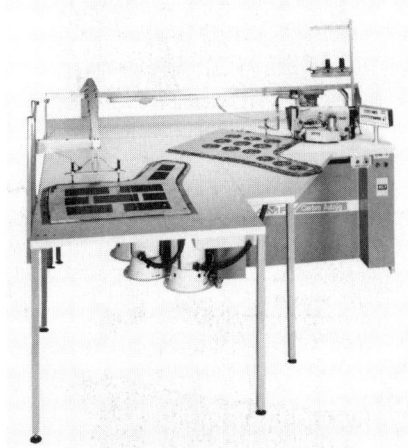

Computer-aided production machinery

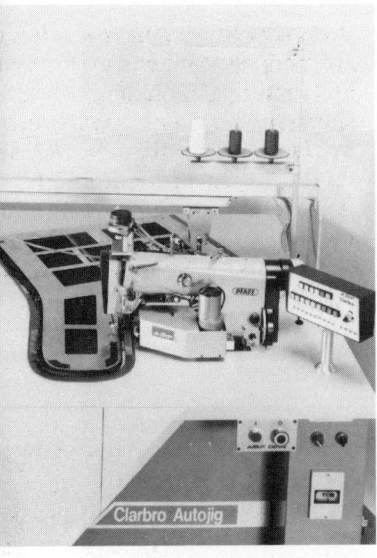

Sewing head of the AMF Clarbro autojig
 (Courtesy AMF Clarbro)

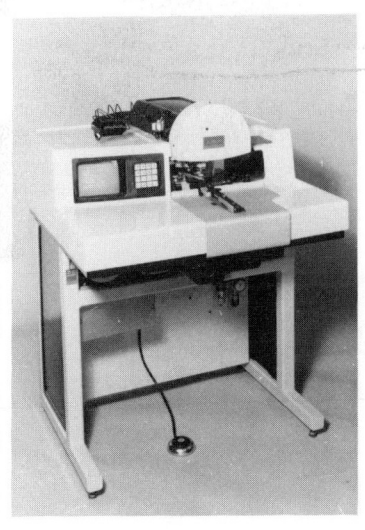

AMF electronic buttoner 'hand sews' conventional or blazer-style coat buttons in eleven different ways — selected by computer keypad and screen
 (Courtesy AMF Clarbro)

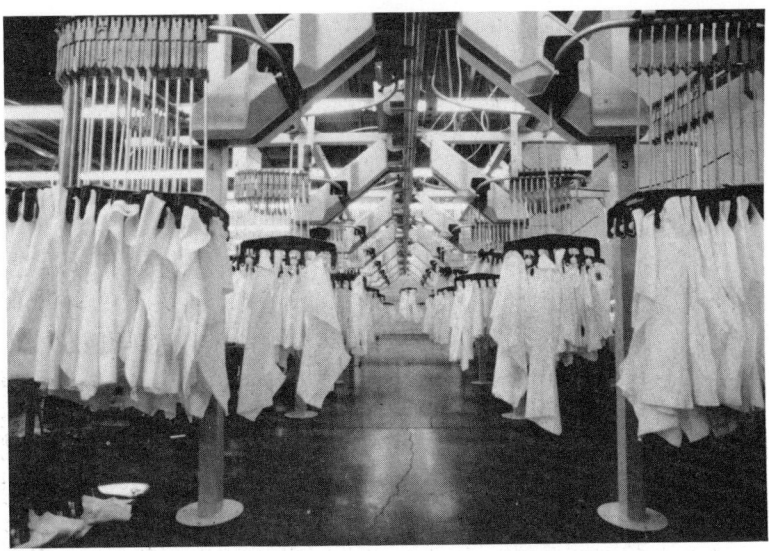

Gerbermover GM-200 for sewing room efficiency, providing advanced unit production operation, utilizing a powerful, multi-user computer and radio frequency technology
  (Courtesy Gerber Garment Technology, Inc.)

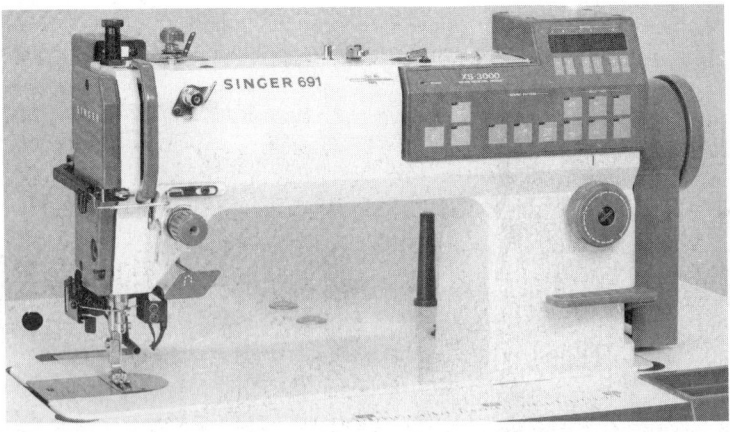

Singer 691 high-speed lockstitch complete with AC servo motor. With advanced thread cutting technology, the 691 virtually eliminates the 'bird nest' at the start of sewing, leaving only 4 mm or less of thread at the end of each seam
  (Courtesy Singer Industrial Products, SDL Limited)

Computer-aided production machinery 173

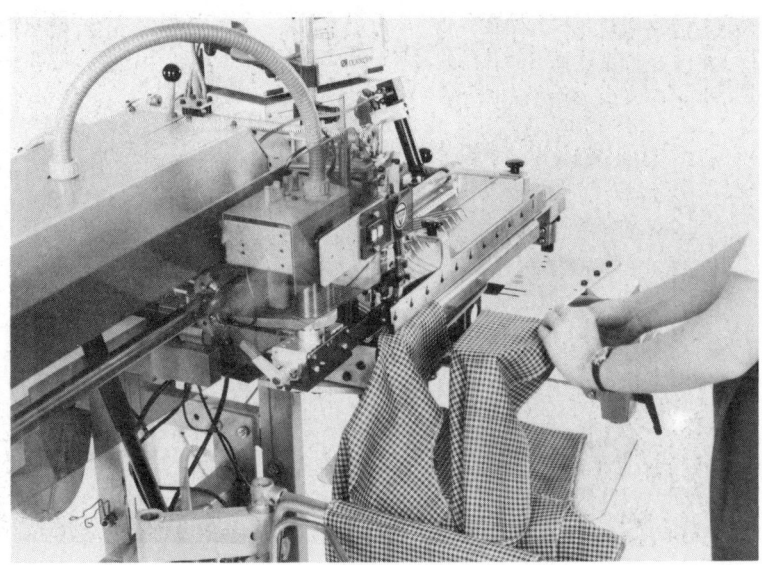

Durkopp 743 sewing unit for sewing darts or pleats
(Courtesy Durkopp (UK) Ltd)

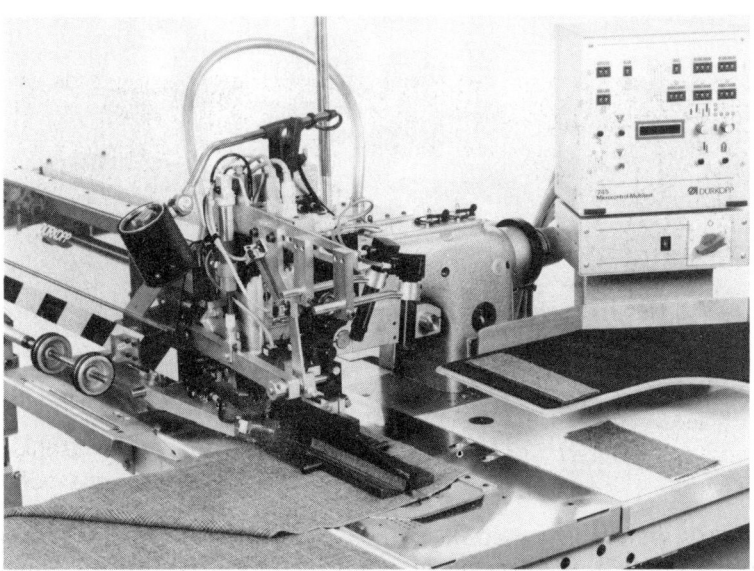

Durkopp 745 sewing unit for sewing and stacking piped and welt pockets
(Courtesy Durkopp (UK) Ltd)

174 *Computers in the fashion industry*

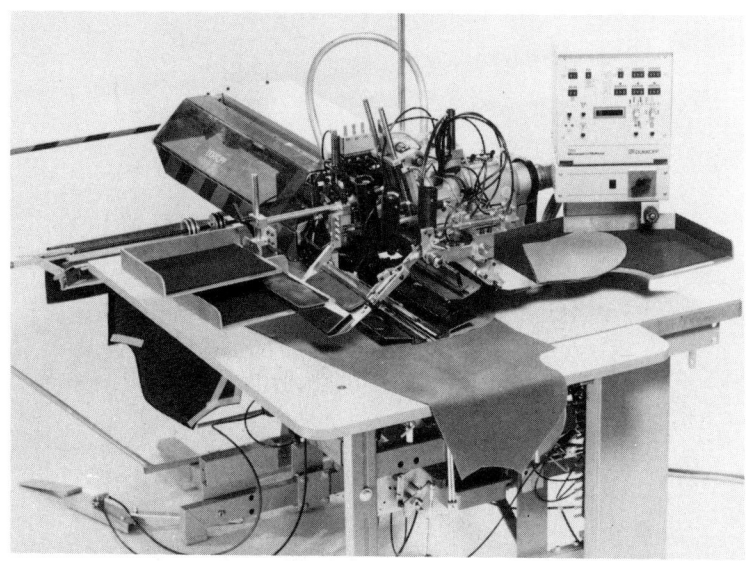

Durkopp 745 sewing unit
 (Courtesy Durkopp (UK) Ltd)

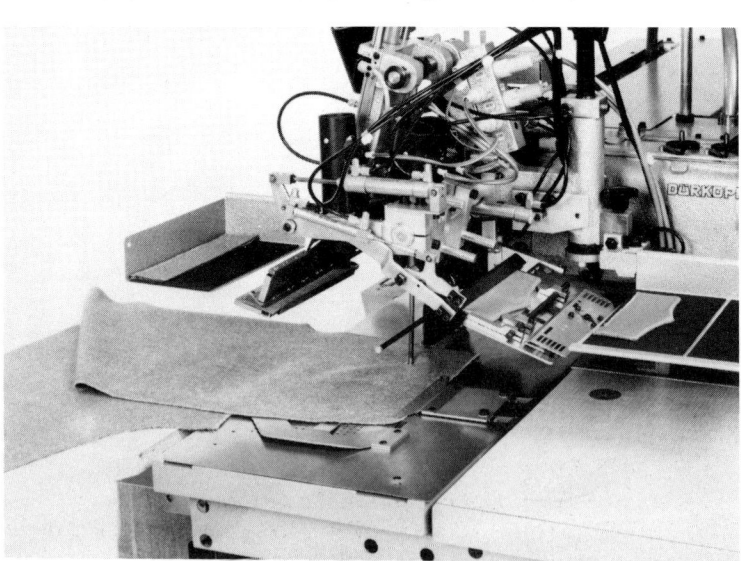

Durkopp 745 sewing unit
 (Courtesy Durkopp (UK) Ltd)

Computer-aided production machinery

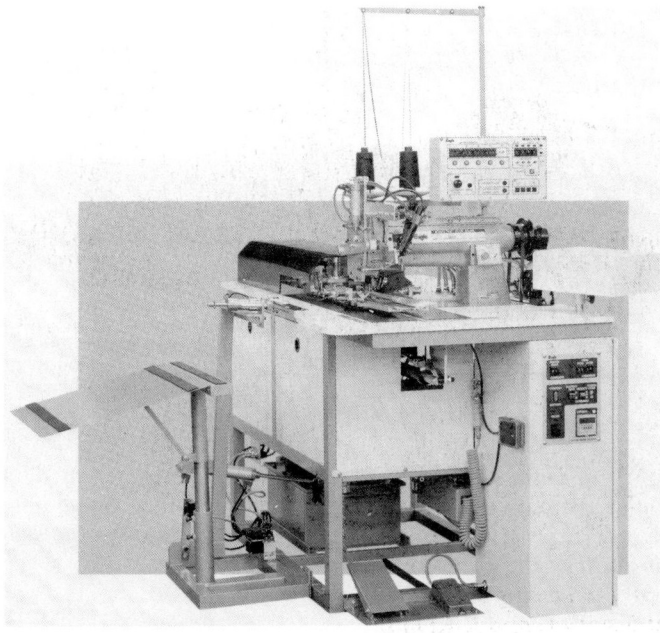

Automatic welting and flap insertion machine
(Courtesy West Bridgford Machine Company Ltd)

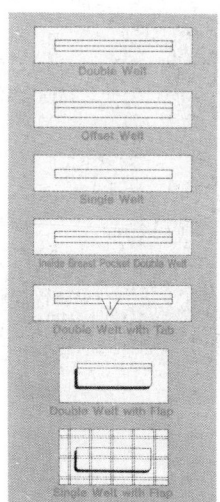

Options for the Eagle welter
(Courtesy West Bridgford Machine Company Ltd)

176   Computers in the fashion industry

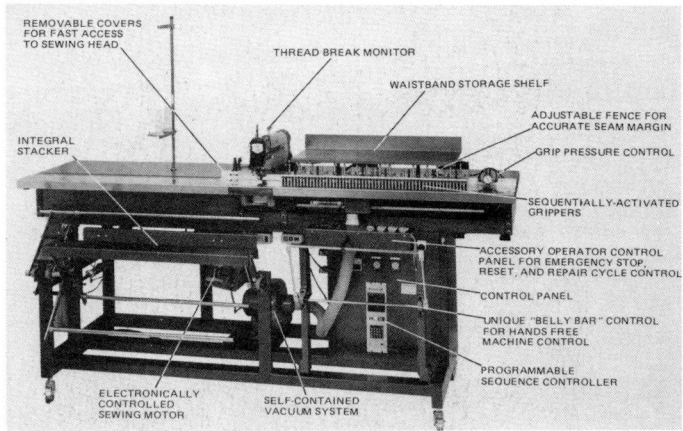

An automatic grip seamer. Seam start and stop are controlled by a photoelectric sensor, so no adjustments for different sizes are necessary. Seam length can be controlled by a proximity switch which allows interruption of the seam at any point. Sewing will resume automatically when required
   (Courtesy West Bridgford Machine Company Ltd)

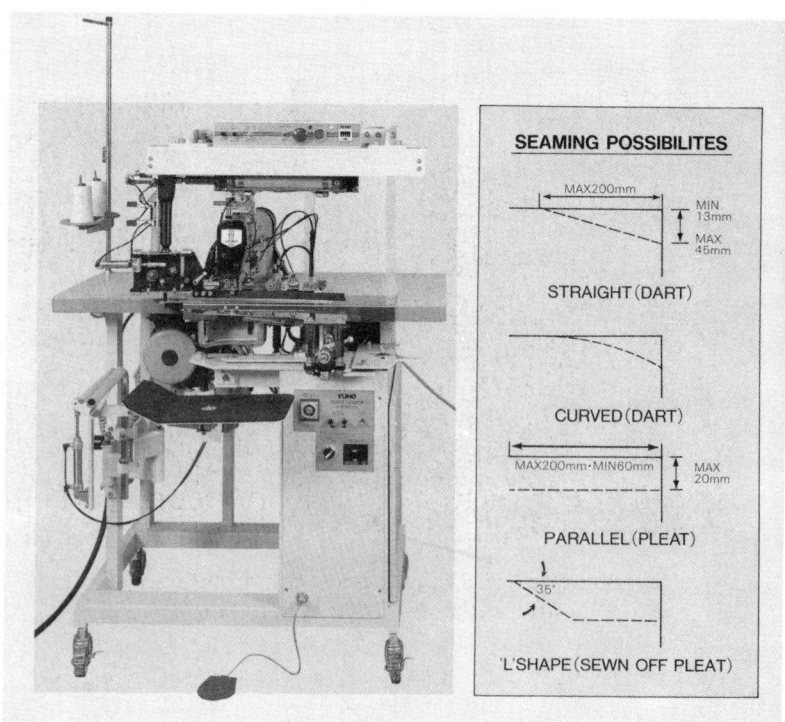

A dart or pleat seaming machine
(Courtesy West Bridgford Machine Company Ltd)

Computer-aided production machinery 177

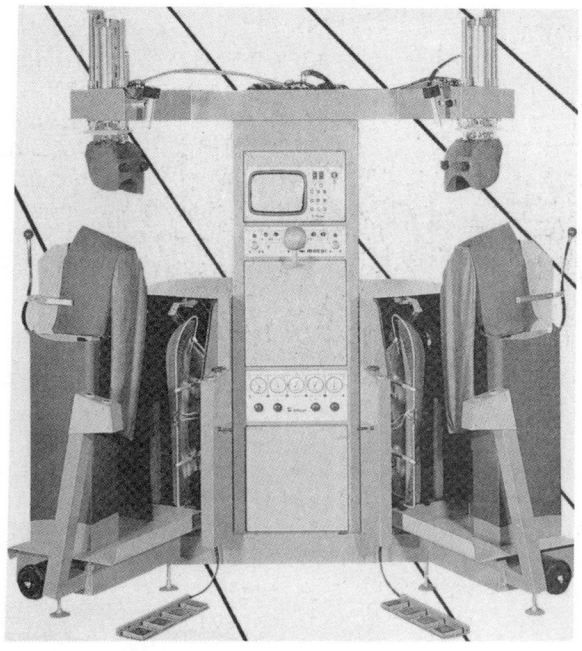

A computer controlled shoulder pressing unit
(Courtesy Macpi UK Ltd)

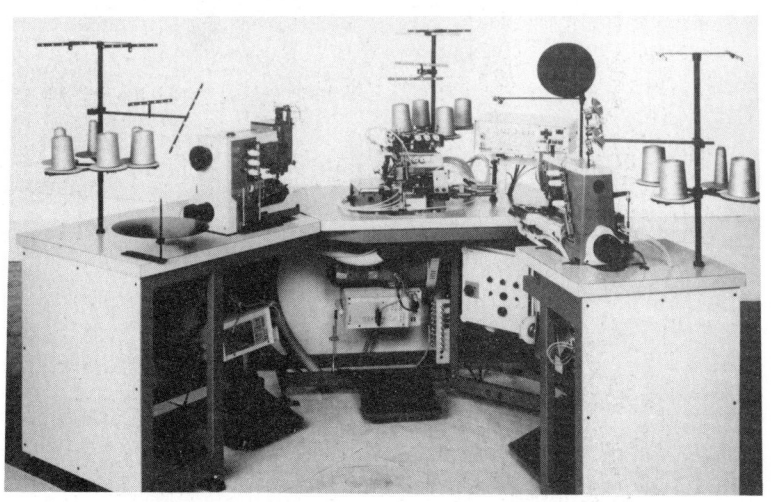

A computerized multi-operational sewing system
(Courtesy Rimoldi Great Britain Ltd)

178 Computers in the fashion industry

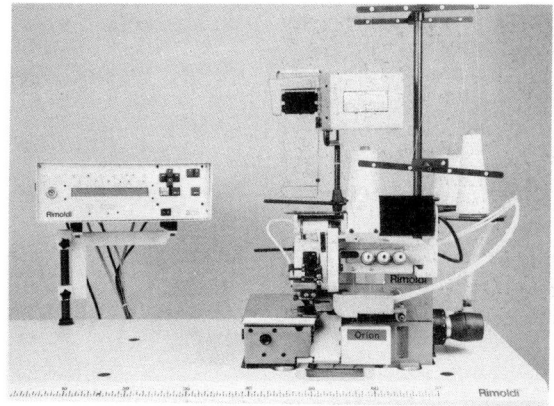

A programmable sewing unit. Some of the functions include: automatic machine start and stop; automatic measuring of strips, laces, etc.; and activation of devices for cut of elastic, etc.
(Courtesy Rimoldi Great Britain Ltd)

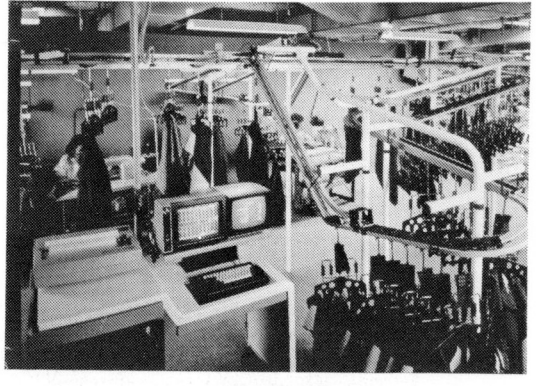

Overhead transport system
(Courtesy Investronica UK)

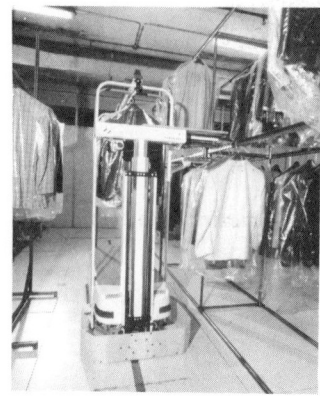

Computer-controlled warehaouse storage 'T' CAR stops anywhere in the warehouse unit with great precision
(Courtesy Investronica UK)

Computer-aided production machinery 179

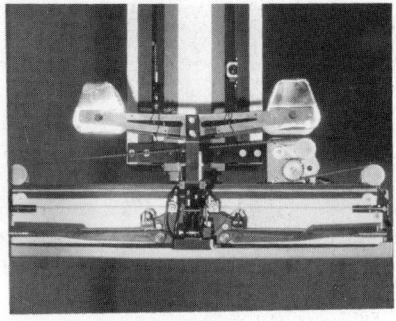

'T' CAR details. It conveys a rail of garment to within 5 cm
 (Courtesy Investronica UK)

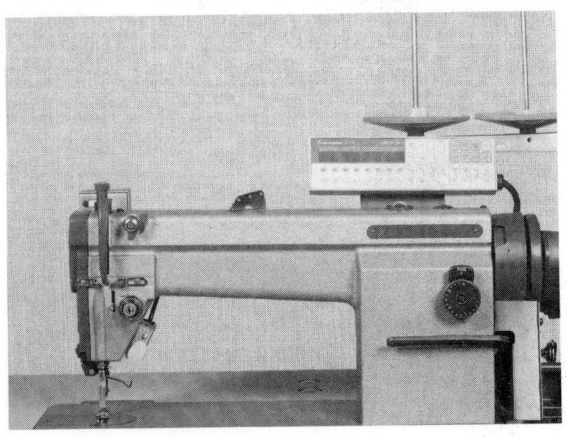

Variable speed, single needle, lockstitch machine with automatic undertrimmer
and non-contact clutch motor
 (Courtesy Mitsubishi)

180   Computers in the fashion industry

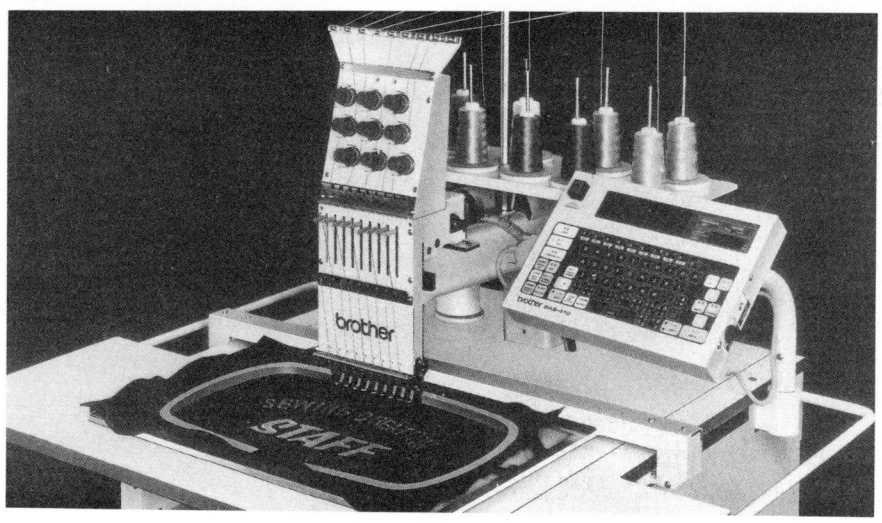

*Programmable nine-needle embroidery machine
(Courtesy Jones & Brother)*

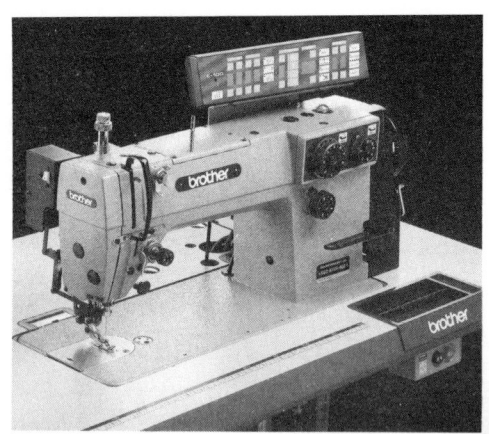

*Programmable single-needle lock stitch machine
(Courtesy Jones & Brother)*

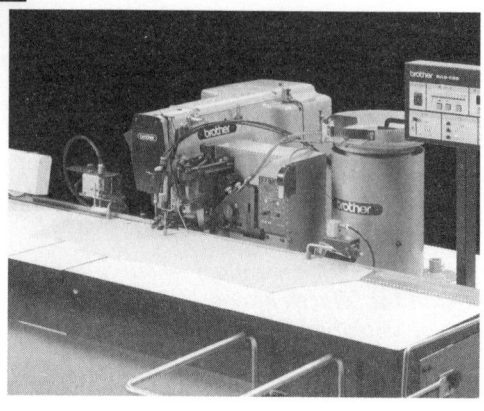

*Programmable automatic lockstitch button-sewing machine
(Courtesy Jones & Brother)*

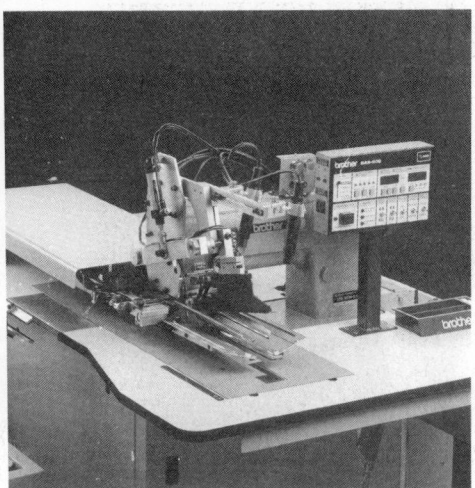

Programmable automatic pocket welt sewer with flap device
  (Courtesy Jones & Brother)

Chapter 11

Computer-aided management and production control

When a company has computerized all the areas of its production, it is logical that they should all be interconnected and able to interact with one another. This, unfortunately, is not the case, since there is no standardization in either hardware or software. Each computer manufacturer works to their own specifications, hoping that the user will become dependent on their products and not be able to bolt on a piece of hardware from one of their competitors. This has had the reverse effect, in that the buyer of a system now looks for the computer manufacturer that offers the best integration and compatibility and will tend to avoid the dead-end option. Basically, this will amount to compatibility with IBM structures, since they are the largest and have the deepest penetration in the user field, of both hardware and software. Most CAD/CAM systems are now based on IBM-type hardware; this means they run on Intel processors, either 80286 or 80386 and variations on these, or the latest 80486. Unfortunately, the software invariably is not compatible across the board of a large computer complex.

The software may be written in a different language or, if it is in the same language, may differ in some small detail that will make it lock up when addressing another program.

It may seem a simple thing for the outsider to expect full and failure-free integration of all sectors, but in fact this is a very difficult thing to achieve in reality.

It is now the aim of the computer producers to accomplish this, and to this end they have invented yet another synonym, CIM, which stands for 'computer integrated manufacture'. When and if it is achieved, it will have to be as bug-free as conceivably possible, since there is nothing more frustrating and infuriating than to spend half the morning wrestling with an unfriendly bug-infested non-compatible system just to achieve something that could have been done manually in five minutes. It will make a great difference when such a system is perfected, as it will save much time making the company faster and more responsive to market changes.

This is the dream of management at all levels, to be able to have at their fingertips all relevant data and to make the necessary calculations and costings plus the ability to see at any time what is happening anywhere in the process – what is called in their jargon 'real time access' (RTA).

However, there is help on hand for the company that has invested a lot of money in systems that are incompatible across the board. Programs are available that will, in theory, interface the various systems.

They are based on the two standards for interfacing that have been developed; the first, by General Motors, is called MAP, and the second, by Boeing, is called TOP. This will mean that systems already purchased may be fully integrated rather than having to scrap the lot and start again.

Ideally, the areas that need linking in the fashion field are the following:

1 Point of sale
2 Retail stock
3 Supply source for item replacement
4 Market analyses data re size and age
5 Market analyses data re consumer fashion demand
6 Style data bank (working sketches), graphic art software
7 Pattern data bank, blocks and styles, PDS system software
8 Grade-rule data, grading software
9 Size-chart library including British and international standards
10 Layplan files; auto and manual layplan software
11 Production cut planning. Computer bulk-cutting software
12 Fabric, in stock, on order and delivery times
13 Fabric suppliers and all relevant information
14 Wholesale order and supply of finished garments, delivery dates and customers
15 Trimmings source data and pricing
16 Manufacturing process breakdown and costs

17 Finished garment stock (warehouse control)
18 Commercial data, all financial ledgers and payroll
19 Production planning and control
20 Costing data for all overheads and non-production staff
21 Costing data for raw materials and trimmings, etc.
22 Product costs for cutting, assembly, finishing and pressing

Ideally, these are the main areas that can be linked for access by the controllers of any part of the process. Obviously, not all personnel will have access to all areas as a lot may be confidential information, and passwords, etc. will be used to control the vast network of data. The retail end of the process is not usually directly integrated with the wholesale and product-manufacturing processes, because they are usually different company interests. If and when they are connected, considerable advantages would be available, in that the designers and the clothing manufacturers would have direct access to the market trends and fluctuations, and could help the retailers to decide what to stock any particular store with, instead of the retailers' total dependence on the buyers.

Before a computer can be of use, it has to be primed with the data with which it is to work. This can take a long time. It is the most important stage as it determines the future efficiency of the system.

The software for each area must be written by, or in close conjunction with, experts in that field, so that the sectors and requirements can be clearly defined in order to receive and manipulate the data correctly.

Above all, 'user friendliness' is of prime importance. These systems have to be used by people who are not computer literate, and are only interested in achieving the successful fulfilment of their work goal. At all times the computer must be of help and not get in the way, making the task easier instead of harder.

Priming systems

There are two difficult stages to plough through when a new system is acquired.

The first is to learn how to use the program and become sufficiently fluent in it to be able to tackle the next stage – which is loading the system with the necessary data.

It is very important that the first stage, which is learning to operate the system, is as short and easy as possible.

A manager will be required to oversee the whole process and will decide how the system is to be organized, as there are usually options as to the layout and distribution of the data.

Point of sale

In the case of large chain stores, the first program will be linked to the point of sale and be controlled at a remote centre. Items will be coded; this will detail the price, description, colour, style number, etc. This will be fed into a central decoder and relayed to other branches of the system, such as retail stock held at the main stores, stock held at each branch including the point of sale, and wholesale suppliers of the item. Each of these data banks has to be fed with the information required, such as names and addresses of suppliers and all the price structures. The program has to be capable of recording delivery dates from the supplier; to plan distribution to the various retail branches; and be able to analyse items' turnover speeds and predict the re-order quantities for each branch.

A program should be capable of analysing all of this data, and presenting a clear picture of the market requirements in each of the areas serviced.

It will show an interesting map of the likes and dislikes of various regions, which will enable accurate predictions for future sales. The areas of interest to the garment designer will include colour preferences, choice of fabric, age groups, size breakdown and general fashion trends in the area. In particular, the age of the purchaser will help enlarge the scenario and permit a more accurate targeting of designs.

The other important area is that of sizing, which is linked to the degree of contouring of the style; in other words, 'the looser the fit the greater the number of bodies it will fit', and therefore fewer sizes will be required for that style. With a close-fitting style, the number of sizes required increases dramatically in order that sales are not lost because of ill-fitting garments. All such information can be stored for future analyses.

Design data file

All data relating to style preferences in the different localities and countries can be continuously updated and made available to the design department of the manufacturer. A style library can be assembled and enlarged over a period of time, so that a fashion trend can be recorded re location and time-span. The library will carry sales data for each style regarding colour, ways sold, type of fabric preferred, the price (wholesale and retail) of the last sales, size range offered, and how many sold in each size and where.

This data will be updated continuously and edited where

required. It is doubtful whether any designer will have the time to do this, so it probably will be done by special marketing support staff.

Pattern data file

This will be linked to the design data and will consist of patterns that have been perfected, graded and used to produce bulk sales. The designer, on the advice of the sales-support section, can choose a style from the data file that corresponds to the current demand, and change it in detail knowing that the design is backed up by a perfected pattern in the pattern file, which in turn can easily be altered to correspond to the new style.

It must be understood that these design and pattern files do not appear overnight, but take a long time to build and assemble. They must consist of only well-tried and balanced patterns that can be altered by an experienced pattern technician without destroying the balance.

Process-costing data file

The design and pattern files can be linked to a product-costing data file. This is collected and assembled by work-study engineers.

The cutting, assembly, pressing, and finishing processes of each part of a garment are closely monitored and timed, which gives rise to a standard price costing.

For example, take the making price of a specific shirt cuff, welt, pocket or a collar and revers. When the designer has access to this information, they can design garments accurately within a specified price limit, and so do not have the production manager breathing down their necks requiring style modifications in order to come down to price. Once again, the setting up of such a file takes the time and effort of experienced work-study engineers. In most cases, a program is purchased that offers a breakdown of all the relevant product costs. But more of this later.

Some CAD/CAM systems, such as Lectra and Gerber, offer a product-costing program as part of the package, which enables the designer to select pre-costed details, parts or whole garments so that an accurate price can be available immediately.

Grade rule library

This is a collection of size-increase rules that are applied to a pattern at various predetermined points and, when required, will change the size, up or down, automatically and very rapidly. These rules are calculated by the pattern technologists and applied by a grader or a pattern technician.

This data file is also available to anyone on the system.

Layplan library

All layplans are stored in a special library file which will be available to the pattern and cutting staff. These will be plans of previous production runs and also current ones. They will show the material costings of the style in question, and indicate the widths of cloth previously used.

Any style changes can quickly be reflected in the layplan and new costing arrived at.

Size-chart library

When operating on an international scale, it is imperative to have the sizing codes and charts for the country being supplied.

These charts are available but need seeking out, and when acquired they can be stored in one of the data banks. When time is available the pattern technicians can calculate all the grade rules corresponding to the different countries' size changes and store them in the grade-rule library. This will take a lot of patience and time but, when done, will be a valuable asset; that is, until and if an international code is brought into use – though this is highly unlikely.

The size-chart library can also contain all the infant and children's charts plus foundation wear. It is highly unlikely that any one company will operate over such a wide range, unless they are combined retailers and manufacturers, similar to Marks & Spencer, who contract all their manufacturing requirements out to other companies. In this case, the more data that is collected the better. A size-chart library would be indispensable to a concern such as M&S, since they, at present, have several what they term their 'bibles' or production-size charts that their contractors work from. In their case, the size charts are finished garment-measurement charts linked to various different types of fabric and garment types. These are used to check the finished garment size by measuring, with a tape, the various girths, on the flat; this makes them quality-control tools as well as pattern and grading indicators.

CTC

This stands for 'Clothing Technology Centre'. This organization has developed a computer system for measuring and monitoring various aspects of sewing assembly operations.

A sensor is attached to the hand wheel of the sewing machine and its behaviour is accurately mapped, memorized and analysed by a computer. It will show stitching speeds related to every part of an operation, and will enable the work-study team to set up their machines accurately to any specific situation and also to measure a machinist's performance. It will isolate a machinist's strong and weak points and measure any improvements related to a time scale, either in a training situation or on the factory floor. It can also be used to test new machinery and to compare existing pieces in relation to performance. This can be extended to testing work aids and assessing their effect. It is a very useful tool, and is easily transported around from machine to machine. This is an example of a refinement that work-study people used to dream of.

Production planning and control

Before going into detail about production methods, it would be useful to outline the bones of the situation.

There are basically two ways to assemble garments. The first is where the complete garment is made up by one machinist, and the second is when the garment is split up into small operations which are carried out by different machinists in a predesigned sequence.

The first has the advantage that it is more interesting for the machinist to carry out the whole process, and for them to see a completed product that they can claim as their own handwork. On the other hand, it has more drawbacks and disadvantages than the other method.

It will mean that each garment will reflect the skill of the particular machinist, good or bad, and therefore will mean uneven completion speeds and varied quality. This can be exaggerated by the way in which the machinist is paid, which can either be by the hour or a price for the whole process. If they are paid by the hour, then the speed of production will be low, but the quality may be higher than if there is a price paid for each garment, which may mean that the work is rushed and the quality could deteriorate. Plus there is the near impossibility of getting a machinist to alter any bad workmanship, as this will cost the machinist money unless there is a rate of pay for alterations. This will all revolve round the price bracket of the garments. If they are at the expensive end of the scale, then quality is of more importance than speed and the employer can afford to pay more for manufacture. In contrast, if the garments are

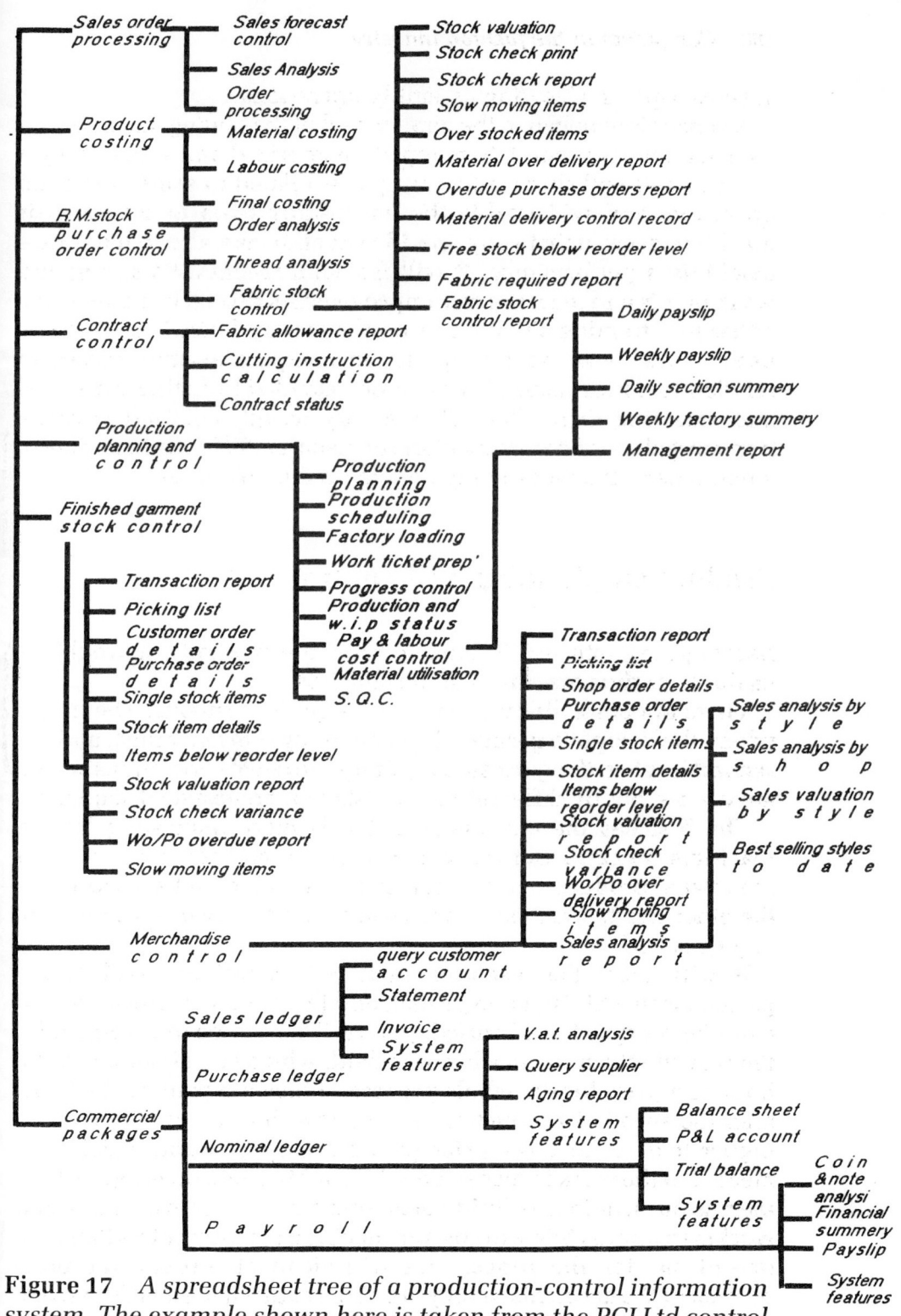

Figure 17 A spreadsheet tree of a production-control information system. The example shown here is taken from the PCI Ltd control system and, as can be seen, covers a very large area and offers around seventy-five different spreadsheets

```
                    GARMENT COSTING SHEET              DATE:   16/12/88
                    =====================              ==========================

STYLE NO.       S34                        CAT/LOT NO.         45835
                                           CAT/LOT NO.
CUSTOMER        C&A                        CAT/LOT NO.

GARMENT DESC:   Skirt                      LENGTH:
****************************************************************************
MATERIAL
========
CLOTH           SUPPLIER   QLTY NO.   WIDTH   RATING    PRICE  % WASTE    VALUE
Cotton          J. Lewis               140    2.000     4.00    4.00%      8.32
Lining                                  90    1.500     2.00    2.00%      3.06
                                                                0.00%      0.00
                                                                        ---------
                                                      SUB TOTAL CLOTH:    11.38
                                                                        ---------
TRIMMING        SUPPLIER   QLTY NO.   WIDTH   RATING    PRICE  % WASTE
Button                                        1.000     0.20    5.00%      0.21
                                                                0.00%      0.00
                                                                0.00%      0.00
                                                                0.00%      0.00
                                                                0.00%      0.00
                                                                0.00%      0.00
                                                                0.00%      0.00
                                                                0.00%      0.00
                                                                0.00%      0.00
                                                                0.00%      0.00
                                                                        ---------
                                                       SUB TOTAL TRIM:=    0.21
                                                                        ---------
SEW THREAD                                    15.00     0.02    0.00%      0.30
PACKAGING (INC HNGRS)                          1.00     0.35    0.00%      0.35
GARMENT LABELS                                 2.00     0.15    0.00%      0.30

DIRECT LABOUR              TOTAL SM           CONVERSI
                               25             0.0394           0.00%       0.99
OVERHEADS                     120%                                         1.18
SAMPLE/FINISHING COST                                                      0.00

FACTORY COST:=                                                            14.71
EXCESS DISCOUNT %           5.00%     ON      14.71                        0.74
LOSS ON 2NDS    %          10.00%     ON      14.71                        1.47
PROFIT          %          30.00%     ON      14.71                        4.41
                                                                        ---------
                                                   SELLING PRICE          21.33
                                                                        ---------
                                                   TRANSPORT COST          0.10
                                                                        ---------
                                                   CONTRACT PRICE         21.43
                                                                        ---------
****************************************************************************

¢m
                              THREAD ANALYSIS¢m

STYLE NO      : A1212       DESCRIPTION  : LADIES BLOUSE¢m
WORKS ORDER NO: 70740     COLOURS       RED  BLUE  GREY  PINK   TOTAL¢m
                          QTY (DOZS)    300   500   650   120   1570¢m

            MACHINE          SEAM LENGTH    BOBBINS REQ/COL    BOBBIN SIZE¢m

LOCKSTITCH                     120 CMS    13   22   29    6    1000 MTR COPS
5 THREAD OVERLOCK (COTTON)       0 CMS     9   15   19    4    5000 MTR CONES
5 THREAD OVERLOCK (BULK)       150 CMS    13   22   29    6    5000 MTR CONES
BLIND STITCH                    50 CMS     1    2    2    1   10000 MTR CONES
CHAIN STITCH                    65 CMS    11   18   23    5    1000 MTR COPS
BUTTONSEW & BUTTONHOLE          10 BTTNS  36   60   78   15    1000 MTR COPS
PICOT EDGE                     100 CMS    18   30   39    8    1000 MTR COPS

TOTAL  1000 MTR COPS  PER COLOUR          78  130  169   34¢m
TOTAL  5000 MTR CONES PER COLOUR (CTTN)    9   15   19    4¢m
TOTAL  5000 MTR CONES PER COLOUR (BULK)   13   22   29    6¢m
TOTAL 10000 MTR CONES PER COLOUR           1    2    2    1¢m
```

```
                        WORK TICKET SAMPLE¢m
QUANTITY 15     ORDER NO 70707     BUNDLE NO 01¢m
LADIES PATTERNED SKIRT¢m
LENGTH 27IN.    SIZE 10     COLOUR BROWN     LM:12¢m

:...................................:..................:.....................................:
: QTY 15    70707     BN 1      1 : 1 LENGTH 27   2 : QTY 15   70707     BN 1      2 :
: MAKE BELT                        : SIZE 10        : OVERLOCK HEM                     :
: SM 1.54 TM 23.1 PAY 69P          : BROWN          : SM 1.24 TM 18.6 PAY 55P          :
:.................................:  LM:12         :.................................:
: QTY 15    70707     BN 1      3 : 3 LENGTH 27   4 : QTY 15   70707     BN 1      4 :
: JOIN SIDE SEAM                   : SIZE 10        : INSERT ZIP                       :
: SM .85   TM 12.8 PAY 38P         : BROWN          : SM 1.25 TM 18.8 PAY 56P          :
:.................................:  LM:12         :.................................:
: QTY 15    70707     BN1       5 : 5 LENGTH 27   6 :                              6 :
: ATTACH WAISTBAND                 : SIZE 10        :                                  :
: SM 1.8   TM 27.0 PAY 81P         : BROWN          :                                  :
:.................................:  LM:12         :.................................:
```

Figure 18 *These spreadsheets are demonstration examples taken from the PCI system*

cheap and cheerful, then 'bashing them out' is the order of the day and 'hang the quality', particularly if business is good and the weather is right for the time of year. In other words, if it is very cold or very hot just when it should be, and everything is selling like hot cakes. Neither the retail buyers nor the public will look closely at the quality of finish, if the price is right. If the weather is not seasonal and the public is not buying, then depression descends on the whole fashion scene and nothing goes right for anyone. All of this will be influenced by the employment rate in the area. If there are plenty of opportunities at other companies, then the quality of the product will tend to fall, regardless of which way the company operates, as the machinists will up and go if they are not satisfied. The attitude of employees to quality and 'pride in their work' varies from country to country, and is reflected in the general character of the population in terms of a higher or lesser tendency to fastidiousness and fussiness. Also, the availability of products within the community and the degree of competition in the native industries will have a large influence on the quality of production. Where countries and communities are poor, then quality is not a consideration; all that matters is producing a product that people can afford.

The second method, sectional assembly, has more advantages than the first. A price can either be fixed for the whole garment and the team share the total equally, or individual prices are fixed for each operation. Whichever way it is done, the general outcome is bound to be an improved and consistent quality and greater output.

Both of these effects are due to the situation of 'immediate repetition'. This ensures that the operator quickly becomes automated to the operation and perfects it to a degree that is not possible when making whole garments. All production methods revolve around these basic facts, but there are many variations on the theme. Some of these will be looked at to give an idea of the implications.

GSD and GAD

These stand for 'general sewing data' and 'general assembly data'. They are both computer programs from Methods Workshop (sewn products) Co. Ltd UK.

They are planning and estimating systems. GSD is recognized as an international standard manufacturing aid in the sewn-products industry, and there are over 600 installations world-wide. GAD is the same, but applies to any product-assembly situation. Other data bases that are available to the work-study teams are DSD and MTM. These offer the same basic data as GST.

These programs contain all timing breakdowns for every process of sewing, pressing and cutting. This enables the work-study teams to calculate in detail the time and cost of any part or the whole unit. They can then design its assembly sequence and production path.

The control of production starts with the cutting schedules. A plan, based on delivery dates, must be drawn up and all the relevant processes keyed into it, such as ordering fabrics and arranging dates for receiving the fabric into the material stock department in time for the prearranged cutting dates. Fabrics must be available in good time for checking and, in the case of some companies, measured and preshrunk with all flaws indicated ready to be recognized by a computerized laying-up device. On the other hand, the company does not want the fabric in too soon as this will clog up the stock room, and who can tell what the future holds? There may be cancellations of orders or any other minor catastrophe that will necessitate cancelling a fabric delivery. Before cutting, it is now possible to predict, with some accuracy, how long it will take to cut a particular order and to organize the output of the cutting department with more precision because of systems such as GSD.

Standard times for laying up, manually and automatic, plus times for manual and automatic bulk computerized cutting have been established; these will give precise time scales and costs enabling planning that can be relied on to work, provided that all goes well and the computers behave themselves. The success of all this sophisticated computerization depends on the reliability of the hardware and the software being bug-free, and of course the ability of the employees to understand and run it without too much difficulty.

Unit-production methods

Assuming that the system of assembly to be used is sectional, then a work path has to be designed and a method of getting the work to the operator must be devised. The cut work arrives at an intermediate place between the cutting room and the production area; here the cut work is organized and sorted, ready to be fed into the assembly system.

Before this can be done, a work-study team will analyse the style that is to be assembled and devise its 'order of assembly'. Every garment has a correct order of assembly and a sample machinist will be one of the team to advise in this area. Sometimes, for speed and ease of assembly, a way of closing a garment is used that is not ideal for the hang and balance of the finished effect, particularly at the cheaper end of the market. But for the majority of companies, who will be catering for an informed market, only the best way will suffice. For example, the sewing of an inset sleeve into the armhole can be achieved by closing the shoulder seam first and then sewing the sleeve head into the armhole on the flat. The side seam and underarm seam is then closed in one long run from hem to the end of the sleeve, instead of closing the under seam of the sleeve and the side seam of the bodice separately and then insetting the sleeve into the completed armhole. This is the correct way to assemble an inset sleeve, and the reason for it being called an inset sleeve. The sleeve will hang correctly only when it is inset into a complete armhole. This kind of know-how comes directly from the pattern cutters and sample machinists, and any production management that ignores their indications in order to follow the 'path of least resistance' does so with some danger.

Having established the 'order of assembly', the total assembly process will have to be divided up into equal segments that will be comprised of small operations that have the same time-span but not necessarily the same skill input. The operators then have to be chosen for the operation that they are suited for, in order to create a balanced team that will ensure that there are no bottlenecks in the production line.

The operators will include underpressers whose job it is to press individual parts during the assembly process. Also, there may be items such as collars that require 'bagging out'. This will need someone to turn the collar the right way and trim the seams at the corners; poke out the tips of the collar; and then pass it to an underpresser before the collar is sewn into the garment. This process can also be done by semi-automatic collar-sewing machines (in the case of a shirt manufacturer where the style is constant), but for the fashion market collars are very seldom the same shape on any two designs so they require human hands to carry out the operation.

Another operation that has to be inserted into the line is 'fused interlining parts' such as collars and fronts, etc. These will be done on a fusing machine; this can be a continuous-feed type, but whatever type is used it is fairly time-consuming, because there is a preset time-span for the fusing process to be completed.

A great deal of experience is needed to be able to design an assembly process that will work without hitches, and very careful analyses are required if production is not to be impaired while the problems are being sorted out because of the lack of detailed forethought.

We will now return to the cut work. This has to be delivered to the assembly line in the correct order. Where the garment is made up completely by one machinist, a bundle of all the parts will be deposited with the machinist or collected by the machinist from the sorting area. This applies only to small companies where there is no automation.

The bundles will contain ten or so garments. When a sectional production line is being used, the parts are fed into the system in order of making and certain parts are fed in down the line to be assembled ready for insertion into the partially made garment. As the garment is sewn it is passed from one machinist to the next, and if there is a gap the work is moved by the supervisor to wherever it is needed. In this type of assembly the work is moved on manually, and each time an operation is carried out the operator registers it on a work docket so that a record is made of work carried out and due for payment.

Until recently, this whole process relied on the team moving the work to where it was needed next. Now there are automated conveyor systems that are computer controlled, moving the parts along overhead rails and delivering the parts and part-made garments at the correct height almost to the needle where it is removed from an easy-release clip, sewn and replaced, and moved on to the next operator. All of this is monitored, and a 'real-time' overview and control is possible that enables immediate response by the supervisor to any problem that should arise. These overhead systems are designed and offered on the market by the major CAD/CAM system manufacturers, and are quite expensive to install. They do tend to take up a lot of space and, once in place, cannot without a lot of time and expense be moved and adapted in any reorganization that is required; however, they are indispensable for a large output.

One of the computer-systems manufacturers, Investronica, the

Spanish company, has produced an optional conveying system using automated vehicles that are guided by floor computer-controlled paths. This type of system is used in other manufacturing areas with success. It means that the system is more flexible, can easily be altered to changing requirements, and is less space-consuming. The other factor that was not foreseen when the overhead systems were designed, involved the isolation of the operator by being surrounded by high-conveying machinery with hanging garment parts. Operators cannot relate with their work colleagues as they can in other systems where they are next to each other. Not that operators have a lot of time for chatting – being flat out trying to make enough money to exist on – but they can at least have a gripe to their neighbour when they feel like it.

It has been calculated that actual sewing time in the assembly of a garment takes only 20 per cent of the total. The rest is made up of a host of other connecting activities such as:

1 Handling the work pieces from bundles
2 Handling work dockets (records of work done)
3 Matching pieces and applying them to the needle
4 Trimming threads
5 Positioning needle
6 Taking instructions from supervisor
7 Rethreading needle
8 Machine maintenance
9 Pausing for a breather and other miscellaneous activities

This means that even if sewing were speeded up 100 per cent, it would make little difference to the total time; however, if all the other activities can be minimized, then considerable savings can be made.

This can be achieved to a large extent by using an automatic conveyor system which presents the work piece at the correct place at the right time, thus cutting down handling time. If the latest programmable sewing machines are employed then savings in positioning the needle, cutting threads and rethreading can add up to considerable time savings. All the latest developments are aimed at cutting down processes that do not entail sewing, the speed of which is more than adequate for any production purpose.

Great savings are made by the streamlining of production control using computer terminals on each machine which registers the exact state of production on a monitor at strategic points of supervision.

Automatic programmable microprocessors, where each machine has a mini computer terminal at the right-hand side, enable the operator to press a button to register the work completed. Where all the machines are related to a central control terminal, the supervisor can see immediately the overall situation on a monitor because of the clear and easily understood graphical representations of the work process. Each of the mini terminals on the machines are also linked to a program which calculates employees' weekly pay packets with tax and deductions, etc.

Finishing and pressing

These processes, in general, cannot be fully computerized as, like the machinist, the handling processes are highly complex and there are not, and cannot be in the foreseeable future, any robots that can cope with the situation in this area. There are areas of automation in the buttonhole-making machines, where the machine can do a sequence of holes at preset distances apart.

The final pressing is done on a variety of steam presses, all of which are operated by humans. The only exception to this is the hanging press, which steams the whole garment and is situated in the conveying system; this enables the finished product to pass through a steam chamber where the creases are relaxed out of the garment without any pressure being applied. This is only suitable for certain products and will not remove any stubborn creases. Most of the pressing is done on varying forms of Hoffman presses that use steam and pressure and a vacuum to remove the steam. Coupled to these presses, there are ordinary steam irons that are used to press the intricate parts that the Hoffman cannot be used for. There are some forms of automation in the form of preshaped presses that are designed to shape and press certain parts of a garment, particularly in the men's tailoring sector.

The garments arrive at the pressing area by overhead tracks or computer-guided vehicles. They are then conveyed to an area for inspection and, in some cases, cleaned off with an air-pressure nozzle. Finally, they are bagged in polythene.

Warehouse storage

Storing large numbers of finished garments in all sizes, colours and styles is a difficult problem to solve. The main difficulty is quickly finding the garments to complete a specific order ready for dispatch by road or to be packed for mailing. There have been many solutions to this puzzle, but most have a major drawback. Stacking garments high into a warehouse on multi-storied rails solves the cubic footage problem (in other words, going upwards gives more capacity), but retrieving them is a major headache. They have to be stored by style colour and size in a carefully recorded system, or else they may get lost and take a lot of finding. If they are stored on rails on one level they are difficult to move because of the weight involved, and in all cases a large staff is required to handle a big warehouse.

There is now a computerized system that can handle storage using electric automated vehicles that are run on batteries; this eliminates power supply wires, and the batteries only need charging once a day. This system was pioneered by Investronica and they have devised a special upright vehicle that has a device for storing the garments in a preplanned layout; this uses a robotic device which can reach in all directions and place the garment very accurately in position so it is able to locate garments again just as precisely. It can then be instructed to retrieve garments off a rail and place them on its own rail. All the stock is stored in preplanned areas using the computer, according to style, etc., and when an order for delivery is required the one operator types in the instructions and the rest is done by the computerized system, collecting the order from the rails and placing it in the dispatch area. It also makes out the delivery notes and informs the central computer that the order has been dealt with and adjusts the stock records.

PCI (production control information)

This is actually the name of the company that produces the software, and is an integrated data base that can present the state of the production at any time. It is similar to SCI (sales control information).

It has overall costing capabilities and can link and define any part or parts and relate and compare all relevant data. This gives rise to as many as seventy different spreadsheets containing all possible information for past, present or future performance.

Costing is divided into three main areas:

1 *Overheads.* These are all non-production costs, of which there are many including non-production staff salaries. These include everyone except cutting, assembly, finishing, pressing and packing employees.

2 *Materials.* These are the costs of everything that goes into the product. Fabric and trimmings of all kinds are included.
3 *Production.* These are all detailed cutting, assembly, finishing, pressing, packing and delivery costs.

All these data can be accessed and brought together in whatever way is required, and a picture of any area is immediately available for scrutiny.

Added to this, there is the ability to read off profit margins related to production flow and output. Also, there is the facility to adjust the entire cost structure to conform to inflation levels; by simply typing in the percentage increases, the rest is automatically adjusted, giving new overheads, materials, and product costs, without having to get out of breath once.

There are many such programs available at the present time and a list of companies offering them is given in Chapter 13. A tree of the spreadsheets available on the PCI is shown in this chapter along with a few examples extracted from it. Most of the programs offered by other companies are very similar to the ones shown here; before buying one, though, be sure it is IBM compatible.

Computer-aided management and production control

A cost and production cutting control system (Courtesy Assyst GmbH)

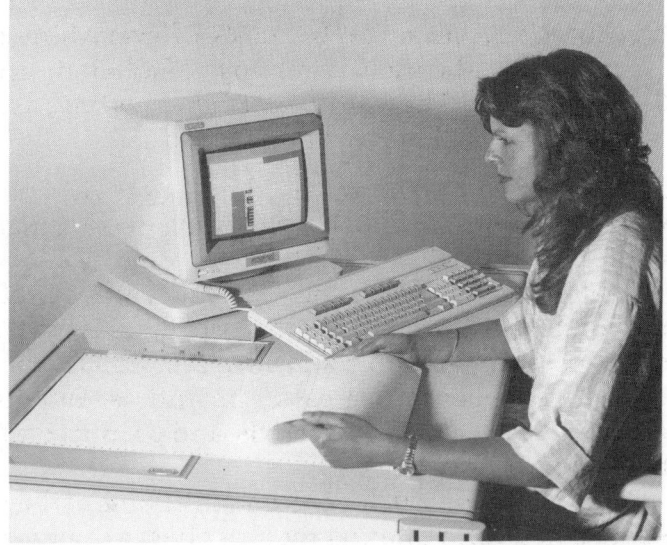

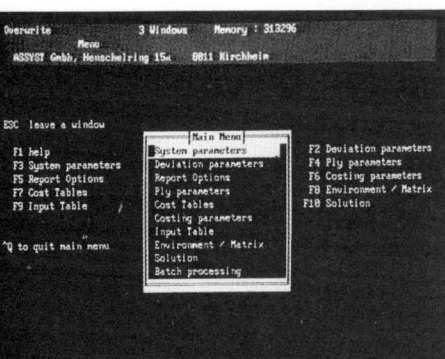

The system's main menu

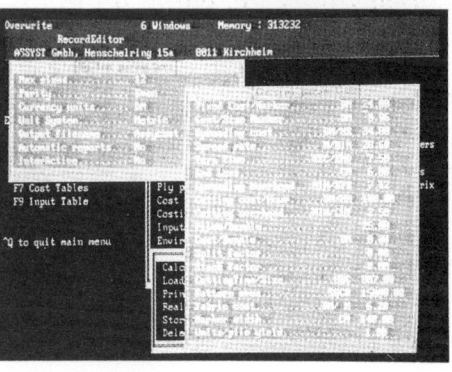

Windows for parameter point

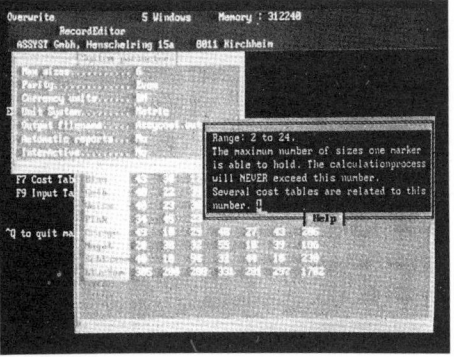

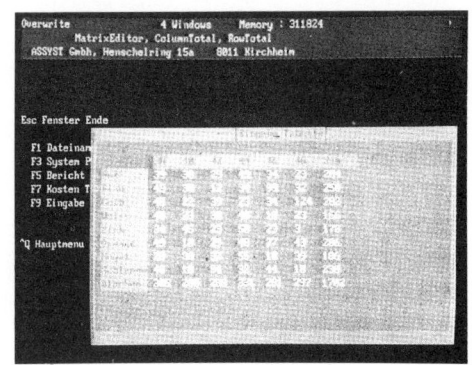

Input of ordermatrix

Help messages for each system function are available at the hit of the button

(Courtesy Assyst GmbH)

200 Computers in the fashion industry

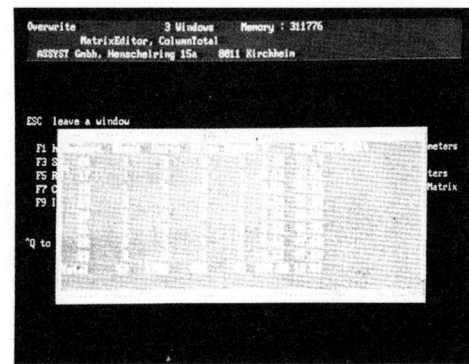
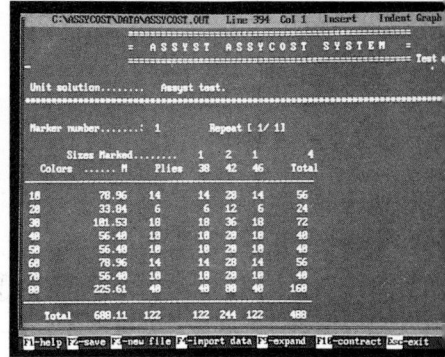

After a few seconds: the solution

Solutions can be checked on the terminal prior to printing (Courtesy Assyst GmbH)

Chapter 12

Projection into the future

The areas where most advances will take place are:

1 PDS computer systems for pattern construction.
2 3D scanning technology for surveying population shape.
3 The creation of solid realistic 3D computer images used for: (a) designing; (b) buying; (c) selling.

1 PDS computer systems

The main drawback with these systems is having to work on a small video screen, which strains the eyes, and the small scale does not enable the pattern technician to see the whole of the pattern at the same time (full scale is available, though). Also, because of having to control the pattern through a series of commands, it is like moving an object at distance using remote-controlled arms and fingers. This gives the operator so many extra problems that details in pattern-construction techniques are sometimes sacrificed in order that at least some sort of result is achieved. At the end of a day's struggle with the system, a technician can be exhausted and feel that a much better way would have been to do it manually and with better results. In general, it can be said that the refinements are lost owing to lack of control. This may be all right for some of the crude pattern work done in some companies, but is unsatisfactory for the more experienced and precise creators of shape and balanced proportional styling that some are aiming at. These pattern systems also assume that the pattern is arrived at solely by flat pattern-cutting techniques, omitting modelling on a stand, which is the source of all the flat 2D pattern-manipulation processes. No pattern cutter of experience will work without a model form at their elbow to enable them to explore any unknown area firsthand. For most pattern cutters, the computer PDS programs, as they stand, are clumsy tools. The only true advantage they give is the superb memory facility, which does away with all the bulky pattern cards that clutter up the pattern rooms of the factories, and the paper patterns in the sample rooms.

If the computer companies want to sell pattern-construction systems, the next generation of PDS will have to be much easier to use and nearer to the natural way that a pattern cutter works. The software for these systems are written by computer programmers who, in spite of the fact that they say that they understand what is required, are not pattern cutters and do not understand the complexity of the problems that confront the pattern people.

Designing software programs for layplanning, grading and cutting are easier to perfect because these processes do not have the almost infinite variability, and at times subtle application, that are present in the construction of patterns. A pattern cutter can spend their whole life working on patterns and still not understand the interaction of the many principles involved. But there may be hope for the future if the following specification could be achieved. But it may be just a dream. As was said earlier, the natural way of working ought to be maintained so that the pattern technician can take to it like a duck to water.

This would require an interactive surface similar to the digitizer, of at least 1 m deep by 1.5 m long, the same as the draughtsman's set-up with tilt and movable drawing tools. Ideally, it would be a LED crystal display but with a much finer definition, capable of producing pencil-thick lines. The surface would be strong to withstand pressure and general rough treatment. To operate the system, there should be a simple menu at the bottom right of the surface, to bring up patterns, and an electronic pencil that can be used the same way as a pencil, to draw, using the usual manual rulers and curves, not displayed ones. The pattern pieces must be easily moved using the pencil by dragging and manœuvring into place. The pencil can be turned into a rubber and used to erase by passing it over the line to be deleted.

Easy dart manipulation, pattern separation, storage and recall would be essential. Whether it would be possible or an economic proposition to develop a system like this is hard to tell. It could also be used by the draughtsman, if it had a high enough resolution; the attraction of working in larger scale than they hitherto have been used to would be a significant one. This might enlarge the market sufficiently to warrant the development time and money. It would also make a good tool for the artist, particularly if colour was introduced. This kind of interactive surface in real size, with direct access and no clumsy sets of commands, would be the answer to a pattern cutter's prayer. It would have all the advantages of the present systems without the eye strain and hassle experienced today. So what is needed is a touch-sensitive crystal display with good contrasted high definition. This could change the whole attitude towards PDS systems and make them a real and desirable alternative to pencil and paper.

2 3D scanning technology

The surveying of a population using a 3D scanner would produce accurate data for generating wire-frame or solid models on screen that would represent any grouping or figure type that the pattern department wished to study or work on.

Who would collect all these data is not clear, and whether they would release them for general use would depend on who they were and whether they had any vested interests.

But assuming that an extensive data bank was set up covering all ages in both sexes and every conceivable shape and size, it would open up the possibility of major advances in all precutting areas.

Work is being done, at present, on developing a facility to dress up a 3D image in cloth, creating a silhouette or draped style and drawing style lines where required or introducing flare and gathering, etc. Parallel to this, work is being carried out on a software package that will enable the pattern cutter to peel off the separate pieces of the design from the 3D shape and convert them into 2D pattern pieces. The program, that converts 3D to 2D, does not produce the final shape that can be cut out and sewn up in cloth. It produces a pattern that has an accurate peripheral measurement, but the internal measurements are compressed and are shown as a matrix of lines plus variable colour to indicate the areas of compression; the extent of compression is indicated by a blended change of colour and a convergence of the lines. The programmers describe this as a stress indication image, which is the same thing in reverse. This is not a true 2D representation; the only true datum on the pattern is the measurement round the edge. To arrive at a true 2D pattern, the image has to be split open to the points of maximum compression, or maximum stress, and spread until the colour is constant and the matrix of lines are all parallel. This requires skill and a deep understanding of pattern construction. Knowing where to open the pattern and insert style lines to conform to the design and at the same time produce the correct 3D representation in 2D, will tax the judgement of the best pattern cutters; and, at the end of the day, there may not be the refinement of shape that makes for a balanced and well-proportioned garment. But all of these new innovations have to be put to the test in the real manufacturing environment to establish their true value. It may be that it will work satisfactorily in the majority of situations and, if not, perhaps the program can be improved. If this program can be improved to a point where all the requirements of pattern construction can be clearly specified before the pattern is peeled off and converted to 2D, then the life of the pattern technician is limited, and designers will not be required to be competent pattern cutters. The designer will then only need to model the garment on the screen and draw the style lines plus pockets and collars, etc. and push a button. The pattern pieces will appear ready to be cut out in cloth, having been through the automatic layplanner and cut out by the laser cutter and passed to the machinist to sew up.

There are, however, many difficulties to overcome regarding drapes and complex design details that will defy all efforts to solve in a way that will enable designers to work more freely than they do now, and yet not add more complexity to an already difficult varied process.

One important aspect is nearly always overlooked, and that is of the pleasure that can be got from manually handling and manipulating cloth, pencil and paper. This direct experience will be more and more submerged in the avalanche of technology that is engulfing everything. It is also true that the technology itself is fascinating and has a place of its own, but it is a second-hand experience through a machine; as such, it is not as rich as the real thing.

The availability of many sizes and figure types in the computer memory will enable the designer to have direct feedback of design features on different shapes and enable him or her to assess the suitability of styling for different age groups and sizes. A facility could be included for selecting an image of a particular figure type in size 10, for example, and then grading the image up to larger sizes by predetermining where the fat will be deposited or the muscle developed and see first-hand the visual effect. This would enable the designer to experiment cheaply and without wasting material and machine time; what effect a particular style feature will have in larger proportions; add to this the function of designing textiles with all the colour options, and a truly three-dimensional environment is available for experimentation.

A disadvantage with all these systems is the miniature size that the operator works with. If the images were full size then the subtlety of creating a design or pattern would be preserved. This coupled to a full-sized draughting facility, where patterns are full-scale, would make the system completely acceptable to the designer/pattern cutter.

3 Design, buying and selling with 3D imaging

The ability to generate realistic images and look at them from different angles opens up a novel means of buying and selling clothing.

The retail buyer would benefit immensely. If full-scale realistic images can be animated sufficiently to imitate a live model, then the dressing of the image in various styles will be done by the flick of a switch; also, the ability to change the material to any predesigned print, stripe or check, and mix the colours to suit the buyer's whims, will make the process of establishing a range of clothes a very economical procedure with a flexibility unmatched today.

There could also be incorporated a facility for changing the size of the image to a standard or statistically average shape of a given girth and height in a selected age group. It would of course make the live model somewhat redundant in the wholesale manufacturing sector. This would make life easier for the people involved, as they would not have the models' usual biased remarks about the styles, and complaints about having to change in and out of clothes all day, of how their feet ache, and how they have to leave at a certain time to meet their boyfriends.

The customer buying clothes in the shop would also confront a minor revolution. Instead of a shop full of clothes, there would be cubicles containing computers linked to full-size image display monitors. The customer could then view a large range of variety of different types of clothing coupled to a huge selection of fabric designs which could be shown on any style at the flick of a switch. These images could, if required, be animated in a realistic way. To make life even better, the customer would already have had a scan of their body shape done at a special scanning centre, and entered on to a customer data base with a personal code; this code would be quoted when they ordered a style in one of the retail-chain ordering centres. Having entered the ordering cubicle and keyed into the computer their personal shape code, they could then proceed to view the type of garments that they were interested in and have them shown on their own animated figure. This would give them a true picture of their exact appearance from all angles in any type of garment from swimwear to a strapless evening dresses.

This would be a strange experience for most people, who are not accustomed to seeing themselves on screen. It would probably be a revelation to most – and whether it would prove popular or not will remain to be seen! The order for the chosen garment would then be forwarded via a modem link to the factory, and the garment cut out in the chosen material and assembled to fit the client. It also would be possible to have the computer terminal in the home, so that all of the ordering can be done without moving an inch. This situation will once again rob the individual of direct contact with the cloth and the finished garment, and require the customer to wait while the garment is made and despatched to them through the post. It will deprive customers of the thrill of trying the clothes on and feeling the texture and weight of the fabric, and also the interaction with the sales persons which, for some, is essential – although the sales staff may disagree with this in some cases.

Probably the situation will resolve itself into a compromise where made-up garments are available to handle, plus a selection of basic fabrics provided in different weights to help selection. There will also have to be sales persons to help in all areas with pressing the right computer buttons, etc.

It may well be that only the more expensive clothing will be offered as 'one offs' and the cheaper garments will remain 'off the peg'. All of this could transform the mass-production scene. Instead of producing large numbers of the same style in predetermined sizes, all garments will be 'one offs', made to the customer's requirements.

The use of bulk computer-driven cutters will diminish, and only single-ply computer cutters will be used. The high-ply cutters would be used only for bulk orders of non-fashion goods, such as overalls, etc. There obviously is a limit to the number of styles that can be offered by any one company, and the same applies to the selection of fabrics.

The manufacturer will need a single-ply cutting device, such as a laser or water cutter, linked to an automatic material feed that can select from a number of fabric styles and colour ways that have been preselected for a specific style of garment, or styles. This is coded and linked directly to the retail sector for activation by the customer.

When the fabric has been cut out it is automatically relayed to a human machinist for assembly. It is highly unlikely that the human machinist will ever be replaced by a robotic device in the fashion areas, since the expertise is so infinitely variable that nothing but a human could handle it satisfactorily. Items like shirts and underwear can be robotized reasonably well as the patterns do not change all that much, and it may well be that these garments will be produced exclusively by robots and automatic devices. Before this can happen, ways of picking up and handling fabric must be overcome, and at the present time nobody can predict how the problem will be solved.

The answer may be that the human machine is the cheapest and most satisfactory way to do the job, but by then will they want to do it?

It could be that, having tried all these automatic procedures, humanity finds that they bring more problems than they solve. In other words, the cost of the systems and their maintenance and the problems of replacing outdated hardware and software, plus the resistance of people to the technology, may tip the balance in favour of the old ways. It remains to be seen what it will be like in 200 years' time.

Chapter 13

List of computer hardware and software companies

GA CAD paint and draw systems

Assyst
Bellow Machine Co.
Concept 11 Research Ltd
Cybrid
Gerber Garment Technology, Inc.
Investronica
Juki Corporation
Lectra
Microdinamics
PCI

CAD pattern-construction systems

Advanced Technology Industries
Assyst
Bellow Machine Co.
Bullmer Works
Complan Technology
Concept 11 Research Ltd
Cybrid
Gerber Garment Technology Inc.

Investronica
Juki Corporation
Lectra
Microdinamics
Moda Cad
Polygon
Terminal Display Systems

CAM grading and layplanning systems

ADM Development Consultants
Assyst
Bellow Machine Co.
Bullmer Works
Carlton Press Knives
Complan Technology
Concept 11 Research Ltd
Cybrid
Gerber Garment Technology Inc.
Investronica
Juki Corporation
Lectra
Moda Cad
Polygon
Stylewear

Computer systems management and production control

ADM Development Consultants
Alan Shelton
Apparel Computer Systems
Assyst
Bellow Machine Co.
Comply Business Systems
CP Programming
Eidon Electronics
Electronic Data Processing plc
Esperus Software Ltd
Eton Systems
Fraser Williams Group
Gandalf Digital Communications

Gerber Garment Technology Inc.
ICS Texicon
Investronica
Jeff Johnson Associates
Juki Corporation
K. Soft
Mass Micros
Methods Workshop
Microcast
MW Scicon
PCI
PDA Management Consultants
PWS
Radius
SMCS International
Software Systems UK
Stylewear
Syscom plc
Terminal Display Systems
Universal (CMS)
Vertex Engineering
West Bridgford Machine Co.

Computer-controlled conveyor systems

Apparel Production Systems
Bellow Machine Co.
Conveyors International
Eton Systems
Eurosew Ltd
Gerber Garment Technology Inc.
Integrated Handling
Investronica
Stewart Gill and Co.
Stockrail Ltd
The Marine Engineering Co.

Computer-controlled bulk cutting

Bullmer Works
Fairhaven Machinery
Geoffrey E. Macpherson

Gerber Garment Technology Inc.
Investronica
Lectra
Machine Technology

Cloth inspection and measuring machines

Alan Godrich
Alan Shelton
Bates Textiles Machine Co.
Beecroft and Co.
Bullmer Works
Emberfern
Fairhaven Machinery
Hill-Lupton
James Bailey
Kennedy Sewing Machines
Laughton Engineering
L. Linz and Sons
L. W. Stutter
Napier Engineering
Phillips and Son
SGS Quality Control

Computer-aided cloth spreaders

Alan Godrich
Ardmel Automation
ATH Clothing Engineers
Bellow Machine Co.
Fairhaven Machinery
Geoffrey E. Macpherson
Gerber Garment Technology Inc.
J. W. Stutter
Kennedy Sewing Machines
Laughton Engineering
Lectra
L. Linz and Sons
Macpi UK
Phillips and Son
Union Special

Computer-controlled plotters

Bellow Machine Co.
Complan Technology
Concept 11 Research Ltd
Cybrid
Gerber Garment Technology Inc.
Investronica
Juki Corporation
Lectra
Xetal

Programmable sewing-machines

Aisin
Alan Godrich
Allide/Willcox
Anglo/American
Bellow Machine Co.
Chapman Sewing Machines
Chris Sewing Machines
Derek Allman
Durkopp & Adler
E. L. Grain
Eurosew
Holgate Machine Co.
J. Davis & Co.
Jones & Brother
Juki
J. W. Stutter
Laughton Engineering
Mitsubishi
Nottingham Sewing Machine Co.
Rockwell/Rimoldi
S. A. Smith
Singer/SDL
Tyson Sewing Machines
Union Special
Vale Sewing Machines
Vertex Engineering
West Bridgford Machine Co.
Yamato Sewing Machines

Index

AM1, Gerber sytem, 23
Amiga, 46, 79
Artists, 62–8
Assembly, 15–17
Atari, 46, 79
Auto layplan, 127
Auto sewing, 161

Band knife, 137
Block construction, 112
Bulk cutting, 14–15
Bureaux, grading, 117
Buyer, fashion, 1–4

CAD/CAM, 9, 22–36, 67–87
Camsco, 23
CDI Inc., 77
Chain stores, 1
Checks, matching, 43
Chemist, dyes, 76
Choice of systems, 25
CIM, 26.
Cloth, inspection, 135
CMT, 126
Code, computer, 45
Computer theory, 37–47
College training, 27
Conveyer cutting, 140
Conveyer garments, 194
Couture house, 7

CPU, 44–5
CRT, 47
CTC, 188
Cutter:
   sample, 10
   stock, 137
Cutting, bulk, 14–15
Cutting room, 14–36
Cybrid, 32–3

Design department, 6–9
Design process, 72–4
Designer:
   fashion, 6–9
   textiles, 9–10
   pattern cutter, 8
Digitizer, 82
Disc:
   drive, 43–5
   floppy, 43
   hard, 43
Draughtsmanship, 68–9
Drill holes, 138
Drum plotter, 91–2, 125
Dyes, 77–9

Embroidery, 8, 79, 82, 164
Energy, 39

214 Index

Fabric:
  characteristics, 16
  inspection, 136
  handling, 160
Fashion design, 6–9, 68–71
Fashion shows, 4
Fibres, 76
Filaments, 76
Finishing, 17, 196
Flat bed plotter, 125
Flat pattern cutting, 88
Floppy disc, 43
Fusible interlining, 196

GA (graphic art), 80–9, 47
GAD (general assembly data), 192
Garment storage, 196
Genesco, 23
Gerber, 23, 31–2
Grader, 12–13
Grade rules, 111–12, 187
GSD (general sewing data), 192

Hardware, 37
Hewlett Packard, 23
Hughes, Howard, 23
Hughes Research Co., 23
Human input/output, 38

IBM, 23–6
Increment path grading, 110
Input/output, 39
Inspection, cloth, 135
Intel, processor, 26
International sizing, 48
Investronica, 33

Knives, manual cloth cutting, 14

Language, computer, 45
Laser cutting, 141
Layplanning, 13–14
Layplans, 105
LCD, 165
Lectra, 23, 35–6
Libraries, 95, 120, 187
Lockstitch, 160

Machinist, sample, 10, 80
Macintosh computer, 46
Markers, 14, 120
Market research, retail, 4
Main frame, 23

Manager, systems, 23
Mass production, 11–21
Matching, checks, 143
M&S, 3
Memory, 41
Men's wear, 5
Menus, 26
Metal cutting, 139
Microdynamics, 35
Modelling, 2D/3D, 88, 203
Models/mannequins, 10
Monitors, 47
Mouse, 90
Multi-markers, 121, 126

Network computers, 2, 46

Order of assembly 193
Overlocking, 163

Pattern cutter, 6–9
Pattern data file, 186
PCI (production control information), 197
PDS, 26, 89–105, 201–3
Photo cell, 164
Plasma cutter, 141
Pleating, 8
Pluto, system, 80
Pressing, 17, 198
Process costing data file, 186
Production:
  area, 15–18
  costing, 184
  control, 188–90
  pattern, 107
Production manager, 9
Profile stitchers, 164
Prototype pattern, 12

Ram (random access memory), 43–5
Ranges, summer/winter, 5
Retail sector, 1–4
  chart, 18
  houses, 5
RGE, 47
Robot devises, 39, 161
ROM (read only memory), 43
Round knife, 137
RTA (real time access) 183

Sales data, 185

Sails, 139
Sample cutter, 10
Scanner, 92, 114
Seasons, 5–6
Senses, 42
Servo cutter, 137
Shoe design, 80–1
  manufacture, 166
Showroom, 5–6
Shrinkage, 135
Sleeve head sewing, 164
Size charts, 12, 48, 66
Sketch, 9
Software, 45
Sports wear, 95
Spreading machines, 138–9

Strands, model forms, 51
Stock cutter, 137
Storage, 191
Straight knife, 137
Stripes, matching, 123, 143
Stylus, 90
Surveys, 48, 66
System manager, 28

Tailoring systems, 117
Textile design, 9–10
Three-dimension body scanner, 114

Unit production methods, 193

VDU (visual display unit), 32